M.

RELATIONSHIPS

Dr Tony Lake

Michael Joseph
London

First published in Great Britain by
Michael Joseph Limited
44 Bedford Square, London WC1
1981

ISBN 0 7181 1967 3

Made by Roxby Press Productions Limited
98 Clapham Common Northside, London, SW4 9SG

Editor: Jana Gough
Designer: Elizabeth Palmer
Picture Research: Caroline Lucas

The author particularly wishes to acknowledge the assistance of Muriel Lewin during the preparation of this book.

Phototypeset by Input Typesetting Limited
Reproduction by Latent Image
Printed and bound in Italy

PICTURE CREDITS

Cover: Tony Evans. E. Arnold (Magnum): 8, 91, 267; Associated Press: 101T; E. Baitel (Viva): 31, 85, 92, 125, 318; B. Barbey (Magnum): 82, 178; C. Barda: 70; I. Berry (Magnum): 194; F. Bourke (Weidenfeld & Nicolson Archives): 67R, 173; R. Burri (Magnum): 120B, 198; Camera Press: 78, 107, 108, 140, 146, 151, 167, 176, 191, 192, 209, 216T, 237, 271, 280, 282, 315; R. Canault (Viva): 155; H. Cartier-Bresson (Magnum): 13, 28, 65, 74B, 100, 160, 174, 184, 219, 261, 304, 307; Central Press: 203; A. Dagbert (Viva): 14, 55, 287, 297; Daily Telegraph Colour Library: 73, 79, 87, 179; A. De Andrade (Magnum): 74TR; M. Edwards: 30, 45, 272; L. Freed (Magnum): 41, 218; J. Garrett: 241; B. Glinn (Magnum): 131; H. Gloaguen (Viva): 61T, 77, 93, 135, 152, 154, 208; R. & S. Greenhill: 35, 41, 49, 58, 72L, 80L, 80R, 96, 99, 110, 113, 123, 126B, 129T, 148, 177, 182, 195, 204, 207, 293T; Greenpeace: 220; Susan Griggs Agency: 76; R. Haas: 94; Robert Harding Associates: 86; J. Hermanson (Viva): 19, 159; F. Hers (Viva): 147, 197, 215; A. Heyman (Magnum): 24, 137, 158, 240; T. Hopker (Magnum): 245; D. Hurn (Magnum): 277; Alan Hutchinson Library: 187; R. Kalvar (Magnum): 120T; Keystone Press: 221; F. Le Diascorn (Viva): 51, 114; G. Le Querrec (Magnum): 59, 168; L. Lewis: 43, 68, 200T; M. Luskacova (Magnum): 66; Magnum: 38, 74TL, 89B, 230; C. Manos (Magnum): 2, 157; A. Miles: 39; W. Miller (Magnum): 46, 256; J. Mougin (Viva): 102, 166, 169; J. Mounicq (Magnum): 1; M. Murray: 34; R. Perry: 36, 47, 72R, 90, 138, 293B; Picturepoint Ltd: 81, 142, 186, 190, 196, 213, 244; C. Raimond-Dityvon (Viva): 11, 88, 104T, 129BL, 202, 210; Rex Features Ltd: 20, 22, 37, 53, 56, 61B, 183, 185, 199, 212, 216B, 233, 239, 250, 290; M. Riboud (Magnum): 50; B. Seed: 83, 130, 134, 193; C. Smith: 149; C. Steele-Perkins: 16, 44, 61C, 67L, 71, 89C, 104B, 118, 129BR, 133, 141, 163, 188T, 308; H. Sykes: 17, 42, 84, 89T, 98, 101B, 119, 126T, 139, 145, 161, 164, 170, 188B, 205, 234, 255, 259, 278, 285, 295, 303, 311; M. Vignes (Viva): 101C; Vision International: 224, 248, 249, 252, 253; Viva: 226; A. Webb (Magnum): 64; V. Wilmer: 236, 310, 316; ZEFA Picture Library: 69, 95, 143, 200B.

INTRODUCTION

This book introduces you to a new way of looking at yourself and other people. Whenever you meet and communicate with somebody you form a relationship, however temporary. Understanding how relationships are set up, maintained and ended is a fascinating exercise. If you are interested in people this book will help you to gain even more enjoyment from observing human behaviour. Yet this is only the start.

Relationships affect everything you do. They cannot be separated from what you are. Developing greater insight into the actions of other people helps you gain not only more skill in your dealings with them, but also a deeper knowledge of your own personality. This is a practical exercise, rewarding in itself and applicable to every aspect of your life.

Contents

SECTION ONE
YOU AND YOUR SYSTEM OF RELATIONSHIPS

This section looks at relationships in general and shows why we make them, what kinds we make and how we can improve our skills with people. Relationships enable us, first, to meet our need to maintain and improve a standard of life which is acceptable to us and, secondly, to have freedom of action, whether our relationship with somebody is based on power, give-and-take or love.

The way we relate to others is seen in terms of simple economic theory. Each person is at the centre of a system of resources, a 'mini-economy' of which he is the manager. He can obtain what he wants only by increasing the value of the resources in his system. Positive feelings tell him when his value is increasing, and negative feelings when his value is decreasing. As a result of early training, people often ignore their feelings and respond to a set of unconscious needs called the 'hidden agenda'. The later chapters in the section examine the effects on relationships of these hidden needs, and explain how they arise.

1 Objectives

The need for skills

We have always been materially and emotionally dependent upon one another. Most of our ancestors lived in small, unchanging communities and met few strangers. They grew up knowing personally almost everybody they would need throughout their lives. It was safe for them to assume that what they learned about relationships as children would serve them well until they died. Today that assumption is no longer valid. There are more people in the world and we travel more widely. The organizations we work for are more complicated, the communities we live in are bigger and some of our institutions – notably marriage – are less stable. We need to go on learning about relationships all our lives, and can no longer rely upon an immature and uninformed response to the people around us. If we deliberately improve our understanding of relationships we can become more adaptable, miss fewer opportunities to have an interesting and happy life and use more of our abilities to greater effect.

Whilst there are many different kinds of relationships, this book will be dealing with those with people you get to know because they share parts of your life. The people concerned may be your husband or wife, your parents, children, brothers or sisters, friends, colleagues or neighbours. Together you belong to the groups and organizations such as families, firms and neighbourhoods where most of your activities take place. It is often easier to see the differences between these relationships, rather than the similarities. Some go smoothly, while others generate anger or anxiety. Some are with people you like; others with people you feel indifferent towards or dislike. They include relationships with strangers – a new colleague or neighbour, perhaps – and also people you know intimately. Because each individual is unique, it seems as if each relationship is different.

Yet there is another way of looking at them. You are at the centre of a set, or system, of relationships which includes everybody you know. Similarly, everyone else is at the centre of another set containing all the people *he* knows. Once this is recognized, two important facts become more obvious. First, each set is designed in an attempt to meet the needs of the individual at the centre. Secondly, in order to meet his needs within this set, and to change it for the better, the individual requires skills.

The first of these facts provides a starting point for a systematic understanding of relationships. All human beings have similar needs. Social scientists have been able to study these needs and how they are met by using surveys and laboratory experiments. Part of the purpose of this book is to describe their findings. Secondly, because we rely on skills in our everyday dealings with other people, it is possible to approach the subject of relationships in a practical way. The main purpose of this book is to help you improve your skills: your ability to communicate effectively; your ability to get to know the people you meet, either for the benefit of the groups you belong to or to serve your private needs more directly; your understanding of your own sexuality and that of others; and your ability to discover and practise new relationship skills for yourself.

This approach requires a change of emphasis from the direct, unthinking response to relationships which we learned in childhood to one which is based on better understanding and self-management. This may seem unnatural to some people. Yet thinking more carefully about someone's behaviour and how you can respond does not mean that you will lose spontaneity in your relationships. In fact the reverse is true. By improving your understanding of yourself and others, you can avoid wasting time and energy on unnecessary conflicts and destructive misunderstandings. This will increase your opportunities to be spontaneous, and will also help you to feel safe enough to act naturally and intuitively with more people.

Even in this informal situation, people are using skills of which they are not aware in constantly adapting to each other's feelings and expectations. We learn these skills in the family.

2 The Economics of Need

Relationships enable people to meet needs

It is difficult to imagine a world without relationships or the benefits of relating to other people. Yet these conditions exist wherever prisoners are kept in solitary confinement, where people are oppressed by extreme poverty or isolated by illness and neglect. Social scientists have shown that under these circumstances people stay alive by behaving as unsocial animals. If you would die of starvation by giving food to somebody else instead of yourself, love becomes a luxury you cannot afford. Every scrap of energy you have must be conserved and used to obtain the next scrap.

The background against which to see relationships, therefore, is that of human need. Some of the things we need are basic to our survival: food, water and shelter, for example. However, we are unlikely to regard our needs as satisfied if we merely survive. To live from day to day at subsistence level is to exist in unacceptable poverty. Need can be defined as the lack of sufficient resources to sustain an acceptable 'standard of life'. Only the individual concerned can decide what is, or is not, an acceptable standard in his own case.

To maintain the standard of living to which we have grown accustomed we need a wide variety of consumer goods (or 'resources'), such as cars, televisions, telephones, and so on. To our ancestors of a few generations ago, and to people living in extreme poverty today, this would seem like unimaginable wealth; they would probably be surprised that we still have needs. Yet this is only surprising if we think of resources in terms of money. A resource is *anything* which meets a need, and we have many needs which cannot be met directly by having money. For example, someone who is poor in financial terms may have other resources, such as a loving family, friendly neighbours or a happy place to live. His standard of living may be low, but his standard of *life* will be high. Equally, a wealthy person may claim to have a high standard of living, but if he is ill, however many doctors he can afford, his standard of life is depressed. In spite of our higher material standard of living, we still need the same things as our forefathers: emotional comfort, to feel valued by other people, to know who to turn to in a crisis, and so on. Our needs probably differ only in terms of the wider range of skills required to meet them.

Since relationships are a way of meeting needs, and depend on the resources available, it is possible to subject them to an economic analysis. Economics is the science of the production and distribution of wealth. A science which investigates the ways in which people produce and distribute non-material resources could be called 'psycho-economics'. During the last twenty years a growing number of scientists have developed and tested psycho-economic theories.

When people are faced with starvation, their relationships are of secondary importance to meeting their need to survive.

Some examples will help to illustrate the similarities between the subject matter of economics and psycho-economics. Each country has different natural (or 'physical') resources, including such things as min-

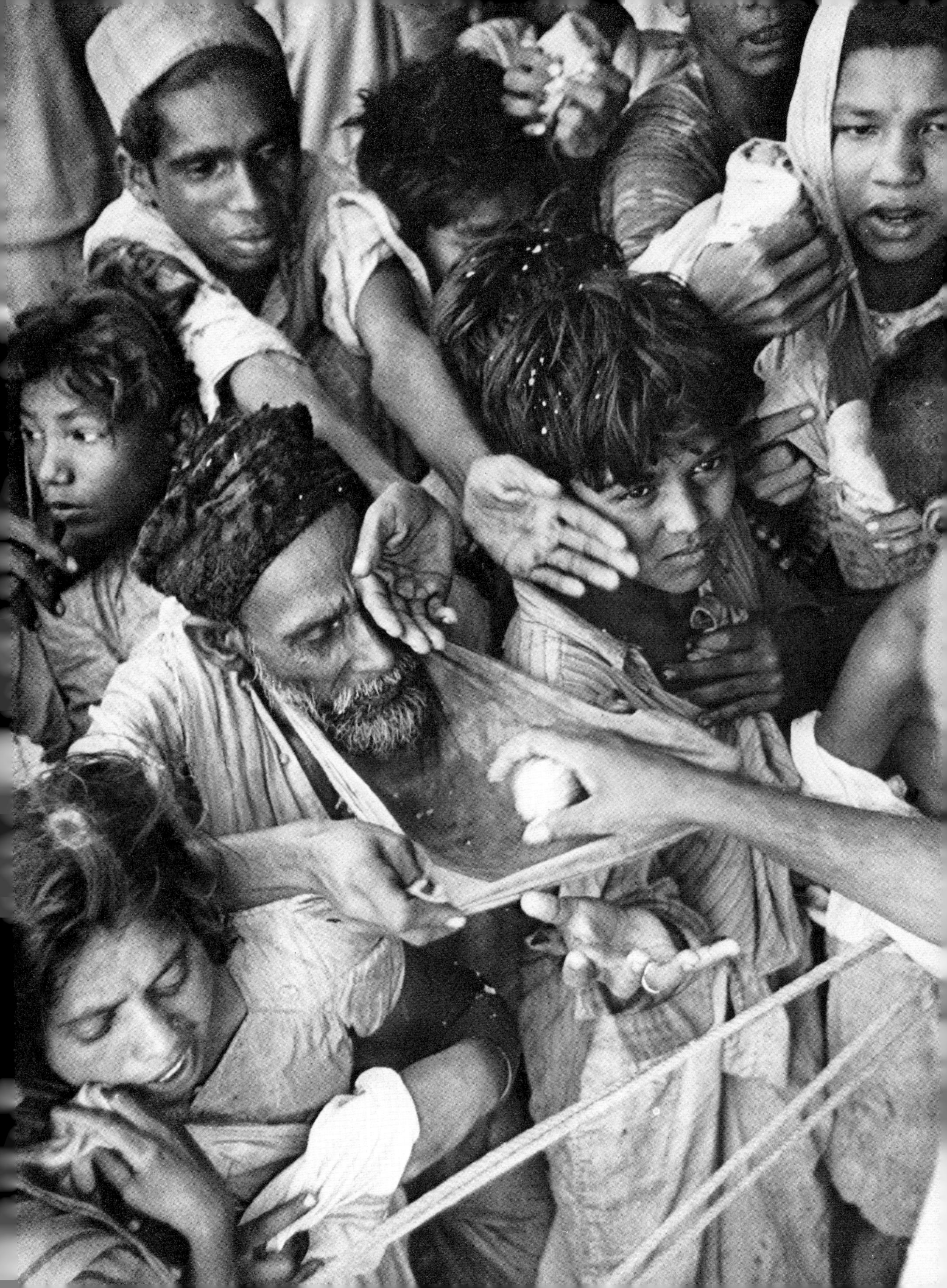

eral deposits, forests and fertile valleys. These resources are developed as part of the national economy and used for international trade. In the same way, each human being has a different physique and uses his physical resources, such as his strength and attractiveness, in his relationships. A nation's resources include the skills of its population, without which the other resources would be underdeveloped and trade with other countries impossible. Similarly, an individual uses skills in his relationships with other people. A nation may belong to economic and political alliances which enable it to protect its access to the overseas resources (such as oil) on which it relies. Equally, many of our relationships protect our supplies of the things we need. For example, children need the security of a good home, and their family relationships help to guarantee this. Friendships are formed which enable us to feel valued – a most important resource, without which we cannot judge our progress. The equivalents of treaties and alliances are found in the world of personal relationships, particularly at work, where we often have to exercise and protect our power over others.

Both the economist and the psycho-economist are concerned with the ways in which resources are used to meet needs, and how people obtain, process and value resources. There are two main differences between economics and psycho-economics. First, there is a difference of scale: one deals with the wealth of nations, the other with the wealth of individuals and small groups of people. Secondly, economics is concerned mainly with money, while the economics of relating are more concerned with invisible commodities, such as knowledge, feelings, skills and perceptions. However, both sciences use similar methods: theory, experiment and observation. Many of the people who have helped to develop psycho-economic theory are social psychologists; others are sociologists, anthropologists and philosophers. Their research enables us to view relationships in a new light, and to reduce the complexity of the subject so that we can learn how to improve our skills with people.

This man does not have the resources with which to maintain an acceptable standard of life.

3 You and Your Relationship Set

You are the centre of a system of relationships

Everybody you know is important to you in a different way. Some people are special because you love them or they love you. Others may be important because they have the power to give you orders and control how much satisfaction you gain from your work. There will also be people who do not fit into either of these categories, but who have a major influence on your way of life – an unfriendly neighbour, perhaps, or even your parents or in-laws. You cannot measure somebody's importance to you, but if certain relationships suddenly ended, it would seriously affect your ability to maintain your chosen standard of life, whether in financial or emotional terms.

Every system of relationships, or 'relationship set', is unique, although each set overlaps with others. Each individual has his own reasons why a particular relationship is important to him. You probably take many of your reasons for granted, and sometimes find other people's surprising when they differ from yours. For example, your parents may be important to you because you love them, and you regard this as natural or inevitable between parents and children; some people do not. You may be married and love the person you are married to; other people have marriages in which they never expected love and never sought it. At work you may never have experienced receiving orders from others; or the reverse may be true.

Some people have a relatively small number of relationships. This may be because they are too young to have made ones of their own, or because they are old and their friends have died. They may lack the opportunity to meet people, as in the case of a single parent on a low income or an immigrant working in a foreign country. Alternatively, they may lack skills, motivation or health, as do people who are shy, lonely or sick. Some people frequently make and break friendships; others keep the same group of friends over a long period. Some systems change faster than others, but the rate of change varies from moment to moment and from individual to individual, as when a person moves to a new job or neighbourhood, or comes into contact with somebody who introduces him to a wide circle of acquaintances. Some systems are more specialized than others: for example, a musician may know only other musicians or a man may know only other men. This often applies to people whose relationships are concerned with power, such as an officer in the police or army, a politician or a business tycoon; and to those whose lives are devoted to caring for others, such as a mother of young children, a kindly grandfather, a dedicated professional care worker (such as a nurse or doctor) or a good neighbour who is always willing to help somebody else with his problems.

Some people find it difficult to see themselves as part of a relationship set. The individual is born into his first set as the result of a relationship

which began before he was conceived. Many of us have never experienced the reality of having no relationship set; we take it for granted that we are never far from people we know, and we are unlikely to question how and why we know them. Even the idea of a relationship may seem artificial and contrived: there are people we know, whom we like or dislike, who come and go, but whom we regard only as something which happens in our own lives, not – except in theory – as people with lives of their own. On the other hand, someone who has experienced loneliness, perhaps as a result of grief, rejection or enforced separation from loved ones, and who has become self-aware as part of the process of recovery, may notice his relationships in detail and be sensitive to his own separate existence and that of others.

Social scientists have studied the way in which we see ourselves and other people. They have found that most of us perceive other people as the source of actions to which we may have to respond, and not as separate individuals – unless we seem likely to form a close relationship with someone. We seem to expect other people to be like ourselves, but with variations, some of which are beyond our comprehension. The most important influence on the way we see others is the way we see ourselves. If somebody's 'self-image' is very different from the way in which he sees other people, he will probably be isolated socially and find it difficult to relate to others. This is because, as numerous studies have shown, we are much more likely to find somebody attractive when we see him as similar to ourselves.

The people in your own set are a vital part of your psycho-economy, for much the same reasons as nations are important to each other: as a market for exports and a source of imports; as potential allies or enemies; and as part of a world economy in which every developed nation is forced to take part if it wishes to stay developed. Similarly, you need to give and receive, make friends, defend yourself where necessary and avoid destructive conflicts. Once you have become aware of your own independent existence (this usually happens in early childhood), you need to grow through the relationships you build for yourself, or you will be unable to reach your full potential.

We each build up a relationship set around us, composed of people who share our aims and objectives. The relationship sets of Hell's Angels (left) and businessmen (right) conform to very different codes of behaviour.

4 You and Your 'Self'

You are the centre of a system of resources

We have already seen that each individual is at the centre of a system of relationships, designed, as far as possible, to meet his needs. The person at the centre has many different resources. Take yourself as an example. First, your body contains 'physical' resources, such as the energy and strength to carry out tasks, and all the internal organs which keep you strong and healthy. Secondly, you have 'behavioural' resources (those related to your mind as opposed to your body), which include such things as feelings, memory, skills and intelligence. Outside your body there are yet more resources consisting of the things you own, such as clothes, money, perhaps a car or a house, and other 'property' resources. Beyond these are resources you do not own, but can use: they belong to the people you know. We can group them together and call them 'social' resources. It is important to remember that, from the point of view of the people you know, 'your' social resources are 'their' physical, behavioural, property and social resources. The part of you which seems to stand in the middle of this system is called the 'self'. In the world of material resources, every nation, organization or system has a leader of some kind, such as the president or managing director of a company. His job is to be aware of the value of all the resources at his disposal and direct the work of the company. In exactly the same way, your 'self' controls your resources.

When a department of your system is running out of resources, you are made aware of this through your feelings. For example, if any of your physical resources are damaged you will probably feel pain. If they are threatened, you will feel discomfort, perhaps even fear or anger. The strength of the feeling gives you a rough indication of the strength of the need, or, in other words, the extent of the threat or damage. When your behavioural resources are not functioning properly, you may experience a sense of failure. For example, you might try to explain something difficult and feel that you lack the necessary skill. Your 'self' regularly checks the value of your property resources. Again, your feelings will tell you if something is missing or not working. Similarly, you will experience changes in the value of your social resources through your feelings towards other people, such as liking or disliking them.

Feelings thus reflect the total value of a person's resources at any one moment. (This is often what we mean by a person's 'mood'.) Sometimes the value appears to be decreasing. This will be experienced in terms of negative feelings, such as pain, fear, anger, misery, unhappiness, stupidity, clumsiness or the feeling of not liking or being disliked. In a depressive illness, the value may decrease so quickly that the individual cannot use any of his resources and withdraws from contact with other people. At other times, the total value of a person's resources seems to be increasing. The result is a positive feeling of some sort, such as pleasure, elation, or simply cheerfulness. When someone falls in love, for example, he may feel that his value is increasing so rapidly that he cannot keep up with the rate of increase. A similar feeling of excitement can occur in a learning situation, when the value of the information is increasing. If it increases very rapidly we may experience sudden moments of insight.

The 'self' often ignores negative feelings. This happens with physical resources when we take no notice of pain or discomfort, and with behavioural resources when we try not to feel inadequate. Sometimes the 'self' ignores negative feelings because it has been trained to do so. A boy may be told not to feel fear, for example, but to be brave 'like a man'; a woman may have been taught to ignore the pain of a menstrual period. Similarly, we may ignore the value of property resources when we are being generous. Many of us believe there are times when we know we are right and have to say so whatever other people think of us. On such occasions we ignore the value of social resources. The 'self' can also ignore positive feelings. For example, somebody may feel comfortable and relaxed, but tell himself that he is being lazy and has work to do. Or he may feel that he has been clever in solving a problem, but suppress the urge to boast, even to himself. If the value of his property rises, he may feel elated but only allow himself to feel satisfaction (perhaps because he considers that the value will rise even higher, and he does not wish to celebrate prematurely). People sometimes suppress their feelings of pride when they meet someone famous, or behave modestly when praised. In order to feel pleasure, many of us have to ignore the feelings of guilt which were instilled in us as part of our early training not to be lazy, boast, celebrate too soon or be snobbish.

A factory worker displays his perception of his own value at a particular moment. His mood is miserable and withdrawn, but it may change even a moment later in a situation in which he can see more point in his job.

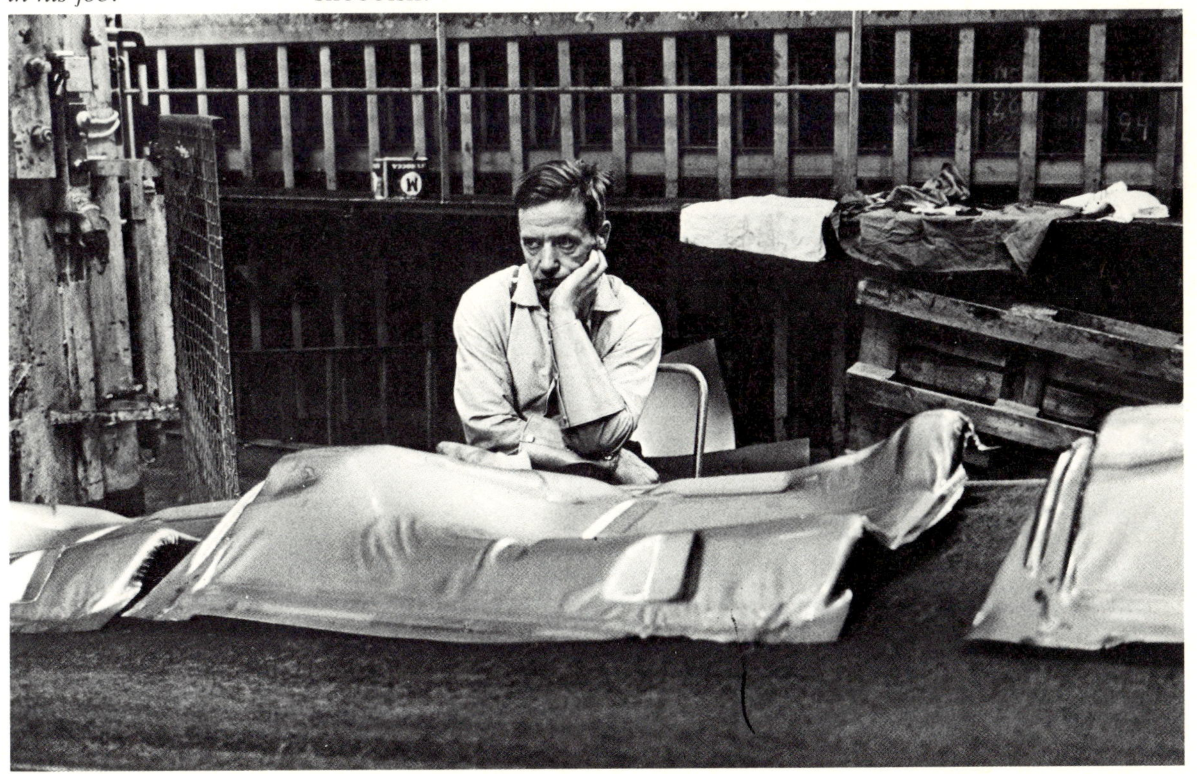

A Soviet soldier takes part in the invasion of Czechoslovakia in 1968. He must ignore any negative feelings he may have in order to carry out his military duty. His impassive face betrays nothing of his inner feelings.

Sometimes we are not sure whether a feeling is good or bad; we need time to see how we feel. Often we do not know how we feel until we know what we want. With physical resources this may happen when we have a vague feeling of unrest, and do not know why until we decide we are hungry. There may also be doubt about the value of behavioural resources, as when we are puzzled about something – a noise, a smell, a taste or something touched or seen, for example – which we cannot identify without concentrating. When we know what we have encountered, we know what to feel. If we are uneasy about whether an object is worth its price, or how somebody feels about us, this shows that the value of property or social resources is uncertain. Worrying is a general uncertainty about values. Many people worry about their own value. Unless the 'self' can accurately judge the value of the resources at its disposal, we have no way of knowing whether we are succeeding or failing in our attempt to maintain our desired standard of life.

5 Freedom of Action

Being free to choose depends on having surplus resources

In economic terms, the difference between the rich and the poor is simply that the rich have more money. Wealth brings freedom of choice because somebody who is rich has a surplus which he is not forced to spend. This is equally true of the psycho-economic system. In all three parts of the system – the self and its resources; each relationship the self has with another self; and the self's full set of relationships – choice depends on having a surplus of resources.

Just as people differ in terms of their economic standing, some people are 'psycho-economically' richer than others. In other words, there is a difference in the value of their physical, behavioural, property and social resources. Many examples could be given; in each case the person who is 'richer' has more freedom of action in using his resources. Physical resources include health: the healthier we are, the more freedom we have to choose what we do with our bodies. Freedom of movement is restricted if we are disabled: we have to rely on other people to take us where we want to go. Physical attractiveness limits our freedom to choose sexual and social partners. The people with the most valuable skills are those who need least help: surplus gives choice.

The same principle applies even to things like time and patience. Suppose you meet somebody you want to get to know. Unless you have spare time, you are forced to let the opportunity go by. The answer is to save up surplus resources (what we call 'making time' for somebody) or make an appointment for later when you know you will have a surplus. Alternatively, suppose you dislike somebody and find you are impatient with him. You can either save up a 'surplus of patience' or a 'surplus of impatience'. For example, you can ensure that you meet him when you are likely to feel relaxed and not under pressure yourself, so that it will be easier not to get annoyed. In other words, you choose to meet him when there is a surplus of patience in your system. Alternatively, you can meet him and try not to show your impatience. You save it up and use it later, perhaps by telling a friend how you felt and letting off steam so that you feel better. If you save up a 'surplus of impatience' you will have more choice in your dealings with the person you dislike: he will like you more and the meeting with him will be more efficient, giving both of you more choice. But when you see your friend later on, you will have less choice: the feelings you have bottled up will have to come out.

There are countless other examples of situations in which a surplus brings extra choice. By contrast, whenever your freedom of choice is restricted, it is because you have an insufficient surplus. Sometimes you are aware of this because of your feelings. However, you may have been trained (or have trained yourself) not to be aware of certain feelings. The principle of 'surplus value' is a fundamental concept in psycho-economics, and underlies all the points made in later sections of the book. Better self-management cannot be achieved without the

NURSERY NEEDS ARE PRIORITY NEED
WHY DEPRIVE THE
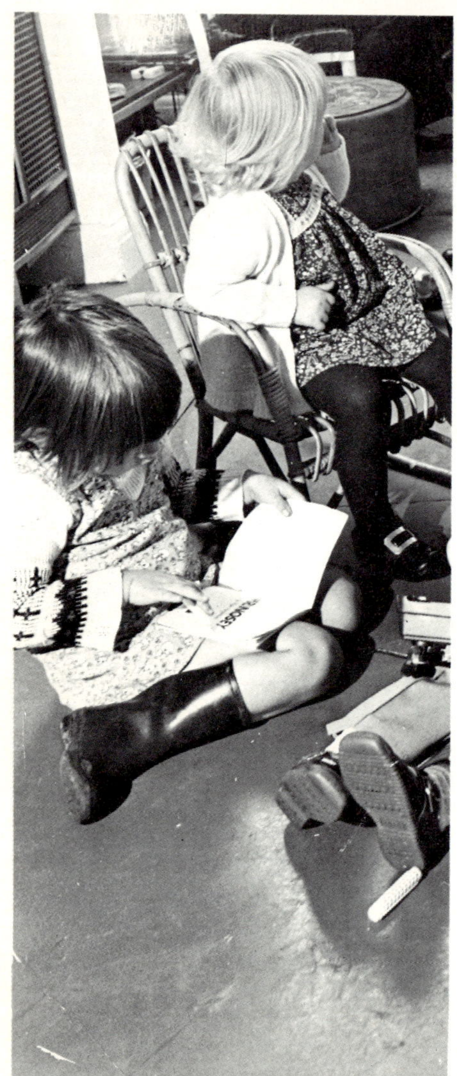

freedom to change yourself and your situation; this in turn depends on having surplus value to spend as you wish in order to get what you need.

'Need' was defined earlier as 'the lack of sufficient resources to sustain an acceptable standard of life'. In order to explain how we improve our standards, we need to understand the difference between a luxury and a necessity. Suppose you see a car which looks attractive. If you cannot afford it, you cannot buy it and it will probably seem a luxury. If you cannot afford *not* to buy it, it is a necessity. Whether we can afford something, or cannot afford to do without it, depends on what we already have. Necessities keep us going in the manner to which we have become accustomed; they enable us to maintain, but not improve, an acceptable standard. Luxuries are things which improve our existing standard of life. When we obtain them, we raise our standard and can change our ideas about what is acceptable. However, we can only do this if we have a surplus.

The activities of each member of the group emphasize a particular stage in the use of some of the available resources. (top right) The placards show the adults' ***identification*** *with a political objective. (top left) The small boy emphasizes his need for* ***security*** *from the two adults. (below left) A small girl looks around, uncertain of her* ***commitment*** *to any activity and displaying a need for* ***security****, while beside her another girl is absorbed in her* ***commitment*** *to reading a book. (below right) The children indicate* ***specialization*** *as they explore the potential of their toys. Through all this varied activity the* ***achievement*** *of the group is to illustrate its point about the need for nursery education.*

You improve your standard of life by obtaining luxuries which then become necessities

If you have no surplus value in your system, you have no freedom of action. Once you have a surplus, you have a choice: you can either save it and maintain your present standard of life, or spend it on improvements. In order to illustrate how people use a surplus to increase their standard of life, we will return to the example of the car. This will then be used to explain what happens in the case of non-material resources.

Suppose you regard a car as a luxury you can barely afford. At this stage you say you 'want' a car, meaning that you would like one but are unlikely to be able to afford it. The next step is to save up for one. This may take some time, depending on how much you earn and how badly you want the car. It still seems a luxury and your ideas as to which car you want will probably be rather general, such as small or big, two-door or four-door, second-hand or new. But when you have made sure of enough money you can identify a specific car, the one you want to own. Imagine that you look around at what is on sale, buy the car which appeals to you most from the range available at the price you can afford, and then drive it away. So far you have decided that you want a car; you have made sure you have the means to buy one; and you have spent your money, committing yourself to the particular car which you now own. As we shall see, these stages in acquiring a new resource always occur, no matter what the resource is. They are known as the 'identification', 'security' and 'commitment' stages.

Now that you own a car, you begin to explore all the things you can do which were not possible before. You can drive to the supermarket and buy in bulk because the goods are easier to carry. You can drive to work, thus saving time and having more freedom to choose when you leave home in the morning. You can take the car on holidays, visit family and friends more easily, and stay longer when you get there because you are not dependent on other people to take you home. The car brings a new freedom to your life, and you enjoy the sense of excitement this gives you. Throughout this stage the car is 'special',

A moment of withdrawal in a busy family. The mother needs to collect a surplus of resources to share with her children.

something which you own and which is not the same as anybody else's. While the novelty lasts, you test the car in order to discover every aspect of its special status and find out what you can and cannot do with it. This is the 'specialization' stage.

Eventually the car turns into a necessity, rather than a luxury. Now that you can drive to the supermarket, you alter your routine and take it for granted that shopping means driving there once a month, say, instead of every week. Your new habit of leaving home later for work also becomes incorporated into the pattern of your life, so that you forget what it was like before you had the car. If it fails to start one morning, you curse instead of doing what you did before: catch the train without even thinking about it. Your family and friends may expect to see you regularly every week, instead of only seeing you occasionally when you could spare the train fare. They, too, forget the old days when you had to leave to catch the last train, and are surprised if you leave early. This is the final, or 'achievement', stage in acquiring the car: you have reached the new standard you once saw as an objective. What was a luxury in terms of your old standard of life is now a necessity to support your new one. The need has been replaced by a resource. Although we have taken the example of a car here, you will be able to think of many other similar instances.

The same five stages are involved in any situation in which you acquire a resource, even if this process lasts only a few seconds. Suppose you want something to write with, perhaps to fill out a cheque. You look around in frustration, unable for the moment to maintain your desired standard of life. You see a pen and spend some of your surplus energy on securing the means to use it: perhaps you ask somebody to lend it to you or you just pick it up from a desk. Now you have committed yourself to using that particular pen, you begin to see what it will do. Perhaps it runs out of ink and is difficult to hold, so that your writing is below your usual standard. But suppose it is so good that you enjoy writing with it. It makes writing a pleasure, not a chore, because of its special design. You begin to examine it more closely. Having identified the resource you need, secured it and committed yourself to using it, you have now reached the 'specialization' stage. The final, or 'achievement', stage is to keep the pen you at first only 'wanted', because you now 'need' one like that. Alternatively, you may go and buy one for yourself, and repeat the same five stages. These stages in the acquisition of a resource were first discovered by psychologist Abraham Maslow. So far, we have considered them only in terms of material resources. However, they apply equally to non-material resources.

Changing values: five stages in the acquisition and loss of resources

You can improve your surplus value by altering the whole of your relationship set, changing only some of your relationships or changing yourself. In order to do any of these, you must acquire non-material resources; whatever you do to obtain them, you will go through the same five-stage pattern.

Suppose you decide to change the whole of your relationship set by cutting yourself off from everybody you know and moving to a new location. The first step is to identify the need: in this case, the need to move to a new place. Next you have to make sure you can go. You will need money to travel and you cannot calculate how much unless you know where you are going. So in order to secure the means, you have to commit yourself to a particular objective. After the commitment stage, the next one cannot be reached until you have explored the possibilities of the life offered by the new area. Some people will be more willing than others to be your friends. As you concentrate on them, the specialization stage starts and you begin to develop a new set of relationships. Soon you will have attained your objective.

Drastic action like changing a whole relationship set may be unnecessary unless people emigrate, or become refugees as a result of a political, social or economic disaster. We may have neighbours who have been in this position; children who are fostered or adopted also go through much the same process. Sometimes people only partially change their relationship sets, as when a person moves to a new job in a strange area but keeps in touch with his old friends, or when a married person accompanies a spouse to a new district. Under these circumstances, the individual has to build his new relationships one by one. He identifies himself to somebody, shows that he is not a threat to him (thus securing the means to develop the relationship), commits himself to becoming a good friend or a good neighbour and then uses his special, individual qualities to maintain the relationship until both people forget that they were once strangers.

Moreover, within the development of each individual relationship, the same five stages are repeated many times. The 'identification' stage of getting to know somebody involves constant reassessment of the kind of person he is. It will proceed fastest where both sides feel secure because they already have things in common, and where they can secure a surplus of time, patience and skill which can be shared. If one feels threatened by the other, the process slows down and may stop. The things they can do better than one another, but which they both need, become apparent; they develop their commitment to the friendship by doing favours and returning them. They may also find that each is a specialist on a particular topic, and they can share their skills. At the 'achievement' stage, each person comes to have a special status for the other, which defines precisely how much, and in what ways, they like or dislike each other. This can change every time they please or disappoint one another.

The development of the 'self' also passes through the same five stages. Self-realization occurs when you extend your personality: you identify ways of becoming the sort of person you want to be. You cannot do this unless you feel at ease with yourself, and secure enough to use any new insights which will arise. You also have to feel committed to changing yourself. Self-realization means you will find a new speciality, something only you are good at in a particular way. Once you have learned a new skill, you tend to forget all the difficulties you went through in learning it and become dependent upon the wider range of choice made available. Some stages may take a long time; others are over very quickly. Success depends upon having this wider choice by gaining new resources and adding to your own value; failure and loss mean that your choice is non-existent. You are forced to adopt a lower standard than the one you wanted.

The sequence of stages by which we acquire resources occurs in reverse order when we lose them. Suppose you have two cars, but cannot any longer afford to keep them both. Until then you have taken for granted the wider choice afforded by having the second car; now you have to manage without it. Instead of seeing the car as a need, you see it as a luxury once more – but one you cannot afford. Where you were once excited you are disappointed, and instead of finding the car special, you think of all the other things you would rather have. Next, you get rid of the car (the reverse of buying it). Once it no longer belongs to you the commitment fades, and you begin to persuade yourself that you did not want it anyway. Eventually you will probably forget you ever had it. The loss of the resource thus follows five stages: you lose the choice the car gave you, the car is therefore no longer special; you are no longer committed to keeping it and therefore lose ownership; you secure the money instead of the car, and thus convert it from something you once needed into something you no longer need.

A similar sequence can be seen when a relationship ends. Our grief works through a phase of anger and frustration, disappointment and misery, the more intense if we were very dependent upon the person we have lost. We are facing up to the fact that we have no choice. Next we remember all the special qualities of the person and begin to realize that we will have to manage without them. We slowly realize that we are no longer committed. Nor are we secure in the same way. We complete the process of mourning by reaching the stage at which our own identity has been successfully readjusted, and we are a different kind of person. We may tell ourselves that it was all for the best anyway. The process can take months or years, or may never be completed.

6 You and Your Relationships

How we use our social resources

People with no surplus resources cannot make relationships. This has been demonstrated by anthropological studies of people living in extreme poverty. The psycho-economic value of our relationships can therefore be seen in terms of surplus value. There are three things we can do to our own, or someone else's, surplus value: increase it, maintain it or reduce it. The kind of relationship we can have with somebody depends on which of these three things we do, and how the other person's value is affected as a result. This is more obvious if we begin by looking at property resources. First, let us examine what happens when a valuable object changes hands as part of a relationship.

In order to acquire something valuable, you can take it by force, buy it or be given it. To take it by force, one person has to be more powerful than the other. The result will be an increase in the surplus value of the 'taker' and a corresponding decrease in that of the original owner. If you buy something, however, the value of your surplus stays the same, because you have exchanged the money you saved for an object of the same value. The vendor's surplus value has also stayed the same as it was before the transaction, although he now has money to the same value as the object. In psycho-economic terms, the value of the object (or of any other resource) is the extent to which it meets a person's needs. Even if the other person has made a profit and you have a bargain, you are both exactly meeting your needs and your surpluses stay the same. Thirdly, you can be given the object as a present. From the 'giver's' point of view, if the present is meant as a free gift, with no strings attached and no obligations incurred, he has tried to increase your surplus resources without counting the cost to himself.

The three types of relationships implied by these different situations are power, trading and loving relationships. In a power relationship one person's actions lower the value of the other person's surplus. At the end of a trading relationship, both people end up with the value they started with. In a loving relationship one person increases the other person's surplus without counting the cost to himself.

Power relationships: making a profit

If two people try to take from each other, the person who is stronger or more powerful will succeed. If neither is stronger there is a stalemate, and the pair are locked in a permanent struggle. Trials of strength are an important feature of relationships; they occur whenever both sides are trying to 'take' in order to obtain a surplus. If somebody is trying to take away your resources you have to defend them, possibly by attacking him. The more important these resources seem to you, the more aggressive you are likely to be. Power relationships are commonly characterized by aggressive or defensive behaviour. Sometimes, however, it is obvious that if a struggle took place, one person would lose

A dispute over who has the most power: the situation can only be resolved by give-and-take.

because he is weaker. The stronger person clearly has the advantage: he has a larger or more readily available surplus of resources, and can survive a longer struggle. So the weaker person shows submissive behaviour. In our culture this often takes the form of childlike facial expressions or body movements, such as widening the eyes and looking hurt, or holding the hands in a foetal position and moving the head to one side. (This movement is reminiscent of the way a baby turns its head by reflex action when lying on its back; the movement disappears between sixteen and twenty weeks after birth.)

Many power relationships occur as part of our membership of organized groups. It has long been recognized by social scientists that people organize themselves into groups both to create surplus resources and to protect them. In any such group the people who have most power are those with most freedom of action. They maintain their power by restricting the freedom of choice of other members (those with lower status). The surplus created by a group is shared out among the members, not according to how much work is done by each member, but according to who has most power. Most disputes are avoided by the use of specialized behaviour designed to trigger off submission, such as uniforms which indicate rank, or the status symbols of larger desks, bigger cars or louder voices. Other disputes tend to be settled by 'give-and-take', a form of trading relationship which leaves both sides with the power with which they began.

Power relationships are also indicated by the presence of duties. These are governed by rules which mean that one person restricts his freedom of action, either voluntarily or because he will be punished if he does not. This kind of power relationship usually involves a formal contract. However, this is not always true. For example, parents often undertake ill-defined family duties because otherwise they will feel guilty. An action which begins as a gift can easily become a duty if other people take it for granted and start to expect it. In some marriages everything the spouse does becomes a duty; there is nothing left to give as a free gift, and expressions of love become meaningless.

Power relationships differ from trading and loving relationships in that they result in a profit on one side and a loss on the other. Whenever you make a psycho-economic gain at the cost of somebody else's surplus (or make a loss which somebody else counts as a profit), the relationship is based on power. Sometimes, for example, you feel better, safer, more certain or less uncomfortable because somebody else feels worse. (Or you may feel worse because he feels better.) However, it is not always easy to see whether a gain or a loss is being counted. For example, we may unwittingly patronize somebody, and because we are not counting our profit, fail to recognize that he is counting his loss.

Trading relationships: breaking even

Relationships often involve 'give-and-take'. This means that the two people concerned reach a compromise, so that neither loses. In psycho-economic terms, the resources on both sides keep the same relative value as a result of a particular transaction. An example will help to illustrate this point.

Suppose two people work in the same room, but have separate desks. One person likes to work with the radio playing, the other dislikes the radio. If they both act as 'takers', there will be conflict. The person who dislikes the radio feels that his accustomed standard of life is threatened, since he cannot concentrate on his work, so he switches the radio off. The one who likes the radio also feels threatened; he finds the music helps him to concentrate. His colleague is apparently trying to stop him from working, so he switches on the radio and puts it on his desk. In order to turn it off, the other person will now have to trespass onto private territory, and, in effect, attack somebody else's property. The stage is set for an escalation of the conflict.

Similar minor conflicts occur in many relationships and can create an 'atmosphere', with hostile feelings and aggression affecting the work or play, both of the people concerned and the group to which they belong. The solution to the problem is 'give-and-take'. This means that the two combatants find a solution which threatens neither of them. For example, the person with the radio can turn down the volume at the request of his colleague. If he does so, his surplus of resources – the extra noise he likes, which gives him greater choice in the way he works – is reduced. But his colleague still has to work in spite of the radio, so his surplus of resources – the silence he prefers – is also reduced.

A London traffic warden and a motorist who has committed a parking offence. Although the driver is aware that he is likely to lose the argument, he attempts to negotiate and so change the power relationship into a trading relationship.

Through a compromise they both give up equal amounts of spare resources. But they also gain equally by avoiding a quarrel which would cost time and energy, and which one of them would lose. By reaching a compromise they show that they like each other well enough not to fight. The gains and losses are equal on both sides. Neither wins and neither is defeated.

Give-and-take enables people to resolve conflicts without either person ending up with resources of a lower value. To reach this solution, you must first recognize that you have spare resources. (This may not be easy. You may be spending them all on being angry.) Even then, the skills you need can be considerable. You must be able to persuade your antagonist that he can meet his own need for choice without attacking yours. It is often necessary to take the initiative by proposing a solution in which you lose, too, but where your loss is equal to his. In fact neither of you lose if you avoid a fight.

On the other hand, you may have reasons for wanting open conflict. These may be unconscious reasons. For example, you may still be feeling resentful about something said to you a few days ago and which you thought you had forgotten; it may make you want to hurt the other person so that you feel better. Or you may dislike someone because you think he is greedy or thoughtless, because he is a certain 'type' of person or because you cannot understand why he behaves in this way. Although you cannot be compelled to like somebody, it is often impossible to reach a compromise unless you understand your own unconscious reasons for not liking him – and his reasons for attacking you.

Many relationships in which one person gives and the other takes involve no conflict. They are known as 'buy-and-sell' situations. When one person buys something from another, they exchange resources of equal value. One of them gives up goods to a certain value and receives money in return; the other gives up money and receives goods to that value. When two people bargain or haggle, they are indulging in give-and-take. The agreed price suits them both.

Some features of buying-and-selling are so obvious that we take them for granted, yet they help us to understand give-and-take. In most straightforward selling at a shop or market, the prices of goods are clearly marked. This avoids possible conflict when a shopper might expect to pay less than the seller wants. Similarly, conflict is often avoided when a person shows clearly how he evaluates non-material resources. For example, if we make sure that our intentions towards other people and what we expect of them are clear and consistent, they feel less threatened.

Loving relationships: not counting the cost

Two people can give to each other and not count the cost. In psycho-economic terms, they both gain in value. Some examples will show the variety of such relationships. Suppose a stranger is lost and asks a local resident for directions. They are freely given, and the stranger thanks the resident and goes on his way. The resident does not give directions in order to receive thanks. Nor is the stranger forced to show gratitude. He loses nothing if he merely leaves without speaking. In this situation, the free gifts of information and thanks constitute an act of *politeness* on both sides.

A keen amateur gardener meets a new neighbour, who admires his flowers. The gardener cuts a selection and makes a gift of them. The neighbour accepts them and shows pleasure. This is probably an act of *friendliness*, rather than politeness. The flowers are a source of pride to the gardener, and he clearly values them. By showing that he values them equally, the neighbour gives pleasure to the gardener. If neither counts the cost of giving flowers, or giving pleasure, both gain.

A five-year-old child is finding it difficult to fasten his coat. His mother could fasten the coat for him, but realizes that this would deprive him of a minor, but important, achievement. She gives him

A caring gesture in which affection is given and received. The girl leans across to examine the man's pendant; he looks with her but does not touch. Neither of them counts the cost of the action.

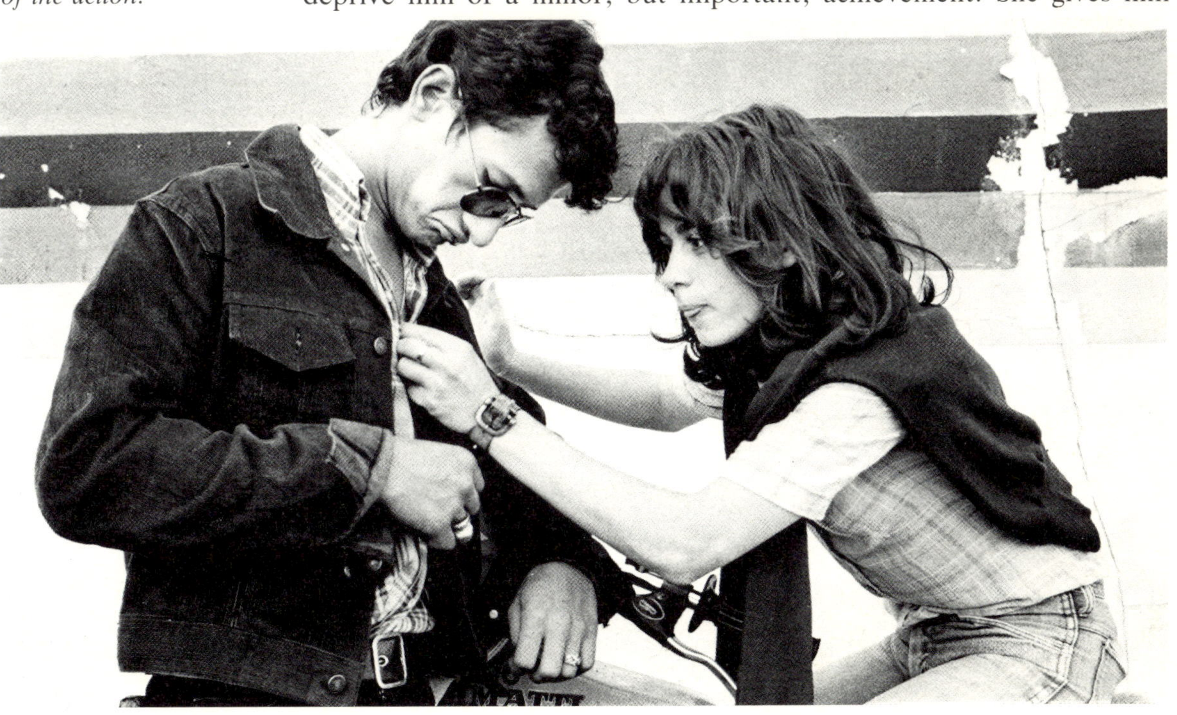

time and shows patience. In doing so, she runs the risk of being late to collect her other child from school. In effect, she has given the younger child a free gift. (Her action was not based on the calculation that it would enable him to grow up more quickly so that he would be less of a nuisance.) This is a *caring* relationship.

Two lovers meet and kiss. They hold each other close and enjoy pleasure through intimate contact. Each tries to kiss and hug so that they will both experience pleasure, not in order to give or receive a gift of equal value. This is intimacy freely given, and the relationship is one of *love*.

It is often difficult to decide where 'politeness' ends and 'friendliness' begins. No precise definition can be given for any of the situations described above. Being polite usually means that the resources freely given are of low value to the donor. Being friendly usually means that the resource which is given has a slightly higher value than politeness demands. It may be either polite or friendly to introduce one of your friends to another. It depends on what might be gained by your friends and lost by you.

In a caring situation, we give away more than would be required if we simply wanted to be friendly. The mother in the example above could have gently told her child to hurry, or she could have used her superior skills and fastened the coat herself. Both actions would have been friendly, but would have deprived the child of a sense of achievement. Many similar examples of caring could be given. For instance, letting somebody take a risk with your property and not counting your anxiety; or allowing others to evaluate your skill, as when you trust a friend to criticize you, no matter how harshly. People also show they care about others by giving physical pleasure, such as a warm embrace or a caress. For most people, the physical resource of the highest value is their capacity for orgasm. In our society this is usually only given freely to those we love most.

All these examples of free gifts show variations in the value of the gift as far as the giver is concerned. The value of things given in return also counts, but not in all cases. Being polite costs very little, so we expect politeness to be returned in equal measure. The same applies to friendly gifts, and to some ways of showing that we care. In our own culture, the higher the value of the gift, the more loving it is not to expect a return. Caring usually means that the giver would prefer to receive equal care or an equal gift of pleasure, but is not distressed if what he gives is not matched by what he receives. If somebody does not return a 'caring' smile, for example, this does not necessarily mean you will cease to care about him. However, loving is only possible as a free gift. In our love relationships we give with no thought of receiving equal love in return.

Psycho-economic analysis cannot be precise about where politeness ends and friendliness begins, or about how caring and loving differ. Nevertheless, it shows that the cost of what is freely given determines how we categorize the relationship, and that where loving and caring are involved, the cost is irrelevant to the giver. We can also see that such behaviour depends on our having something to give. Without a surplus, not even politeness is possible. Caring and loving require the largest surplus.

7 You and Your Resources

Taking stock of the system

As the designer of your relationships, you control a resource system which has an internal and an external economy. The internal economy consists of your body (your physical resources) and what it can do (your behavioural resources). The external economy consists of your property and social resources. It is time to take stock of your system and see how you can achieve better self-management. The first step is to look more closely at the value of the resources available to you.

The purpose of the economic system is to encourage us to increase the value of the things we own. We live in an acquisitive and materialistic world, where surpluses are generated by converting labour into cash, to be spent on the products of other people's labour. Our economic activities are generally of two kinds: obtaining a surplus of money, and spending that surplus to improve our standard of living. However, this is a narrow view of our lives. Alongside this system there is the psycho-economic system. Its purpose is to increase the whole value of the person, thus obtaining a surplus of physical, behavioural and social wealth rather than one of property. This surplus is then spent on relationships to improve our standard of life.

When our standard of life is good, we feel healthy, we value our skills, we enjoy the things we own and we are able to love our friends freely. We are in charge of our own internal resources and can use them either to maintain the kind of life with which we are content, or to make it more interesting by saving and spending surpluses in order to achieve a higher standard. If attacked, we can defend ourselves.

When our standard of life is poor, we have more negative than positive feelings. We fail to achieve what we want, and we cannot accept our present level of achievement. We feel negatively about our physical resources, and regard our skills as insufficient. We own things without enjoying them to the full, and we cannot obtain those we think we might enjoy. We have difficulty in giving and receiving love. Most of our time is spent grudgingly on things we do not want to do. We cannot defend ourselves without attacking others; we feel unsafe unless we are constantly defended.

We often function adequately in economic terms, whether or not our psycho-economy is healthy. However, we cannot function adequately in the psycho-economy unless we have, or seem likely to obtain, a surplus of positive feelings. This does not mean to say that the objective is always to be happy. Psycho-economic growth is often risky and painful. It may entail changing the relationships which surround us, or even changing ourselves. Nor can we ever be totally in charge of our own psycho-economy. Events beyond our control – the loss of, or injury to, people we love, natural disasters and geopolitical conflicts – all affect us and we must adapt to the consequences.

Nevertheless, we already have a large measure of control over our internal economies. We could probably be more in charge of them, and

A market stall in Ghana. The stall-keeper increases the economic value of her wares by adding psycho-economic value in her display of good humour.

use the resources they contain more efficiently. Parts of ourself which are undervalued and therefore not being used can be looked at again, and a new use found for them. We are probably wasting energy by containing negative feelings; or we may have been trained to ignore feelings, thus preventing us from using sections of our economies which had no value when we were children, but can now take on a new value. Negative feelings occur normally as part of the process of adaptation because deciding what we want also means deciding what we do not want and knowing what we can do means correctly evaluating the things we cannot do.

Negative feelings sometimes arise, not from adaptive behaviour, but as a consequence of maladaptive behaviour. Suppose you enjoy painting but think you are not very good at art. As a result, you do not paint as often as you would like, and hide your pictures because you are certain they will be criticized. Or perhaps you enjoy making up tunes but feel you are no good at music. As a result, you never tell other people that you enjoy composing, because they will probably expect more from you than you can deliver. Such types of behaviour are maladaptive: you end up doing something in a particular way (or not doing it at all) because you are adapting to what you imagine other people's reactions will be, and not to what they really are. You are anticipating a reaction which never takes place.

Maladaptive behaviour is the result of the way in which we learn a skill. We adapt to the circumstances at the time, and then continue to perform in the same way even when they have changed. A child who enjoys painting may find that his teacher or parent never likes the results. One who makes up tunes may offend the adults around him. They will be pleased if the child fails, so the child tries to please them by failing. What the child saw as a loving relationship was a power relationship to the adult. Long after this power has ceased and the child has become an adult, he declares that he is no good at art or music.

We all do things unconsciously to please people who are no longer there, or to take account of events which have not happened and never will because the circumstances have changed. We are responding to what is called the 'hidden agenda', the things we have to do but do not know why we have to do them. These unconscious needs may prevent us from obtaining the full value of our resources. In the next few chapters this idea is examined in more detail.

A helping mother. In situations like this, children learn a wide variety of attitudes and skills. Here the little girl is trusted with a sharp knife and accepts the kitchen as a warm, friendly place where people co-operate.

8 Early Relationships

Children depend on their parents' resources

When a child is conceived, two sets of resources are joined together, physical and behavioural. The sperm and the ovum are physical resources, and if the pregnancy proceeds these cells will grow into a human body. Throughout its life in the womb, the foetus is dependent upon the physical resources of the mother; her health mainly determines the ability of her body to support the pregnancy. The foetus is also dependent upon the mother's behavioural resources: her ability to use her skills, intelligence, memory, and so on, to help her maintain the standard of life she wants for herself and her baby. Her property supports both of them: if she has warm clothes, a safe place to live, regular supplies of food, and all the other tangible resources which make her capable of maintaining a good standard of life, the baby will come to less harm and develop better. The quality of her social resources also affects her baby, for she will need support of many kinds from family and friends while she is pregnant. In countries where physical, behavioural, property and social resources are in short supply, the infant mortality rate is very much higher than in rich countries.

In our society, most babies are born to women who are married and live with their husbands. Conception therefore is not only the joining together of the physical resources of two people; it takes place within a pool of surplus resources created by two individuals who have formed a lasting psycho-economic unit. A husband and wife share each other's physical resources every time they touch each other or make love. They rely upon each other's resources of skill, intelligence and information, in other words, all their behavioural resources. They own property jointly and tend to have the same friends, as well as being part of the same family groups (the ones into which they married as well as those

Family closeness: a mother talks to her baby. They share each other's resources with no self-conscious awareness of ownership.

Left to himself, this deprived child in Kampuchea can only use the limited resources available to him. He has managed to find something to play with, through which he can learn about the properties of his environment.

into which they were born).

The baby is born into the psycho-economic system of its mother, and usually that of its father, too. Throughout pregnancy, however, although the foetus benefits from all the resources of its parents, it receives this benefit directly through being physically part of its mother. It has no resources of its own which it can control, and cannot vary its standard of life by its own actions. All it can do is react to variations in its mother's standard of life. Once the baby is born, however, its physical resources slowly start to become its own. As it grows, it also begins to collect a surplus of behavioural, property and social resources. Some of this surplus is freely given, as the result of love relationships between the baby and other people: its family, friends of the family, and people such as neighbours, doctors and nurses, and even strangers who stop to admire the baby in its pram. Any act of politeness, friendliness, caring or love is a gift of free resources to the baby, and will be used to the extent that the baby is able to act on its own behalf.

The child receives free gifts to add to his surplus, but he also gains resources for himself through trading and power relationships. This may not be immediately obvious, but parents will be familiar with many situations in which there is a power struggle between them and their children, or between different children. For example, when a baby cries because it is hungry, some cries are interpreted as a need to be fed, others as 'wanting' to be fed. In other words, the mother often has to decide whether it must be fed at once or can be left for a short time.

Suppose the mother hears her baby cry, but does not immediately pick it up and feed it. Each cry is a statement of want – a demand for choice, rather than an expression of need. However, the baby can only obtain what it wants when the mother provides it. Her own surplus resources are limited: she may be short of time, patience, love or skill. At that moment, for example, she may be frustrated by the need to do

A mother comforts her baby. While they communicate they will both react to subtle variations in the amount of contact.

something in a hurry which she cannot manage because her skills are not as great as she would wish, or she may have other children who are making demands on her spare love. If the baby continues to cry, it will probably modify the noise it makes so that it sounds more desperate, perhaps hungrier or angrier. Its own choice about when it will be fed has already been limited, and it has cut down its wants to take more account of what its mother can afford to give it. This phase shows a kind of bargaining – the start of give-and-take – and is a trading relationship. Suppose the mother attends to the baby only when the cries change from angry to tired. She has won a power struggle, although she may be unaware of this; the baby has partly succeeded in getting what it wants and partly failed. A baby which always wins power struggles is often called a 'spoiled' child. Power struggles, however minor, begin at birth. Even the way a mother and her baby find the most comfortable positions for feeding and changing is a trading relationship, because each is learning to co-operate with the other. Some babies get their way more often than the mother; some never win.

Each of us is different, simply because we have different resources available to us from moment to moment throughout our lives. These differences are often greater between members of different families, because behaviour becomes specialized according to the resources which are most immediately available. Some of these resources are genetic in origin, the free gift of a highly specialized set of cells with a unique chromosome structure. Others, perhaps the majority, are social in origin and form the environmental pool of resources into which the baby is born. Children from the same family tend to be alike because they use many of the same resources.

Early in childhood the baby becomes aware of its existence as an independent being, capable of controlling its own resources. It develops a 'self' which can begin to exercise more choice, obtain what it wants, use it to expand choice even further, and then become dependent on these choices so that it has new needs. How it learns to do this is limited by the opportunities available at the time.

Two adults try to teach a small child to accept a dog as a friendly, cuddly creature.

9 The Hidden Agenda

Hidden reasons which help us decide what is acceptable to us

A group of students were asked to write down six adjectives which described the families they grew up in. More than half of them began the list with words like 'caring', 'loving' or 'protective'. One list began with 'large', one with 'clean' and another with 'clever'. It was immediately apparent that one student had grown up in a family which tended to over-react to the accusation of being dirty, and another student was sensitive to family size. The student who wrote 'clever' at the top of his list was probably designing his life so as to avoid at all costs being seen as stupid.

What was not immediately apparent was that the majority were also from families which had probably over-reacted. They knew they were cared for, loved and protected, but since they accepted this as normal, they overlooked the fact that it was also a reaction to a struggle of some kind within their families. The special feature of their families was that they cared. Why did this seem so important to them? Further questioning revealed that those whose families were reported as 'caring' had parents who fought with each other, but then took special care to show that they still 'loved' their children. In several cases, the parents had nearly broken up, but stayed together for the sake of the children. Two students who described their families as 'protective' added that they meant 'over-protective': their parents had deliberately shielded them from problems, and they had felt unprepared for adult life.

Children cannot be insulated from the difficulties which their parents face. Like all adults, parents run out of love, patience and understanding from time to time. These difficulties set the scene for the skills their children learn. However, the child knows his own family best. The circumstances he encounters there seem to be normal because he has no way of knowing otherwise. The skills he acquires seem to be like those of everyone else. It is only when he examines these skills in later life that he realizes that he may still be responding to special features in his own family which were not as common as he had assumed. Once we have attained a skill, we forget the difficulties we went through to acquire it, just as we forget the identification, security, commitment and specialization stages when we turn something we need into something we take for granted. As a result, we all incorporate unremembered factors into the ways we respond to people and situations. These factors are called the 'hidden agenda'.

In the case of the students above, many were working hard to be caring, loving and protective. In fact, they were working harder than most people, since they were all students on a refresher course for community nurses. The nurse who saw her family as 'large' had become particularly interested in family planning. This was not, she said, because it would help to prevent large families. She saw it, rather, as a response to the difficulties some mothers have in caring equally for all their children, even when some are unwanted. She had understood her own hidden agenda, for she now recognized that, as the youngest of six children, she had started life as an unwanted pregnancy and then become a much loved baby.

A person's hidden agenda plays a large part in determining the standard of life he finds acceptable. This usually begins as what is acceptable to the family he was born into. In adult life, it is apparent as an avoidance of what he was taught to regard as unacceptable when he was a child. Learning not to be the sort of person your parents dislike is often a painful experience. Many families punish unacceptable behaviour severely; either by corporal punishment or by banishing the child from the family for what to the adult is a short period, but seems interminable to a young child. Once the lesson has been learned, the pain and distress are often forgotten. The child does not repeat the behaviour, and will be just as intolerant as his parents when other people behave in the same way.

Throughout childhood and adolescence, the individual is building up his own stock of resources and learning how to manage them for

Hidden agenda. (above) The adult protests at being accused of unacceptable behaviour, using a response she learned in childhood. (below) The child on the left learns to encourage, but not to interfere, while the child on the right learns self-sufficiency. Such lessons influence the way we reject or accept other people's views in later life.

Against the background of urban warfare in Belfast, Northern Ireland, children are unconsciously absorbing many facets of the world around them. Such experiences will form part of their identity for the rest of their lives.

himself. He develops an identity of his own, as a result of power, trading and loving relationships with the members of his family, his teachers, class-mates, neighbours and friends. The psychologist Alfred Adler has suggested that the power relationships in a family tend to give more authority to the eldest, or only, child than to the second or younger children. Being the eldest is often a form of identity as important as one's name. A child is often introduced as the 'eldest girl' or the 'eldest son'. Childhood features of identity often last all one's life.

The growing child also learns how to defend himself, by producing submissive behaviour, learning to bargain or attacking others before he can be attacked. He may form alliances with one parent against the other, manipulating their lack of unity to his own advantage. Or he may grow up in a family where defence is never necessary, and in later life wonder why he is so vulnerable. The child also learns how to belong to a family, using his own family as the pattern, and decides in what ways he is special or ordinary. These also are lessons learned for life. We all learn these skills the hard way – by experience – and then forget we have them. As adults we take them for granted, but they leave an indelible stamp upon the way we evaluate our own resources and use them in our relationships.

10 Physical Resources

Your relationships are affected by how you value your body

Perhaps you do not think about your body very often. However, many psychologists believe that the way in which you evaluate it has a profound effect on the way you make relationships. There is a psycho-economic basis for this belief. Your body contains all your physical resources and can therefore act as part of somebody else's social resources. If you think somebody is stronger or more attractive than you are, you are less likely to see him as an equal, or to expect a close relationship to develop between you.

A girl unselfconsciously displays her confidence in her sexuality and attractiveness.

A crowd watches a topless dancer. Notice the wide range of expressions shown by the men, some approving, some disapproving, and many showing uncertainty. These expressions probably reflect their feelings about their own sexuality.

Physical resources often form part of the hidden agenda. In the psycho-economy, the value of a resource is equal to the extent to which somebody needs it. In theory, each part of the human body contributes equally to the health of the individual. Yet most of us do not regard all the parts as equally valuable. This is because we have a social need to see some parts as more or less attractive, stronger or more important, than others. Some body parts, particularly those connected with sex, are frequently regarded as the least attractive. For example, many men regard the penis as ugly and women find the vulva unattractive. This may be the result of early sexual training. Other people regard the sex organs as just as attractive and varied as the human face. Parents are often embarrassed when their young child masturbates; they use expressions of disgust which teach him to regard his sexual parts with distaste. This makes the parents feel better because the child gives up pleasure. When masturbation later becomes a normal part of the adolescent's sexuality, it tends to be practised in secrecy, often with feelings of guilt and shame.

The more at ease we are with our sexuality, the more we are attracted to other people who feel the same way about themselves. People who place a low value on the pleasure of sex, because they have been taught not to feel such pleasures, tend to avoid anybody who seems too sexy for them. They are suspicious of experts who regard sex as important to health or see it as the mainspring of most human activity. They often see sex as dirty and are shocked if somebody says openly how much he enjoys it. This may be the result of a cultural taboo against masturbation. Similarly, some of the ways in which we express our sexuality are the result of a taboo against homosexuality. Although this taboo is fading in some parts of our society, it is still common in others. As a result, some women reject their faces as too masculine, and some men control their bodies so as to avoid looking feminine. A hidden fear of bisexuality may lead a man to grow a beard instead of shaving, and a woman to use make-up to stress her femininity. Facial hair is common among women, but many are embarrassed by it and have it removed.

Our culture tends to be competitive about sex, treating it as another form of power rather than the basis of love. As a result, there is a generally accepted standard of male and female beauty against which many people measure themselves. Surprisingly, many women who are widely regarded as beautiful do not think of themselves in this way. Within the cultural stereotype of beauty the face, breasts and legs are the focus of attention for the female, and a woman sometimes feels that her own are plain or ugly. A man often rejects himself if he feels that his penis is smaller than average or if he has been circumcized, although these make no difference to his capacity to enjoy sex. Rejection of the face varies in intensity. When someone is depressed, he often experiences a feeling of disassociation from his face, and looks at it in the mirror as though he were looking at somebody else. This often relates to a childhood experience of rejection; it is as though the depressed person is rejecting himself. Sometimes a person rejects only part of his face: for example, he may feel that his nose or ears are too big.

There is a widespread taboo against nakedness, not only in public, but also in private. A recent British study showed that tolerance of nakedness in the house (in other words, parents allowing their children to see them undressed) was a better predictor of middle-class status than the occupation of the father. Intolerance of parental nakedness was an equally good predictor of being working-class. Cultural tolerance of nakedness is selective. It is 'acceptable' to show breasts but not nipples, facial hair but not underarm or pubic hair, and so on.

The way in which a person evaluates his overall physical resources can be called the 'body image'. Studies suggest that a poor body image can be enhanced by attention from an attractive person, provided he is seen as sincere. However, if the approach we receive from somebody is very different from our own view of ourselves, we are likely to mistrust him, even though we may feel flattered.

The hidden agenda also affects our view of our strength and health. In many families a child wins more attention by being weak and failing, or being clumsy and provoking anger, than by quietly succeeding at what he wants to do. The youngest child in the family can often manipulate older children into completing tasks he is physically capable of doing himself. If a parent suffers from a long illness the child may have to take considerable responsibility for nursing him, and thereafter be open to manipulation by a partner who says he is easily hurt.

Members of a Danish commune bathe in a river. Nudity is so thoroughly accepted in the group that neither the nude bathers nor the man wearing clothes appear self-conscious.

11 Behavioural Resources

What your body can do affects all your relationships

Behavioural resources are the actions produced by the body and mind together. They include such things as intelligence, memory, agility, adaptability and creativity. They also include the self-control system, which will be discussed later in detail. We design our behaviour so as to attract people who are similar to us, repel those who are different, help us win certain kinds of power struggles, and avoid offending people who we think might attack us. Many of our doubts about the sort of person we are become firmly resolved in childhood, and thus grow into a hidden agenda which we have to meet without knowing why. The presentation of behavioural skills is often carefully controlled by this hidden agenda.

Learning new skills. (left) An informal lesson in bicycle maintenance: although the younger child is not being taught in a formal sense, he is learning as he watches. (right) A formal violin lesson in a playgroup. All the children are following precise instructions from their teacher by copying her actions.

In adult conversation, for example, displays of intelligence which might provoke a power struggle are often reduced by a technique known as 'pre-apology'. This takes the form of an apology for having an opinion before the opinion itself is expressed. An argument may be avoided by making a statement seem more authoritative by using name-, place- or experience-dropping, as in: 'As the President told me. . .', 'Back in my Harvard days. . .' or 'I've only been doing this job for twelve years, but. . .'. These techniques may be used tactically and insincerely. Alternatively, they may reflect a hidden feeling that people with lower status have lower intelligence – a view fostered in some families where the parents feel threatened by a child who is cleverer than they are. People who grow up in such families may feel compelled to reduce their evaluation of their intelligence whenever they feel respect is due to somebody more important.

Agility and dexterity are also commonly affected by hidden self-evaluations. A child is sometimes regarded as 'slow', either physically slow or slow to learn. In power relationships with his parents he may be told to hurry or to learn more quickly; he is accused of a lack of agility and dexterity. He comes to accept these labels for himself as he learns the skill of being the kind of person his parents evidently believe he is and want him to be. Some children do not resolve whether or not they are left-handed until they are three or four years old. Until then they have tried to imitate right-handed parents and siblings. Unless they receive encouragement they may accept themselves as 'not clever with their hands', and when they become adults they will have forgotten why they see themselves this way. Similarly, childhood obesity can lead to hidden self-denigration, even if the child later grows into a slim adult.

Some people see themselves as less adaptable than others. This may be the result of growing up in an authoritarian family where only one way of doing something is acceptable. Variations of skill and unorthodoxy of belief are frowned upon, games must follow the rules, painting is done by numbers rather than by imagination and mealtimes are ritual occasions. There are other families where 'anything goes'; here the child learns to fend for himself early. The adult who grew up in an authoritarian home will probably give free gifts of duty to show that he loves somebody, while the 'jack-of-all-trades' makes a present of his spontaneity.

In a money economy, creativity is prized most when it will sell. The creative artist, poet, writer or musician has to struggle to earn a living. Many children's artistic efforts are not encouraged at home, because it will not enable them to earn their living. Artistic talents have to be of the highest order to be praised. They are judged as performances, not as a recreation worth doing for its own sake as part of the love relationship a person has with himself, not counting the cost. Consequently, many adults undervalue their own creative abilities in order to meet the long-forgotten requirements of their parents. Similarly, it is not uncommon for one of the partners in an adult relationship to avoid displaying a level of creativity or intelligence which might threaten the other and make him feel inferior.

One common example of how a hidden agenda affects behavioural resources is the way people say they have no memory for faces or names. Psycho-economic analysis of this phenomenon suggests three likely explanations. One is that someone who is preoccupied with details of his own identity places a higher value on it than on that of other people. Secondly, it may be a symptom of shyness. A shy person tends to overestimate or underestimate the value of parts of other people's behaviour. Only when he has had time to relax do his evaluations start to become constant. Thus he may find it difficult to remember names because they are mentioned when people first meet and his perception has not yet stabilized. The face and the name are not connected in his mind. Thirdly, an inability to remember names and faces can be selective. In other words, it only applies to people who are of low value to the person who says he forgets.

As a child grows up he is taught not only to accept his own limitations, but to design ones which suit the people who bring him up. Learning to be the sort of person your parents wanted you to be (and accepting that this is sometimes not possible) is not easy. Our behavioural resources are all founded upon the way we learned to suit our parents. The less love they had to spare for us, the more power they will have used to force us to control our behaviour and to design a personality which suited them, but may now be maladaptive.

12 Self-control

We learn to take risks by controlling our fears

An economic system must have a form of government if it is to function effectively. Some governments are oppressive and authoritarian; others are less so. The individual is an economic and political system, too. Most of us learn early in life that to function effectively we need to govern our own behaviour. In other words, we require self-control. Some of us use 'strong-arm tactics' on ourselves to carry out our hidden agendas, preventing ourselves from looking like the sort of person we have decided we should not be. We may suppress 'subversive' thoughts and feelings, using a system of guilt and self-directed anger. Alternatively, we may govern ourselves more lightly, employing the tactics of good management, rather than those of dictatorship, and allowing ourselves to feel extremes of pleasure and pain.

We can begin to understand our system of self-control if we start by looking at the way in which physical resources are protected. When part of our body feels unexpected pain or pleasure, the whole body responds automatically, using what are called reflex actions. This is due to the work of the autonomic nervous system. When a baby is born it has no control over its nervous system; all its actions are reflexes. By the time it becomes an adult it has learned to control its reflexes and to win sufficient time to calculate any risk to its system. There are two parts to the autonomic system: one keeps a stock of energy ready at all times for use in emergencies (the sympathetic nervous system); the other conserves and restores bodily resources (the parasympathetic nervous system). As we grow older we learn to control parts of these systems, and to tolerate a certain amount of pain or discomfort in order to receive bigger rewards. At first all these rewards come from our

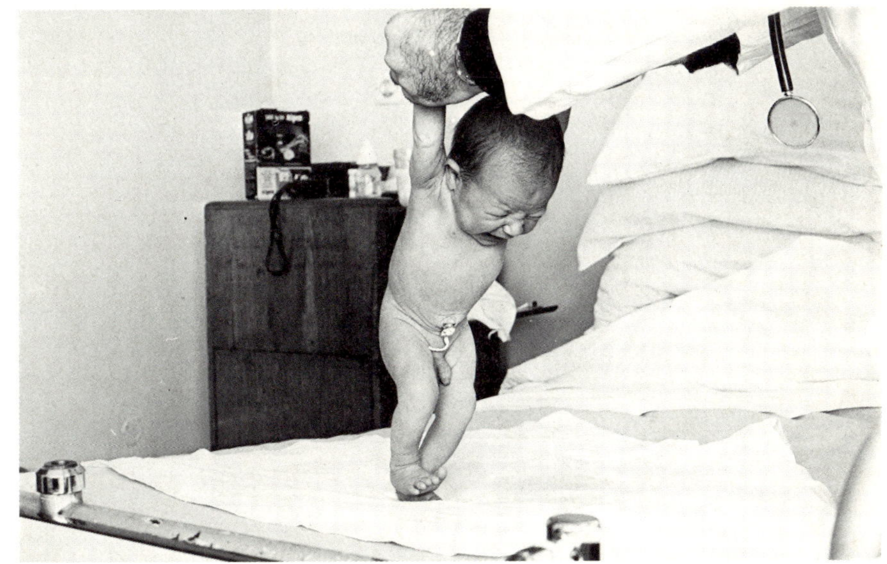

The walking reflex in a new-born baby: the little boy moves his legs and feet as if walking. This response will disappear in a few days' time, only to reappear when the child begins to walk.

A workman painting the Eiffel Tower in Paris. With the benefit of long experience, he takes for granted – and can even enjoy – the risks which most people would find intimidating.

parents, so we learn to put up with the kind of discomfort and receive the kinds of rewards to which they are accustomed.

The part of the body which suppresses feelings in order to take risks is not yet fully understood by scientists; it is the part we have called the 'self'. It is known that this system develops during childhood, and that deposits of a substance called myelin appear throughout the child's nervous system as it grows, apparently connecting up the cells which the child uses most often. This suggests that each individual develops a unique system, designed to suit his circumstances and experience.

Most of us think of self-control as something we use to prevent ourselves running away from something that frightens us, or stop ourselves being so angry that we lose control over our actions, but we also use it every time we calculate a risk. There is a limit to the amount of protection a body can achieve by using physical resources. Behavioural resources extend our protection beyond the body, giving us the skills we need in order to conserve and use our surplus resources. Beyond this, we have the protection of our property resources and the extra line of defence afforded by our social resources. To use any of these we have to calculate risks. When we do so, we are using responses we have learned, although they often feel as though they are instinctive and innate because they involve the use of the autonomic system.

The calculation of risk means weighing up positive against negative factors, costs against rewards. For example, every time we wonder whether we are getting the most out of our lives we are calculating the risk to our own value. Should we be content or try for something better? We might lose what we have and be worse off. The larger the surplus we have to spend, the easier it is to take small risks.

Sometimes we are not aware that we have a surplus. This is because, as we grow up, we are taught to suppress some of our feelings and evaluate them as negative, or even harmful (worse than negative). As a result, these parts of us either stop growing or only grow in secret. If we use a very rigid self-control system we never question our own values. Yet we may have been taught these values in power situations which we thought were loving relationships. For example, a parent who feels better because his child stops masturbating will tell the child that it is for his own good. As a result, the child may grow up to regard sex as something he does not feel strongly about, and never be able to understand that he has the capacity to enjoy it. He mistakenly sees himself as having a low sex drive.

A person is using self-control every time he tells himself he ought to, should or must do something. He is also using it when he evaluates his resources and decides what he can or cannot do. Self-control is particularly useful in power relationships, because these are where we count the cost, and we cannot calculate any risk unless we do so. However, self-controls are inhibiting in a loving relationship; they prevent us from giving without counting the cost. We also use self-control by behaving in a 'correct' manner to please somebody else. In trading and power relationships this helps the other person, because our self-control makes it easier for him to predict the part we play in his life.

On a ghost train, children learn how to extend their tolerance of fear. Experience can increase our ability to take risks as we get used to the feelings engendered by them.

13 Roles People Play

Each relationship can be seen as playing a part in someone else's life

From time to time nearly all of us feel obliged to adopt a particular role as a result of circumstances or in response to the way we are treated. For example, when we visit a doctor we feel less out of place in his surgery if we accept the part of Patient. If we are stopped by a policeman we may find ourselves acting as if we were guilty, simply because of the way we are dealt with. Someone who asks us for help or advice may get us to answer in the role of Expert because he seems to know so little compared with us.

Social scientists have used this idea to develop 'role theory', currently one of the most sophisticated and widely accepted ways of understanding relationships. We each have a set of resources and a set of relationships. Each relationship can be seen as a set of roles. Role theory does not assume that a person is deliberately acting a part or pretending to be somebody he is not. We adopt most of the roles we play unaware that we are doing so, just by being ourselves. A case history will help to illustrate this point.

Carole was married and had two small children. Like most people she unconsciously played many roles, often changing from one to another in a comparatively short period. One afternoon, for example, her husband telephoned to say that they had been invited out that evening and asked her to find a baby-sitter. She was able to do so, and when her husband arrived she was showing the girl round. Carole and her husband changed and left for the party. They enjoyed their evening together and came home. Carole paid the baby-sitter, looked in at the two sleeping children, locked up and then went to bed.

During this time Carole first had to switch back and forth between acting the parts of Mother and Wife while she coped with the children's interruptions during her husband's telephone call. It was an unexpected call on a noisy line, and she needed to behave differently towards the children from the way she spoke to her husband. When he arrived home, she was acting as Friend to the baby-sitter. (Her husband mildly criticized the very informal way she treated this girl, whom they had not met before.) While getting ready to go out, Carole twirled round to show off her dress to her husband as a Little Girl might, and then, unasked, straightened his tie for him in the role of Mother, while he behaved as Little Boy. They spent the evening being Companions. When they returned home, Carole acted as Employer and paid the baby-sitter, speaking more formally than she had done before. She was Mother again briefly as she looked in at her sleeping children, then locked up as Janitor and tidied the room as Housekeeper. Upstairs she took on the role of Little Girl in order to attract her husband's attention, climbed into bed and became Lover and then Wife before going to sleep.

The roles we play are first of all a response to what other people

A young Afghan tribesman is photographed in his soldier's uniform. The photograph will legitimize his role as a hero, and in future he will feel a stronger need to live up to the expectations of others in fulfilling this role.

expect of us. Society expects mothers to behave as Mothers, doctors as Doctors, policemen as Policemen, and so on. A policeman who took off his jacket while on point duty and did a tap-dance would be regarded as very odd! There is a more serious side to this point, however, for our relationships usually depend for their stability on agreement about what is normal in a particular role. Each society has its collective view of what is normal. Wherever we are we will be expected to conform, and be regarded as odd if we do not.

In addition to these general expectations, there are particular expectations attached to each relationship. The way in which people see us depends on the part we play in their lives. The more closely we stick to their idea of each role, the easier it is for them to know where they stand with us. For example, the 'good, dependable employee' is the one who conforms to the rules and always delivers what is expected of him. Yet it does not always suit us to be predictable.

Roles help us decide how to share out tasks. Certain duties, rights and privileges accompany each role. For example, two secretaries in the same office need to know who types which letters, who does the filing and who deals with certain kinds of inquiries on the telephone. They each have their own desks and accept that neither has the right to interfere with personal items left there. They may also both feel privileged to be able to talk to each other in a certain way; if an outsider uses the same familiarity he will be snubbed.

Sometimes it is difficult to know what is expected of us because we have several roles at once. Carole's first response to the baby-sitter is a case in point. She was talking to the girl as one of the family; her husband expected her to act as an Employer. Two roles may conflict, as when Carole was trying to talk to her husband on the telephone while the children were making a noise. She found she could not be Wife and Mother at the same time. The people we know best are probably those with whom we have many different roles. They are also the people we are most likely to come into conflict with, simply because where there are more roles, more is expected of us and this increases the likelihood of failure.

Failure to agree about expectations

When a relationship comes under strain, it is often because the two people concerned cannot agree about what they expect of one another. So far, we have looked at such situations as 'trading relationships'. Role theorists suggest several ways in which bargaining can occur. For example, two people may have opposite views about how to behave in a particular situation. Mr Smith was leaving his job at the end of the month and Mr Green had been promoted to take his place as head of department. A week before he was due to leave, Mr Smith was horrified to find Mr Green sitting at the desk where he himself usually sat. 'You have no right to sit here,' said Mr Smith. 'I have every right,' replied Mr Green.

Similarly, a husband and wife quarrelled about how to punish their teenage daughter. The mother felt the girl was still very young; she wanted to take no action. The father felt that his daughter was 'old enough to take the consequences'. They disagreed about their role as parents because they had opposite views as to what was expected of them in the situation. The mother's view emphasized the protection of the child, while the father's was more concerned with teaching her to be independent. One parent wanted her to grow up more slowly, the other more quickly.

When two people have opposite expectations, the conflict cannot be resolved without them redefining their roles. Through give-and-take they negotiate a new agreement. Mr Smith told his successor firmly that his job was still to act as deputy and not as head of department. 'You can take over when I've gone, but not before,' he told Mr Green. The husband and wife, however, could not agree. They failed to resolve their conflict, and temporarily avoided it by the father refusing to help 'ever again' with their daughter's discipline.

Misunderstandings about expectations can arise in several other ways. Sometimes people disagree about whether they are obliged to carry out a certain task or allowed to decide for themselves. At work, clear job descriptions lessen the risk of such disputes. In the family and neighbourhood, obligations are a matter of custom and practice. For example, a mother may find herself expected to do some things (such as tidying away a child's toys) because she has 'always' done so, but she will protest because what she once did as a favour has become a duty. If a neighbour is ill, not everyone feels obliged to help. Sometimes people avoid volunteering: it can too easily be taken for granted, and become an obligation.

Failure to agree about which is the most important task in a relationship is another source of conflict. This can happen within the same role. For example, an employee may be torn between the need to act swiftly and the need to obtain permission. If he decides to act, he may later be told, 'You should have asked me first.' The more roles there are in the same relationship, the more likely it is that there will be disputes over priorities.

Many disagreements arise over which expectation applies to which situation. There can be a right and a wrong time and place to exercise the role. A wife may object to being treated as Lover in public; while she accepts a peck on the cheek from her husband in company, she draws the line at a passionate embrace from him. He may be happy to let her straighten his tie in private, but object to this in public because he feels it makes him look like a Little Boy.

Two people may disagree as to whether certain behaviour is permitted or prohibited as part of their relationship. For example, friends are allowed to say things to one another which would be unacceptable from more formal acquaintances. (Criticism and personal remarks often fall into this category.) In courtship, adolescents in many Western countries permit some kinds of familiarity but not others: they may allow petting and 'heavy petting', but prohibit sexual intercourse. As the relationship changes there is often a progression from total prohibition to complete permission. Changes in what is permitted and prohibited can also be seen when a woman divorces or separates from her husband. Men she

The changing role of the father today. Whereas the father was once the distant head of the family, he may now be closely involved in bringing up the baby, even at the earliest stages of its development.

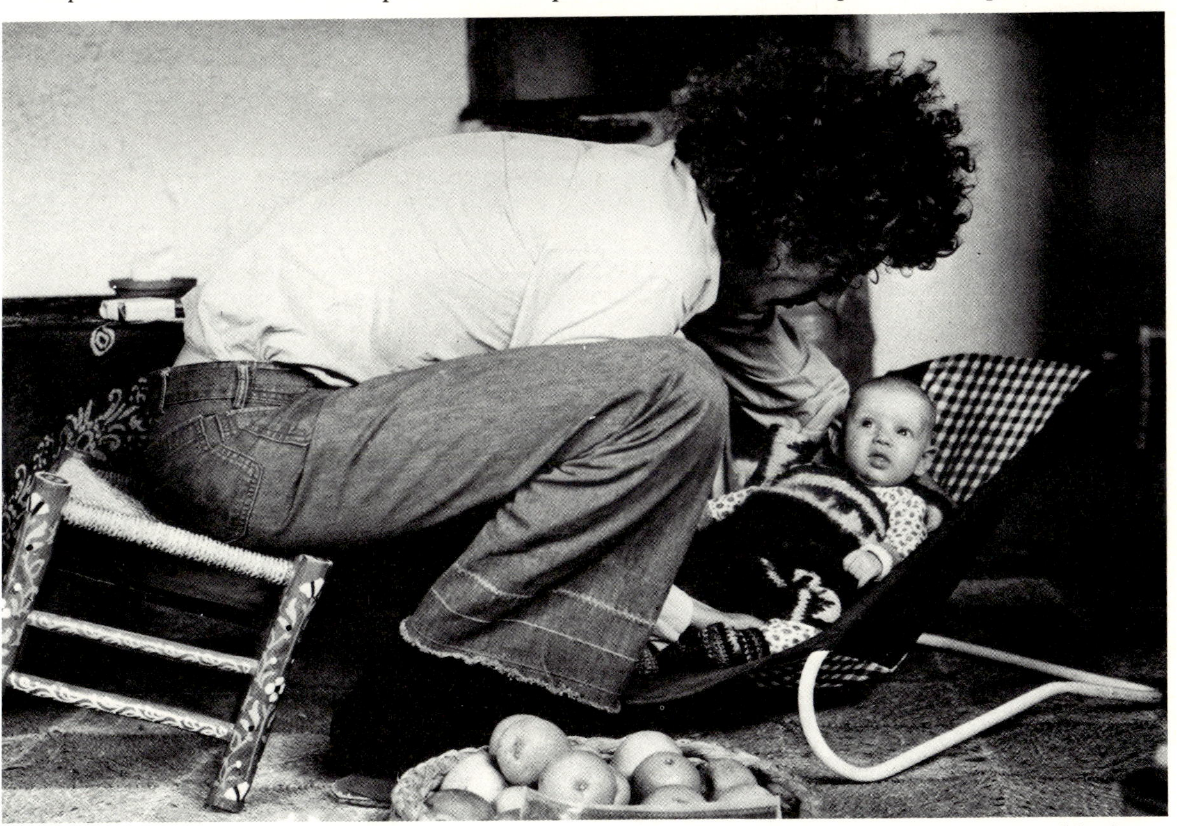

has known as non-sexual friends may now see themselves as potential lovers, so she has to lay down new rules about what she will allow.

Expectations are a part of all roles. At work, or in the role of Client or Customer, most of us would expect to have a contract which clearly stated the rights and obligations on both sides. Informal relationships also have contracts, but they are not written down, and there may be confusion over expectations and obligations. There are often 'hidden contracts', with people expecting others to carry out duties which have never been discussed but are assumed to be obligatory.

A conflict of expectations may lead people to question the terms of their contracts. As a result, they may form a new contract, reaffirm the existing contract or terminate the contract and not replace it. Role theory shows how important it is in power and trading relationships to be aware of what has, and has not, been agreed.

A group of guerrillas pose with an English policeman during the truce before the Zimbabwe elections in 1980. Each man's role in this situation is mirrored in his pose and facial expression.

14 The Nature of Relationships

All relationships depend on the mutual use of resources

So far we have considered relationships mainly from the point of view of the 'self'. This perspective was necessary so that the system could be looked at from a fixed point and therefore simplified. However, it is easy to overlook another point: relationships meet the needs of both the 'selves' involved. Role theory provides a partial explanation of this: some of the parts we play depend on the other person also playing his part. A doctor cannot behave as a Doctor, for example, unless his patient acts as a Patient. Nobody carries conviction in his claim to be a Leader unless somebody is following him.

Yet it is difficult to apply this theory to many everyday situations, for several reasons. First, roles are usually seen in a stereotyped fashion; that is to say, Doctor means the generally accepted idea of what a doctor does, and Leader means the accepted view of leadership. Yet there are many doctors and leaders who do not conform to these stereotypes. If we apply role theory in real life, we may base our reactions to people on what we expect to see rather than what we really see. Secondly, the way people behave is often hard to fit into a role. We often have to invent names for what they are doing and thus reflect our own limited experience rather than extending it. Thirdly, role theory applies best in power situations, where a contract can be assumed to exist and conflict is resolved by give-and-take. It is less helpful in understanding loving relationships, where there is no contract because at least one of the people concerned is not counting the cost.

To understand how relationships meet two sets of needs, we have to accept that only the individual concerned can meet his own needs. Other people may provide the resources he uses, but only he can make use of them. In the psycho-economy a person satisfies a need by using a resource. Someone else may use the same resource to satisfy a different need. For example, two people can look at the same painting and see different things. A parent can enjoy watching a child play with a toy; both are using the same resource to meet different needs. Several million people can watch the same television show and enjoy it for different reasons. When a resource is used simultaneously by more than one person, all who use it are said to have 'mutual access' to it. All relationships depend on mutual access to the same resources. Two people cannot come face to face without using the same room or street, or reacting to the same set of circumstances.

Not all relationships use mutual resources to the same extent. For example, two lovers will grant mutual access to many more physical resources than will two casual strangers or two people of very different status. A kiss means that lips become a mutual resource. We will not usually allow our most valued resources to be used mutually unless we trust the other user. This is because, by allowing somebody else to use them, we may lose control over them. If the other person values them less than we do, he may damage them; if he values them more, he may

A child's birthday party. The family and its guests make this a special day by sharing extra resources in a protected environment: there is more than enough to eat, the children wear their best party clothes, grandmother is treated as an honoured guest and father is on hand to help the children enjoy themselves.

keep them and prevent us from using them. For example, if somebody makes love with a person he does not love but who loves him, the second person is likely to become emotionally dependent on the other and to wish to monopolize the first person's capacity to make love with anybody else. Each has a different understanding of the extent to which their relationship is mutual. This is the psycho-economic basis of jealousy, which is examined in more detail in chapter 70.

Families use many mutually owned resources. The members indicate this to people outside by the way they all use the same terms to identify their membership, adopt the same methods to defend the family, have the same commitment to it and show the same recognition of each other's special status. Yet because each member of the family is also satisfying his individual needs, he requires resources of his own, and the right both to grant and withdraw these from mutual use. This is his right to privacy. Unless he has something he owns for himself he cannot give without counting the cost. He will either have to be victim or victor.

As mentioned previously, we tend to find people attractive when we judge them to be like ourselves. They have similar resources to us and set similar values on them. This makes the mutual use of these and other resources much easier to establish. But people who have very different resources and see things differently are less likely to think it worth the trouble to find mutual ground – unless this is part of a power relationship, and they need to give the impression of agreement in order to trick one another.

The concept of mutual resources also helps to explain crime. A role theorist would have to explain the role of Thief as requiring the role of the 'Person who is robbed'. They are both playing complementary parts. This is misleading. The thief and the victim may have no relationship in the true meaning of the term. No resources are mutually used unless the two people meet. The thief who robs your house while you are out makes no relationship with you. If he mugs you in the street he does make a relationship, however, and it is an intimate one because physical resources are used mutually.

Intimate relationships depend on the mutual use of high-value resources. Most of us control the intimacy of our relationships by the way we permit or deny other people access to the things we value most, for example, personal information, treasured objects (including money) and physical resources, such as the ability to experience orgasm. The most intimate relationship of all – that between the fully formed unborn child and its mother – depends on mutual use of the whole body. In our adult relationships we may often feel the primal urge to return to that same maximum mutuality.

Sharing a joke: a sense of humour becomes a mutual resource in an intimate group.

15 Self-management

Skills help us manage resources

All relationships depend on the use of skills. Psychological analysis of skills shows that they are complicated forms of behaviour. We often have no idea how much skill we use in performing what we see as a quite simple task. Because all skills contain common elements, they can be analysed in order to help somebody improve his performance.

We use skills in order to attain our purposes, but we must first know what we want to achieve. Within 'taking' relationships, the main objectives are the use and preservation of power over other people. Within 'giving' relationships, the objectives are mostly concerned with sexuality: liking, being attractive and being loved. The objectives of power and sexuality may easily be confused, as when somebody tries to achieve love by 'forcing' others to love him, or to gain more power while attempting to retain his popularity. Either way, he will increase the likelihood of failure unless he can increase his skill. Problems in relationships also arise when somebody is unaware of his objectives because he is responding to a hidden or suppressed need, like the objectives he had to meet when he first learned the skill as a child.

Skills depend on having surplus resources, particularly energy, time and equipment. Energy is necessary because trying to gain an objective involves us in a certain cost. Life is often a gamble and this means we need a stake of some sort; if we lose the gamble, we lose our investment. People often try to gain a bigger surplus by investing too few resources. At times we all try to get more from a relationship than we want to put into it. Many relationship problems arise through 'lack of investment' or 'over-investment': expecting too little or too much of ourselves and other people. We need extra skill to solve the problems created by these mistakes.

The equipment we need depends on the kind of relationship we want. A power relationship requires different equipment from a loving one. When we use our skill on behalf of a group, our most important equipment is the power of the group, since the resources belong to others, as well as ourselves. Thus, when we negotiate a business deal for other people, it is a mistake to commit them beyond their power to carry out their side of the contract. When we threaten somebody because his behaviour might endanger the group, we have to be certain that the group will support us and enable us to carry out our threats. If we exceed our authority or use too little power, we will need even more skill to put matters right. In our loving relationships, however, our most important equipment is our sexuality: our attractiveness, our capacity to be polite and friendly, to like or love somebody and to trust and be trusted. Our whole personality is involved: everything we are and all we own can contribute to our ability to please somebody, because it is all part of his social resources. If we believe we are unattractive (as many shy or lonely people do), we will not feel properly equipped for effective personal relationships.

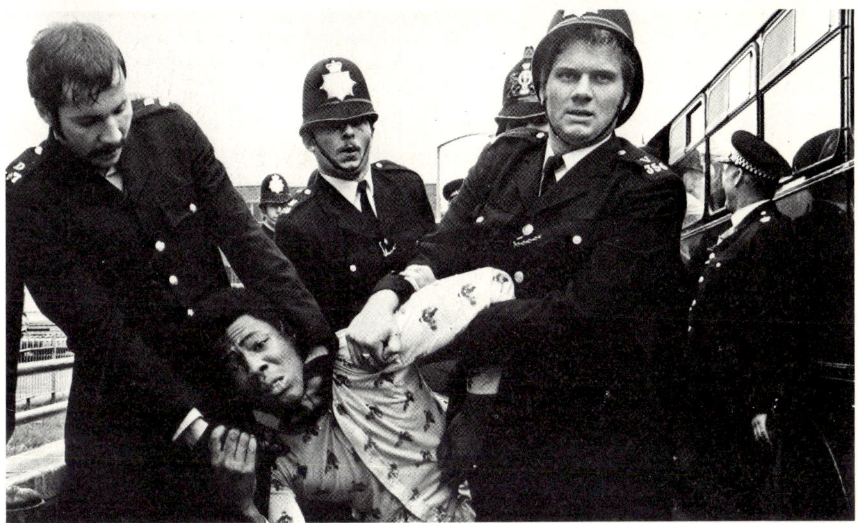

People control their resources to protect their interests. (top) During a verbal dispute at work the men restrain themselves in front of the manager to avoid making the conflict worse. (centre) Three policemen impose control on a demonstrator, so depriving him of the choice as to how he uses his self-control. (bottom) Two people share the same seat and control their body positions to avoid contact.

In addition to purpose and resources, all skills require flexibility of response – the ability to know how we are getting along and to alter our tactics when things go badly. This depends on what is called 'feedback', a stream of information which tells us whether we are succeeding or failing. In relationship skills, the process of communication is the main form of feedback. It tells us whether we are increasing or decreasing the contact on which our relationships depend. Obviously, we need to be sensitive to the feelings of other people, or we will not be able to judge their feelings about us and how they will react to what we do. In our power relationships, feedback helps us anticipate whether somebody will accept or reject our authority. In our caring relationships, it tells us whether we will be accepted or rejected on a personal basis.

The skills somebody uses to organize an economy are called 'management skills'. Similarly, effective skills are the basis of self-management in informal relationships. A manager has to ensure as far as possible that his aims, and those of the group, are attained through the most economical use of available resources, whatever the circumstances. If there is a waste of time, effort or resources, the group's surplus is squandered. The group is poorer as a result and the person responsible is disliked. A manager monitors the group's progress in order to have the best available feedback. For example, the manager of a company might check weekly sales figures, staff turnover or profit and loss accounts, and a housewife will check her housekeeping money. The manager also plans ahead, so that he can be sure of obtaining the resources he will need in the future. In exactly the same way, the individual needs to have accurate feedback and to plan ahead.

The best manager is the person who is most aware of the official objectives of the group. He uses his power to make sure other people stick to the plan, use resources economically and are well motivated to achieve the group's objectives. Similarly, in self-management we have to know what we want, and be realistic and economical. The more skilful the manager, the easier he makes his job look. However, his skills may have been hard to acquire. Although he now makes fewer mistakes and recovers from them more quickly, it has taken him a great deal of hard work, practice and experience to become skilled. He is often not aware of 'conscious effort' in using his skills, but initially he felt self-conscious and was more worried by his mistakes. This also applies to self-management.

A good manager does not waste his powers. If he reacted to every crisis by driving himself or his staff harder and controlling them more rigidly, he would soon lose their support and face continuous crises. Control of the group is important, but control for the sake of it is self-defeating. It forces people to act against their own judgement, and limits their choice of action so that they begin to feel that the benefits of membership are less than the price they pay for belonging. In the same way, too rigid self-control shows bad self-management.

The needs of the individual are essentially the same as those of any group. In your own relationships, you have the choice of being a good manager or a bad one. The skills of self-management are the best foundation for managing your own relationships, whether you need to take or give-and-take. Otherwise, when you want to give and not count the cost, you may find you have nothing to give.

SECTION TWO
COMMUNICATION

If we cannot communicate with someone it is impossible to relate to him. This section explains why communication is so important and how it works. Through words and 'body language' we draw attention to the value of our strengths and abilities, and to our needs. The variations in the ways we do this enable us to build connections with other people which meet their needs and ours simultaneously.

These chapters show in detail how we use our bodies and the senses of touch, sight and hearing to receive and give out a continuous stream of signals, by means of facial expressions, gestures and changes of posture, touching, looking, tone of voice, and so on. When these subtly varied patterns of behaviour are combined with more awareness and skill, we can improve our ability to talk and listen, and thus meet our own needs by building relationships based on a deeper understanding of the other person's experience.

16 Communicating with Others

Why is communication so important in relationships?

Whenever there is a problem within a relationship, difficulties of communication will be found. The ability to communicate is the most valuable of human skills, and the one upon which all relationships are founded. Yet we often fail to develop our full potential as communicators and rely instead on the unsophisticated ideas about communication we learned during childhood.

Communication is a fundamental part of all relationships because, first, it links people together so that shared activity becomes possible. Secondly, the way in which people communicate provides important evidence as to how they value each other. Lack of communication reduces the amount of sharing in a relationship and gives the impression that the relationship is unimportant.

Failure to communicate can arise for many different reasons. There may be simple reasons of geography. People often make friends as a result of working together or being neighbours. When one of a pair of friends leaves the firm or moves house, it is natural for both people to promise to keep in touch. They note down addresses and telephone numbers, and may fully intend to contact each other so that the relationship will continue. A letter or phone call seems such a simple task. Yet nearly all such friendships fade away through lack of regular communication, and those which start well often dwindle into a once-a-year exchange of greetings because the distance is too great to allow a casual chat on a daily basis. The former friends may also find that they no longer have the same experiences to share and discuss, and differences

Communication is essential to start a relationship. This conversation struck up in a queue could last five minutes or develop into a long friendship.

A family lunch outdoors. They communicate their pleasure in the shared activity.

in outlook which were previously ignored become more obvious. The old relationship becomes less important than it used to be. New relationships are formed with other colleagues and neighbours. As communication between the original friends becomes worse, this reflects the fact that they now mean less to each other.

Problems also arise when members of the same family are separated by long distances and fail to keep in touch. Old people often feel deeply hurt at being abandoned by their busy, middle-aged sons and daughters, who are now preoccupied with their careers, homes and children. The occasional reunion is particularly awkward when the parent and child have not shared the important emotional and intellectual development of the middle years, so that the elderly person still treats his son or daughter as a teenager. If the son or daughter protests that the 'child' has now grown up, this only makes matters worse. Kindness, patience, understanding and physical contact are ways of overcoming the difficulty. In cases where the gap is too great for these solutions, the pain

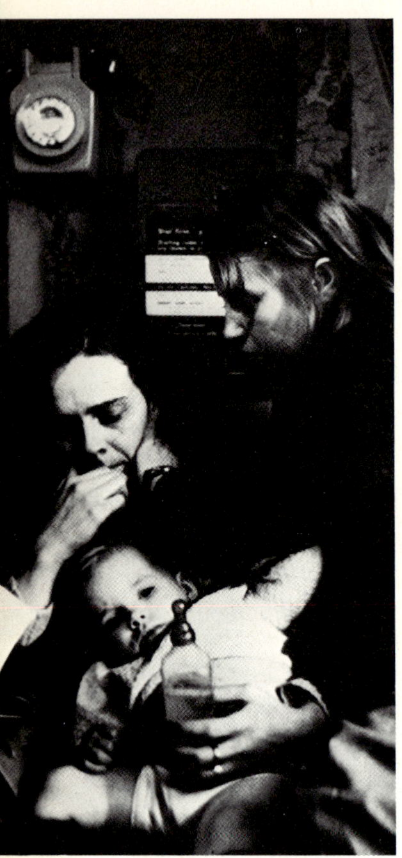

The difficulties of separation. In a refuge for battered wives, telephone calls from husbands are not usually allowed. In this case the call got through and the resumption of communication only caused greater distress.

must be endured and accepted.

Close relationships always come under strain when loved ones are separated and the longer they are away from each other, the greater is the danger of estrangement. Contact by letter or telephone lessens this danger, but it is a poor substitute for being together. Within a close relationship, the partners share many trivial experiences without being aware of it; they often take for granted the fact that they witness the same events. Separation means that they have to explain what has happened while they were apart, and shortage of time usually forces them to concentrate on the most important happenings. Maintaining the relationship is therefore more difficult, and people who are parted often fear that they will lose their value to one another during long periods of separation.

Communication breakdown also occurs between people who are not separated by great physical distances. Sometimes this is the result of a minor misunderstanding which can easily be put right within the relationship. Disputes within the family commonly occur when one member feels that he has been downgraded or taken for granted. From time to time, we all feel that we must insist on recognition for our efforts on behalf of others. Sometimes we expect gratitude or praise, but will settle for some minor sign of appreciation instead. An apology or a word of thanks restores our hurt pride. Too much reliance upon unspoken assumptions shows that people are taking each other for granted. When this happens, a person will often seek reassurance that his value in the relationship has not changed. Everybody has different ways of doing this. Some of them merely make communication more difficult – for example, sulking, or bottling up angry feelings and withdrawing from contact.

Serious breakdowns in communication within a family or marriage are usually the result, rather than the cause, of a deeper rift. Unless people are committed to sharing a significant part of their lives with their partner, communication itself becomes pointless. Alternatively, it turns into a one-way process in which each person ignores or rejects the feelings of the other. In such cases, the lack of willingness to share is reflected in the way the partners communicate. Arguments and disagreements turn into fierce verbal battles in which words are used as weapons, designed to wound and maim. Instead of talking *to* each other, the partners find they are being talked *at*, or given orders about what to do and, even worse, about what to think and feel. One-way communication means people have stopped listening to each other. They show no evidence of valuing what the other person has to say, and from here it is a very short step to showing that the other person is despised.

Relationships differ enormously in the extent to which the people involved accept that they are both of equal value. You may feel superior, or dominant, in some relationships and inferior in others. These feelings can be changed by communication. If you know that you have become more valuable to somebody, this increases your self-confidence. On the other hand, if you feel that you matter less than you realized to somebody who is important to you, it can damage your self-confidence. Improved skill in communication can help you find new ways of rewarding people so that you collect more rewards yourself.

17 What is Communication?

Relationships depend on communication.
What sort of process is it?

Communication involves more than just speaking and listening; it is not simply a matter of sending and receiving messages, in which the main task is to transfer factual information from one side to the other. Since the advent of the video tape-recorder, scientists have discovered a great deal about what happens when two people converse. We now know, for example, that looking is just as important as talking and listening during conversation, and we are in a far better position to explain how and why communication problems occur.

To understand communication, we can start by seeing each person as a 'signal source', somebody who is constantly giving out signals, whether he is sleeping or waking, talking or silent. These signals can then be picked up by other people. So many different signals are being broadcast at any one time that the observer cannot receive them all. In order to notice somebody or something, he must therefore select a few signals out of the thousands available and ignore the rest. A transistor radio can pick up many different stations, but only tune in to one at a time. People communicate by using a 'tuning-in apparatus' to select the set of messages which makes sense and to reject those which do not.

This approach helps to explain how people communicate information about themselves before a single word is spoken. For example, suppose a middle-aged man is sitting in his car waiting for his wife to return from the shops. Naturally, he watches the passers-by. They are all broadcasting information about themselves: who they are, what they are doing and how they feel. First, they are showing other people what sex they are, roughly what age they are and often to which class of society they belong. Some will have chosen clothes which show that they are comfortable mothers, harassed parents, eager lovers, big or little sisters, or too old to be interested in how they look. Others will be broadcasting the fact that at this moment their sexuality is unimportant to them. A young man getting out of his car broadcasts his

An image can be cultivated to broadcast style and intention. The appearance of the 'Rocker' (below) stresses masculinity and aggression. The posture and dress of the race-goer (right) display his self-assurance.

sense of purpose by carefully reading the piece of paper he is clutching, then peering deliberately at the name-boards above the shops. A little girl being tugged along by her mother displays her anger and stubborn rebelliousness in the face of her mother's frustration and impatience. None of this random information is important to the man in the car. He keeps looking at his watch and tapping his fingers, wishing his wife would hurry up. He is not 'tuned in' to all the messages being broadcast, but is simply watching for her. The only message which will get through to him is the sight of his wife hurrying towards him.

Most of the messages which reach us before the start of a conversation only get through because we are looking for them. If we did not separate all the items being broadcast into those we want to receive (the 'signals') and those we want to ignore (called 'noise'), we could not focus on the important factors. Of course, some messages are of such intensity that we are forced to notice them: a loud bang or shout, for example, or a touch when we do not expect one. Sudden unexpected signals startle us at first, but if they are repeated we soon become used to them. We can then ignore them and treat them as noise. Some people seem to do everything noisily; they talk, gesture, move, and even dress in a 'loud' way. Other people are so quiet that they almost fade into the background. With noisy people, we adapt to the level of their signals by ignoring much of the noise. With quiet people, we amplify their signals. But this takes time. Usually we are only ready for certain kinds of signals and we ignore those for which we are unprepared.

At the 'receiving' end, communication is a matter of selection: we tune in to some signals, deliberately treat others as noise and fail to notice many others. All the human senses – sight, hearing, touch, taste and smell – can act as receivers. Each can be used to scan generally for signals or to focus on details, in much the same way as binoculars can be used to look at a wide area of landscape or to help the viewer pick out just one object and study it closely. For example, we can listen generally for sounds or concentrate on one; and we can use our fingers to search the surface of an object, then pick out a particular place to feel more carefully. Taken together, the senses and the 'tuning-in apparatus' form the human attention system. This system can switch from one sense to another and back again. It can treat a bit of information as noise one moment and signal the next.

Let us look next at the 'broadcasting' end. Selection is important here, too. We can each try to control what other people are aware of, even though many of the signals we send out will not be noticed. The amount of control varies; some of us use more control generally than others do, while we all take particular care over what is noticed when there is a lot at stake. For an interview, for example, we dress more carefully than usual and use more control over the way we speak. Sexual attraction also alters the way we select and present our signals. Selection can be hard work, particularly when someone does not trust himself or the person to whom he is talking. At other times, however, control is relaxed. On these occasions, we are just 'being ourselves'; we do not have to worry about controlling our image.

When two people are communicating, they are tuned in to each other. If they are both relaxed and trust each other, their two separate attention systems can combine to become one joint, or mutual, system. They help each other to select the signals which are important to them both, and to ignore the items they both wish to treat as noise. The distinction between 'receiver' and then 'broadcaster' disappears.

Two people broadcast their sexual availability and await a response. A New York 'hooker' advertises her trade (opposite). A man displays 'cool' masculinity as he lounges at the bar ready to spring into action (right).

18 Emphasis and Attention

Each item communicated has the power to keep someone interested

A good communicator must constantly check that his audience is paying attention. He must try to make this easy for the listeners, so that it becomes a rewarding experience, rather than one which is frightening or exhausting. People who are intimidated or bored are usually more concerned with their own feelings than with somebody else's message. Getting the message across means keeping the other person interested; it also means being interested in what he is saying. In a truly satisfying conversation, both sides become so involved that they are quite unaware of themselves and only aware of each other. This happens because they keep one another's attention by subtle variations in emphasis.

We can illustrate the use of emphasis by means of a simple example. Take the sentence, 'The train stops here.' If somebody asks what stops here, the answer will be, 'The *train* stops here.' On the other hand, if somebody asks where the train stops, the emphasis will be placed on '*here*', and so on.

Emphasis also occurs when a particular topic is selected for conversation. For example, if people of the same profession meet and chat at a conference, the first part of their conversation will usually emphasize the work they do. Each will tend to ask the other where he works, what his position is in the organization and whether he knows certain colleagues. People who are meeting for the first time at a wedding reception place their early emphasis on why they were invited, and their relationship with the family of the bride or groom. Strangers who want

Artur Rubinstein. The pianist uses a wide range of touch and emphasis to draw out the subtleties of the music.

A busy classroom: but the teacher has failed to arouse interest in either the subject or his performance.

to pass the time on a long train journey will be likely to mention the time the train is due to arrive, whether a particular seat is vacant, what time the buffet car opens, and so on. In each case, the emphasis is on experiences which both parties have in common. Personal feelings, particularly those of a distressing nature, are commonly avoided unless the two people concerned already know each other well.

Emphasis is a way of drawing attention towards certain sets of signals and away from others. The signals which are emphasized spring to the foreground and those which are underemphasized act as the background against which the others are seen. When emphasis is placed on a particular item being communicated, it makes that item seem more important than others which could be noticed instead.

Human beings like variations in emphasis and are bored by lack of variation. A monotonous voice which never rises or falls, is always equally loud, and goes on without pauses of varying length is very difficult to listen to and sends people to sleep. Bright colours catch the eye more readily than dull ones and supermarket display staff use this fact to tease us into buying goods on impulse. However, the variations between items matter more than the intensity of any individual item. A speaker who shouts everything at the top of his voice will lose his audience, but one who weights his emphasis so subtly that each item seems to have its own importance will keep the attention of the listeners.

Emphasis can also be used to divert attention away from something important and towards something unimportant. A deliberate lie will often succeed if the liar manages to sound unconcerned about the thing which concerns him most. This is even more effective if he also appears to be very concerned about something which he alone knows is unim-

Visual noise: the competition between a number of messages makes it difficult to focus on one of them (above). Visual over-emphasis: this outfit seems designed to shock rather than just attract attention to the wearer (right).

portant. Diversionary tactics of this kind play a much greater part in day-to-day communication than is commonly admitted. People hide their feelings from each other to save time and trouble, and to avoid undesired increases in intimacy. Parents may fight and then hide their anger from their children; triumphant pleasure may be hidden under the cloak of false modesty; a deep sense of self-rejection may be disguised by false *bonhomie*.

If people were not such good liars, it would be easy to understand the way emphasis and attention work together. In principle, what happens is as follows. First, the amount of emphasis placed on an item indicates its importance to the communicator: the more an item is emphasized, the more important it is. Secondly, the amount of attention an item attracts is equal to the amount of emphasis placed upon it by the person 'broadcasting' it. In practice, however, people deliberately alter their emphasis in order to mislead others. They may do this for a variety of reasons. Moreover, the amount of attention given to a signal often depends, not on the strength of a signal, but on how much attention the receiver wants, or is able, to spare at that moment.

A good communicator recognizes that children, as well as adults who are tired or under stress, have less attention to spare than happy, healthy grown-ups. He will therefore take particular care to maintain their interest in the conversation. He will approach busy people in ways which help them stay busy, rather than stopping them in the middle of their business. He will time his changes of emphasis to enable people to spare him attention. Above all, he will get into the habit of rewarding people for listening to him. As a result, he will collect more attention for himself.

19 Verbal Communication

Words can be used both to aid and to hinder communication

Although we tend to think of words as the basis of communication, they are often used in order to *avoid* communicating. One effective method is to choose words the listener does not understand. Any group which wishes to remain separate from the rest of the population can do this by the use of a private language. Experts use their own jargon partly to extend, and partly to preserve, their special knowledge. The technical terms help them converse rapidly with each other, but also effectively insulate them from non-specialists. Similarly, teenage cultures keep a distance from the parents' way of life by using a private language which is changed every few years so that the parents will sound out-of-date. Lovers often have their own special 'baby-talk', and many families use their own internal jargons and nicknames.

Words can also be used as a form of defence. Some people seem to live behind a thick hedge of words, as though everything that happens to them must be converted into a funny story and told to somebody else. It is as though they were afraid it might otherwise not count as real experience. Yet they also give the impression that they do not believe anybody is listening. They come across as lonely and empty, constantly trying to keep themselves busy. Nothing surprises them more than when someone actually listens to what they are trying so hard not to say – in other words, that they are anxious and alone, and wish they were liked for themselves and not for the stories they tell.

Other people defend themselves by choosing words with great care.

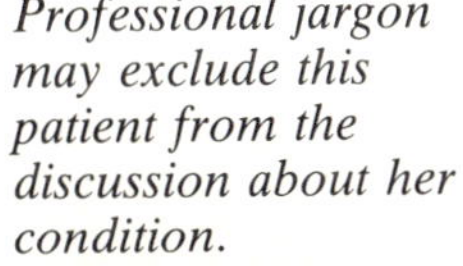

Professional jargon may exclude this patient from the discussion about her condition.

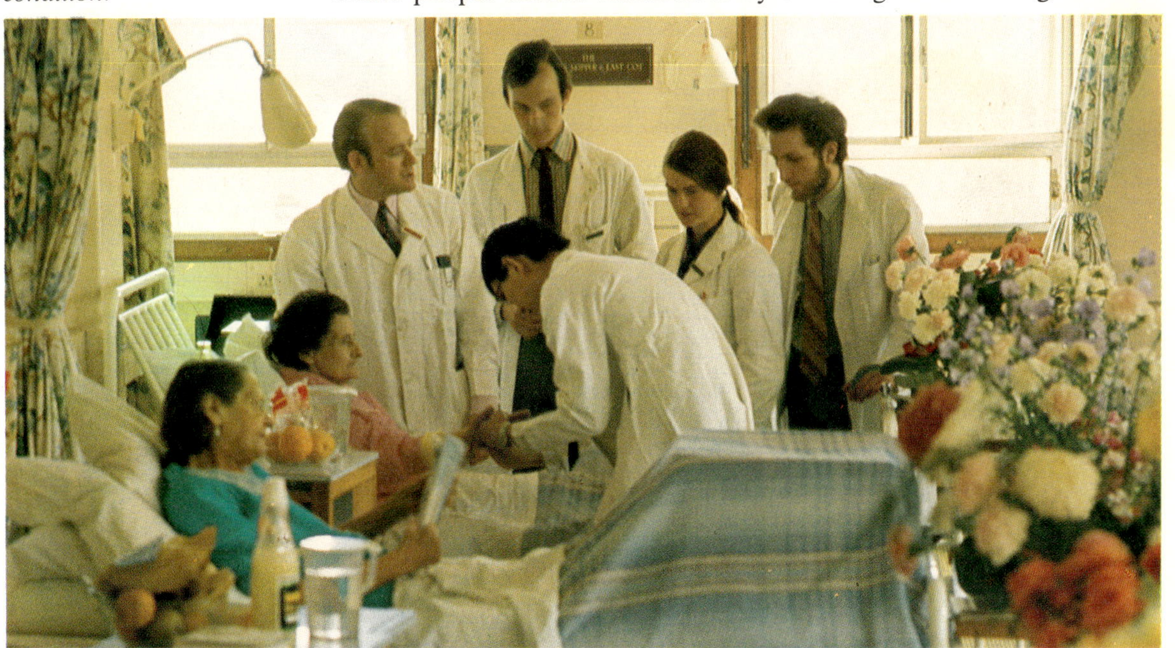

DING
ESA
ENTRADA

Each question receives a polite 'yes' or 'no', and little else. People who say too little about themselves seem untrusting and suspicious, as if they had something to hide. They give the impression that they despise either themselves or those who wish to talk to them. They are often too frightened to think of anything to say.

Many people have doubts about themselves because of what they see as their lack of skill with words. Western industrialized societies place a high value on verbal skills and, for the last hundred years or so, most state-run education systems have been based on the virtues of literacy. It is widely believed that people who are not good with words are the less intelligent members of society. Many parents who are ambitious for their children make the situation worse by insisting that the *form* of a sentence should be correct; they use this as an excuse to ignore the *content* of the message. Parents who correct their child's grammar, instead of listening to what he is saying, only teach the child how to fail as a communicator.

At times, even the most proficient speaker is tongue-tied. This often happens when we try to express our feelings, since many of us are unused to talking honestly and accurately about how we feel. A poetic phrase frequently sounds pretentious, and a man who wants to talk about his feelings in the company of other men will probably do so in a few overworked expletives. Within many close relationships, the partners expect to be able to read each other's minds or, at least, to guess at each other's feelings. It is important to put one's feelings into words, but this requires an advanced level of skill, because of the nature of most European languages.

The language expert B. L. Whorf has pointed out that most European languages use metaphor in the description of feelings. For example, a pain can be said to come and go as if it had legs and could walk. We talk about big feelings and little ones, as if the feeling were an object of a certain size. Our language can impose the need to talk about feelings as if they were objects in space which followed the laws of physics. For example, we say we are 'overflowing' with joy, as if the joy were a liquid which had filled up the space inside us. Talking about feelings can seem so awkward and artificial that it is easier not to speak of them at all.

Another common problem with words is found in sexual relationships, where the four-letter words, such as 'fuck', are widely considered improper. During the early stages of a relationship, a couple may have a happy sex life without ever having to put their sexual needs or problems into words. But when they need to ask for sex and to talk about it, the words often seem offensive and crude. On the other hand, words like 'penis' and 'vagina' seem clinical and impersonal. The answer to this problem lies in an improved programme of sex education and the reintroduction of the four-letter words, with the medical profession setting the example.

Although the choice of a word is important, it is also essential to understand the many different ways in which a word can be said. Verbal communication brings more precise levels of meaning to the messages we are broadcasting all the time. It is therefore less important than non-verbal communication, which will be considered in more detail in the following chapters.

Words can be used to communicate friendship (top left), anger (top right) or persuasion (left).

20 Non-verbal Communication

Most people have heard of 'body language', but what use is it?

We are all constantly broadcasting information about who we are, what we are doing and how we feel. Some of this information takes the form of speech: most of it does not. When someone speaks, his words constitute his verbal communication behaviour. All the other clues he gives out constitute his body language, or non-verbal communication behaviour. Many of these clues are unconscious; most of the time we are probably not aware of what we are telling other people about ourselves.

There are three main differences between non-verbal and verbal communication behaviour. First, non-verbal behaviour is continuous, while speech is not. Secondly, non-verbal communication generally conveys meaning less precisely than speech does. Thirdly, speech is usually directed at a particular person, while non-verbal signs and signals are often not directed at anybody in particular. If we understand these differences, we will be able to use non-verbal communication more skilfully.

Because non-verbal behaviour is going on all the time, anybody who looks at you can select some of what he sees in order to make guesses about you. If he does not know you, or is only just getting to know

Shared triumph: the unity of the team is symbolized in a joyful embrace.

A girl reacts to the camera. Her tough, masculine dress contrasts with a mock-compliant feminine invitation.

you, most of his guesses will concern the extent to which you are likely to fit into his world. For example, he may be interested in you because of the sex you are or the age group to which you belong. (These two questions will often be settled at a glance.) Or his interest may be aroused by the fact that you look important in a particular situation – you may be behaving as though you are in charge, for example. If your non-verbal communication gives him the impression that you are not likely to fit into his world, there will be less chance of him starting a conversation with you.

You can therefore use your non-verbal behaviour to control the likelihood of someone speaking to you. For example, if a stranger tries to talk to you on a train, you can use your body to show that you are not the kind of person who chats to casual strangers or, on the other hand, that you are quite willing to be friendly. You can also use non-verbal behaviour deliberately to show that you are too busy to talk, or that you will probably be very abrupt if somebody speaks to you. A shop assistant or a bank clerk who carefully looks away from you may be deliberately trying to seem uninterested, in the hope that you will ask somebody else to serve you. In addition to such conscious uses of non-verbal behaviour, we often unconsciously put people off, as, for example, when we are lost in thought and do not notice someone, or are too busy to have time for him. By revealing who we are, what we are doing and how we feel (whether this is done consciously or unconsciously), we can also show how easy it will be for someone to continue talking to us. The harder we make his task seem, the less likely he is to want to continue the conversation.

A detailed knowledge of non-verbal behaviour can give us more control over the effects of our behaviour on other people, but since non-verbal communication is far less precise than speech, guesswork is involved whenever non-verbal clues are used. We may misinterpret the other person's feelings and intentions and, equally, he may make wrong

Opposing non-verbal messages: while the man looks for an opening for conversation, the woman controls her posture so that she does not give out any false sexual signals.

assumptions about ours. For this reason, it is important that any such guesses are checked verbally. At the very least, we should not simply jump to conclusions about the other person and assume we have understood, as often happens. For example, when meeting a shy person who is reluctant to talk, many non-shy people jump to the conclusion that the shy person does not like them. Often, however, the reverse is true. When a shy person likes someone, it can make him more tongue-tied.

Non-verbal sexual signals are a common source of difficulty. Many men jump to the conclusion that if an attractive woman smiles at them or touches them, this is a sexual invitation. In many cases, the woman is just being friendly and has no intention of becoming sexually involved. There are many women who reject signs of friendship from a man because they mistakenly see them as being sexual in intention. False sexual signals can also arise between people of the same sex. For example, if a man who does not like being touched by other men meets a man who enjoys touching, the first man may falsely label the second as homosexual. The remedy in all such cases is to recognize that our interpretation of non-verbal sexual signals depends on guesswork and always check the guess verbally to see if it is accurate before acting on the message.

Whenever someone dislikes you, or seems to over-react to something you say, it is worth taking the trouble to think about your own non-verbal behaviour in case you have inadvertently given the wrong impression. For example, you might make somebody think you are angry with him when you are upset about something which has nothing to do with him. Although non-verbal behaviour is often not directed at anybody in particular, it can easily be interpreted as a personal reaction to a specific individual.

The next few chapters are designed to help you extend your understanding of the many kinds of behaviour which transmit information about who you are, what you are doing and how you feel. First, we will consider the face.

21 The Face

Making the most of one's face is an essential part of learning to be a better communicator

In communication, the most important facial structures are the muscles under the skin which enable a person to alter the shape of his face. There are three main sets of muscles. One set surrounds the lips, enabling them to be moved into a wide variety of shapes. The most important muscles in this group are at the corners of the mouth. To find them, you simply pull your mouth into its widest shape by saying 'Meee', and then press your fingers against the bulges which appear at the corners of your mouth. Someone who is not used to smiling nearly always has small or flabby muscles here. Another important group of muscles is found around the eyes. These muscles enable a person to open his eyes very wide or shut them tightly. They also cause the wrinkles which lie at the corners of the eyes in a mature face. The third main set of muscles is to be found between the eyebrows and under the skin of the forehead. Lowering the eyebrows often produces a vertical crease at the top of the nose, or, in some faces, two creases. Lifting the eyebrows has the effect of creasing, or 'corrugating', the forehead.

In many faces, these three important sets of muscles are neglected. Yet they are vital to communication. Many people can become better communicators if they practise some form of 'facial jogging'. The exercises are simple. To strengthen the mouth muscles, you should repeat

The poet, W. H. Auden. The complex character of the man is mirrored in his face.

long-drawn-out 'Meee' and 'You' shapes until the muscles tire. You can exercise the eye muscles by slowly opening and closing the eyes in a smooth movement and stretching them as widely as possible. To exercise the corrugator muscles of the forehead, slowly raise and lower the eyebrows several times. Facial exercises enable you to increase the range and subtlety of your facial expressions.

Many people will find the idea of deliberately pulling faces in order to exercise their muscles absurd, and even immoral. It is worth considering the reasons for this reaction. Some adults were taught as children to think of themselves as plain, unattractive, or even ugly. Physical beauty is highly valued in Western society, and the mass media reinforce the myth that behind an unattractive face lies an unattractive personality. This ridiculous belief can have serious consequences. A person who has been taught to feel that his face is unattractive may seriously underestimate the attractiveness of his personality as well. He may dislike having attention drawn to his face. When he was a child, he was probably told not to pull faces. As a consequence, he may now use a very restricted range of expressions, and fail to make the most of his marvellous facial equipment. Such people often defend themselves against their deep feelings of insecurity and self-rejection by resisting the idea of becoming better communicators. Their defence can take the form of regarding facial exercise as cheating, or as something artificial and immoral. Yet many women are quite happy to use make-up, and many men take great care to cover up spots and to trim their beards or moustaches to suit the image they wish to put over to other people! None of these methods is seen as cheating.

A face does not have to be conventionally beautiful to be attractive. The faces of a smallholder in Nebraska (below) and a Californian housewife (below right). show warmth and experience.

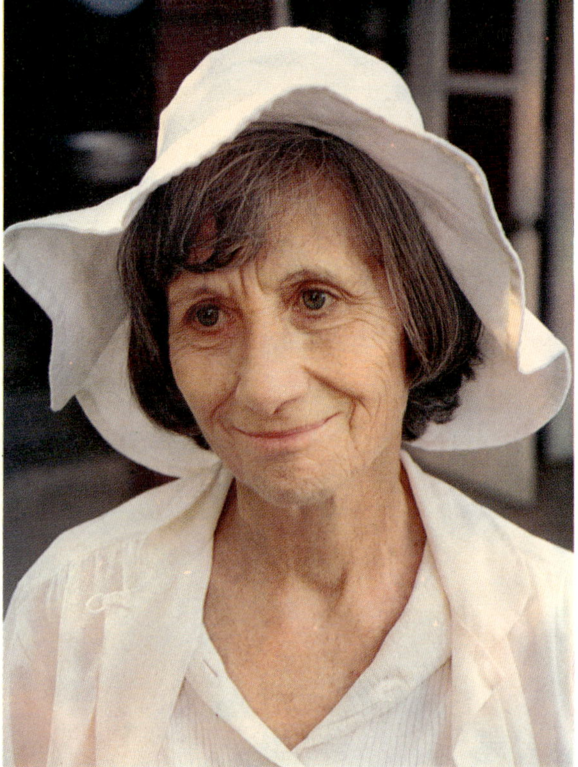

An early lesson in communication: the sharing of a facial expression gives pleasure.

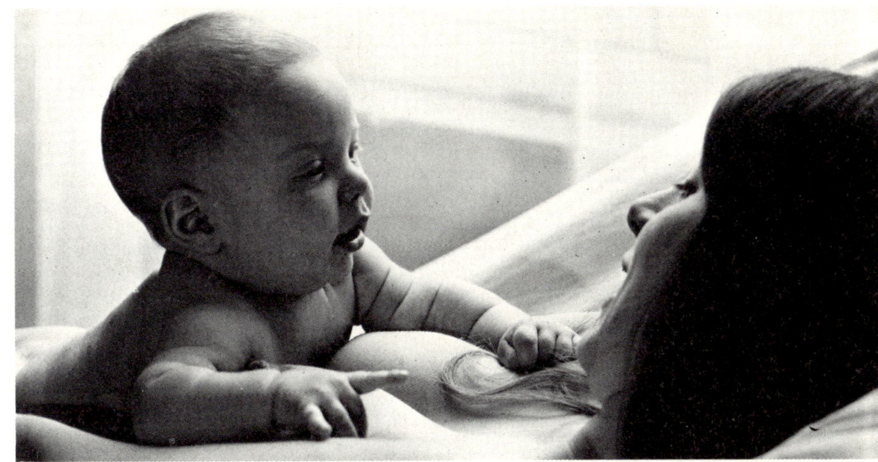

The association between the face and general attractiveness is due to the role of the face in sexual behaviour. The connection between the face and human love begins soon after birth, when a mother first looks at her baby, and the baby at her. The loving feelings of both the mother and the father are expressed in the way they look at their baby. Happy babies respond by returning the same look of delight. When the child grows up and falls in love, he will repeat the same signals with his mate, helping the two people to form as close a relationship as the one which existed between the child and his parents. As he grows up, the child learns to make faces which help others feel sorry for him or angry with him. Most of us continue to use the facial shapes we learned in childhood throughout the rest of our lives.

Human sexuality takes many forms. We each play the part of son or daughter, father or mother, lover, brother or sister, grandfather or grandmother with many different people. These roles depend upon which sex we are; we use them to give people special kinds of pleasure so that they will like us. Our looks and the way we use our faces determine whether they see us as sincere, loving people. Within a marriage, for example, a husband may use his 'little boy' look with his wife when he feels vulnerable and helpless, and his 'father' look when it is his wife's turn to be comforted. When he wants sex, he will sometimes look like a hungry baby, at other times like a devoted mother. The full range of human sexuality can be used within one relationship, so that the whole person is involved. The face signals all a person's needs in different ways; it therefore functions as a major sexual organ.

Giving and withholding pleasure by means of facial expression is used to control how fast we get to know others, and how far a relationship goes. Unfortunately, many people are afraid of their own sexuality, and reluctant to give facial pleasure for fear of being hurt. People who neglect their own faces often fail to enjoy the pleasure shown on the faces of others. If the face is controlled so that no emotion shows, feelings are not shared and communication fails.

A person's face is his 'shop-window'; it shows what he has to give to the world and what he wants in exchange. When his face is blank and immobile, he is living alone in an inner world which nobody else can enter.

22 Posture and Gesture

What do people say about themselves through their use of posture and gesture?

Posture means the way a person arranges his body when he stands, sits or lies down; it can also refer to the way he walks. Gesture is the use of body movement to add emphasis or meaning to speech, or to signal information in the place of speech. Both posture and gesture are concerned with the patterns created by moving the body, and with the way these patterns convey information about the person.

When we look at someone, we look first to see what he is doing. But at the same time as we are taking in this information, we are also making judgements about what he appears likely to do next. Posture shows intention. The way someone stands provides clues as to whether he is relaxed or tense, and whether he is likely to move suddenly or not move at all. For example, if a person is upright and slightly crouched, with clenched fists and an angry look on his face, it usually means that he is ready to hit someone. Yet if we look for further clues we may see that, although this is how he feels, his anger is directed at himself, not at us. His feet are being pushed into the ground to prevent movement forward, and his clenched fists are shaking towards his own body. His face shows that he has not selected us as the target for his anger, for he is looking wildly around, seeing nothing, trapped inside his inner world of anger. Posture shows whether someone is open to receive signals from other people.

The clenched fist is universally understood as a sign of defiance.

Posture is relaxed and approachable in a friendly conversation.

Communication relies upon clues about people's intentions; unless one person can accurately predict how the other will behave in the next few moments, there can be no peace and relaxation between them. If someone feels angry and tense, this produces unsettled feelings in everybody else who comes into contact with him. Even if the anger is not directed at other people, they may still feel threatened unless words are spoken to relieve the tension and give reassurance. A calm, relaxed body shows that its owner is approachable and not threatening. Someone who does not signal his intentions clearly is hard to trust and his behaviour may have serious consequences. For example, a child who never knows whether to expect a cuddle or a cuff grows up untrusting and afraid. His ability to communicate suffers and he often becomes maladjusted, unable to achieve his full intellectual and emotional potential.

The way a person uses his body shows how he feels about himself and other people. When we are unhappy with our bodies, our posture shows it. We use our hands to cover up parts of ourselves, particularly the main sexual parts, the face, breasts and genitals. Very often, an adult in distress arranges his body into the shapes he used in childhood to sulk or withdraw, to display aggression or disappointment. When we are angry with other people or feel hurt and rejected by them, we struggle to contain our feelings, and shift our posture rapidly from one

Some gestures can stand in the place of words in any environment. Italian art experts supervise the hanging of frescoes for an exhibition in London.

set of angular shapes to another, jerking from pattern to pattern, with no smooth continuity. If we accept someone, on the other hand, we relax and open up the whole body, showing that we trust that person and accept his intentions.

In Western society, a child is taught how to sit, walk and stand, in order to be the kind of person his parents approve of. For example, a little girl is taught not to show off sexually by a use of posture which is natural in a three-year-old, but unacceptable in a well-brought-up young woman. Boys are taught to sit up straight and not slop around, in keeping with the military traditions of self-discipline which still dominate our culture. Other cultures produce different models for their children, such as the graceful walk of the Nigerian or the carefree swagger of the West Indian.

In many of us, these controls are so deep that when we meet people who use postures we were taught not to use, we become as angry as our parents were during our own posture training. A manager may find himself having to suppress rage and indignation when a candidate for a job slouches in as if he had not a care in the world, and an older woman may feel threatened by the overt sexuality of a younger one.

Gesture grows out of posture. The signals a person can make with parts of his body are restricted by the position of the body at any one moment. Some gestures stand in the place of words. But for the most part, gesture adds and extends meaning which is already being conveyed by the body or by speech; it is not a separate signal system.

You should not become self-conscious about your use of gesture and posture, however. Learn to trust the other person, and direct your feelings of liking and trusting *at* that person through your face and your eyes. Your body will follow this lead if you can relax and let it behave naturally. The body control which we all learned in childhood is something to be understood and accepted, particularly in extreme cases where people find themselves angered by the 'attitudes' of others for no apparent reason. They are often coping with a very rigid set of internal controls left over from childhood, and would be amply rewarded in their personal lives if they could discover why they try so hard to repress particular patterns of behaviour. Such people may still be reacting to their own repressive childhood by unconsciously repressing other people.

23 Co-ordinated Body Movements

When people are communicating, they synchronize their body movements

When two people are paying attention to each other, particularly during conversation, they are often more aware of one another than they are of themselves. They lose self-awareness and in its place gain 'other-awareness'. This happens most when each is giving the other his undivided attention, as, for example, in a very intimate conversation between two close friends. The same thing happens to a lesser degree when two strangers are talking. The extent to which other-awareness takes over from self-awareness is a good measure of how close a relationship is. How can a person tell that he is getting through to someone else, and how does he know when he is not communicating successfully?

While someone is talking, he constantly makes small movements of his body. He sways backwards and forwards, for example, or moves to a more comfortable position. He nods or smiles, and moves his fingers, hands, arms and legs. These movements are called 'incidental body movements'. Experiments using slow-motion film have shown that two people who are talking and listening to each other co-ordinate, or synchronize, these movements in a kind of continuous dance. The dance of conversation can be slow and gentle or fast and furious, and it can also change tempo. But if one person is out of step, the other knows immediately, because self-awareness takes over from other-awareness.

Suppose that there are two sisters, Jane, who is happily married, and Sarah, who is not. Jane has been worried for some time about her sister, and is trying to persuade her that it would be better if Sarah left her husband. The two women are very close and they discuss the problem in detail. Jane is doing most of the talking. How does she judge the effect of her words?

While Jane is talking, she watches her sister intently. Sarah is looking

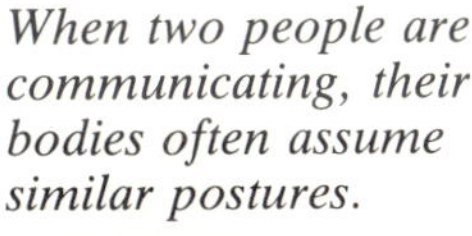

When two people are communicating, their bodies often assume similar postures.

The similar posture of the two players shows their loss of self-awareness during a tense chess game.

down towards her clenched hands, but sees nothing. She sits very still. Every now and then, at the pauses in Jane's speech, or when a word is particularly emphasized, Sarah nods slightly. From time to time, she has to shift her body position, for she could easily become stiff and cramped. But she only moves when it will not act as a distraction. The same is true of Jane. While she talks, she tries to experience in herself what her sister feels, and to frame her words through her awareness of these feelings. She does not wish to say anything which her sister cannot accept, and with each phrase she 'reads' the whole of her sister's behaviour to look for signs of rejection. Her own body movements are tiny, almost imperceptible. If Sarah makes any movement bigger than Jane's, or which interrupts her while she is speaking, Jane will know that she is no longer in touch with her sister's feelings. The size of the movement will distract her and break her concentration, forcing her to be aware of herself instead of trying to feel as her sister does.

The size of any discrepancy between the two sets of body movements shows the extent to which Jane is out of touch with her sister. It will help Jane (the speaker) adjust her approach so that it is on target once more. Or it may force her to stop talking for what will seem like an unusually long pause. Then Sarah will probably say something, trying to get Jane to understand. Are people like Jane and Sarah aware of all this? At the time, people are probably aware of the way they co-ordinate their body movements, but their awareness depends on a part of the mind which stores information for only a few seconds at a time. So although they are controlling their bodies consciously and with great care, they are not likely to remember the details.

Body movement co-ordination is just as important in communication between two strangers. They will both be aware in the short term of the extent to which each is involved with the other, because the dance of communication will tell them. If is difficult for the human body to be still for long, even in sleep. We all need to readjust our posture to avoid discomfort. But if we wish to show that we are really listening, we control our fidgeting to produce less distraction for the speaker.

From time to time, nearly all of us have wanted to get away from someone who is talking to us. Study of the way people end their conversations shows that the friendly way to do this is gradually to increase the sort of movements which disrupt synchronization of body movements. Strangers who do not like each other turn away very abruptly. If we suddenly reject attention from another person, cutting him off completely, it can produce intense anger or fear.

An understanding of co-ordinated body movement helps in many situations. For example, timing is important when it is necessary to break into a conversation between two people. The skilled communicator chooses a moment when the couple are changing the tempo of their conversational dance; this will often be at the end of one phase of their conversation. He therefore looks for big movements, or for the moment when *both* talkers are changing body positions. If a conversation is becoming more intimate, with the body movements getting smaller and more co-ordinated, but the interruption is necessary nonetheless, it is better to butt in early; this will cause less trouble than when involvement has become even more intense.

Proximity and a shared view of the world lead to co-ordinated body movements.

Teachers, lecturers and public speakers know they are losing their audiences when fidgeting increases during sentences instead of at the end of them, or when an audience goes very quiet for long periods. A change of position by the speaker, or a change in the tempo or loudness of his speech, will often put this right. A good speaker varies the pauses he makes, giving long ones now and then to allow his listeners to move into a more comfortable position.

The most intimate forms of communication depend upon full body movement co-ordination and upon the ability of each partner to lose self-awareness in exchange for other-awareness. This is most apparent in mutual love-making, which is very different from being made love to or making love to someone.

24 Touching

The kinds of touching people use show how they feel about each other

The way people choose to touch each other and be touched shows what kind of relationship they have, or would like to have. If they are complete strangers and do not wish to get to know each other, it is unlikely that they will touch except by accident. People who are crowded together in public transport or in a queue, for example, tend to avoid touching. If they touch accidentally, they withdraw as soon as they can. If this is not possible and they are aware that their clothes are touching, they try to keep still, and to avoid skin-to-skin contact at all costs. When strangers have to walk past each other so that they are likely to touch, they tend to defend certain parts of their bodies from accidental physical contact. A careful study of people using a very crowded street-crossing has shown that men are likely to cross with their arms in front of their genitals and to face the people they are passing, while women tend to fold their arms in front of their breasts and to face outwards.

People who wish to get to know each other, and who are therefore ready to take the first step towards establishing a relationship, often use ritual or stylized forms of touching. In Western society the most

Old friends can greet each other without eye-contact, by touch alone, when the centre of interest is elsewhere.

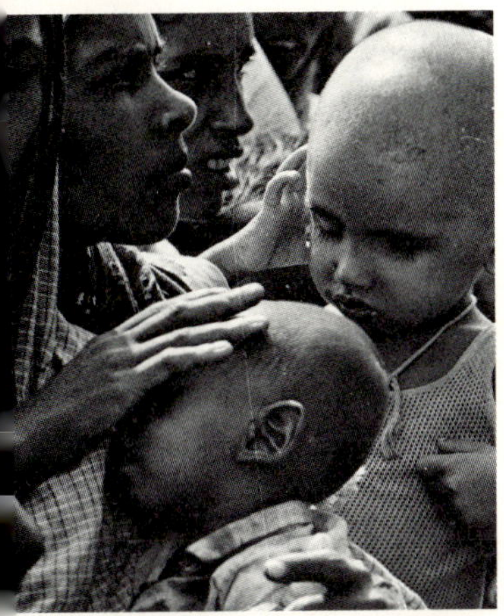

Different kinds of touching used to show friendship (top), to give comfort (centre) or as a sign of intimacy and companionship (above).

important form of ritual touching is the handshake. It varies enormously from place to place. In some areas, it is expected to be brief and very formal; in other places it is accompanied by prolonged shaking or hand-holding. The rituals used when a man meets a woman are often quite distinct from the way the same man would greet another man. And some groups, such as the Freemasons, use a special form of handshake so that they may recognize fellow members by this means alone.

Not only does the way people shake hands vary according to where they come from; it also indicates what kind of relationship each person is seeking to establish. Two people meeting at a business conference, for example, will often use the handshake to try to impress each other with their decisiveness, honesty and sincerity. A different way of shaking hands is used, however, if one of the two people is of very much higher status than the other. A commoner who is meeting a queen would not expect to grip her hand firmly, shake it slowly up and down while squeezing it, hang on to it as long as possible, and finish up with a lingering caress! Such a handshake would suggest a relationship so improbable as to appear impertinent.

A handshake can also be used to indicate how you feel, both about yourself and about the person you are meeting. It is widely believed that someone's handshake says a great deal about his character; a weak handshake, for example, indicates a 'weak' character and a strong handshake suggests a 'strong' character. The truth of this can never be proved – it is based on a rather naive view of personality and human behaviour. Moreover, in forming our first impressions of somebody, most of us take into account many other features of his behaviour, such as his appearance and general attractiveness, the way he moves, the distance he chooses to stand away from us, the amount of eye-contact and smiling, and his facial expression. We also react favourably or unfavourably to his voice and choice of words.

There are various forms of hand-to-hand touching other than the handshake (hand-holding, for example) and each has its own particular meaning. In many Western countries, if a handshake goes on too long – particularly between men – it can become embarrassing, for it looks very similar to hand–holding. This would add a sexual dimension to the contact, giving onlookers the impression that the two men were sexually involved with each other.

Although people can touch each other with many different parts of their bodies, the hand is the main instrument of touch contact. It is particularly important in establishing and maintaining relationships, and in showing and judging feelings within a relationship. This is because it is such a versatile and sensitive part of the body. A blind person's hand can become so sensitive that its owner can read by following the tiny raised dots on a page of Braille print. Naturally, not all hands are equally sensitive or capable.

An experienced palm-reader can guess correctly a great many things about a person simply by studying the shape and versatility of his hand. The palmist will test its sensitivity by touching it in different ways and watching the reactions of the client; he will notice the way the skin may have been affected by different kinds of work or by accidental damage. All this is possible even before he looks at the lines on his hand! The secret lies in the fact that each hand is unique, just as its owner is; the limitations on what the hand can do and feel help us to judge the limits on what the individual is capable of doing and feeling.

We have many names for the things a hand can do. Holding, gripping, pinching, squeezing, pressing, pushing, pulling, lifting and dropping are all varied by increasing or decreasing the *pressure*. The tap, slap, punch, hit and poke depend on different amounts of *impact* for their effect. Rubbing and scratching are, like stroking, forms of *caress*; they produce changes in the level of pleasure or pain from moment to moment. Pressure, impact and caress touching can be used separately or in combination.

For example, a man may be showing kindness and affection to his nephew, who is aged sixteen or seventeen. They sit face-to-face in chairs a short distance apart, and the older man reaches out and touches the younger man's knee (impact). He follows this by a squeeze (pressure), which tails off into a firm but gentle stroking movement (caress) as the hand is withdrawn. The touch sequence is designed to prevent giving the wrong impression as well as to give the right one. The impact, by coming first, suggests a man-to-man approach. If the caress had come first, it would have suggested a more 'motherly' approach on the part of the uncle. Pressure first would have suggested, perhaps, a need to attract the young man's attention or a fatherly kind of criticism, thus failing to respect the fact that the nephew is almost grown-up. Pressure followed by impact would have suggested criticism and punishment. By ending with the caress, the older man is showing affection, but he is also in effect saying that, now that the boy has grown up, respect comes

Professional touching: just the right amount of pressure and caress are needed in order to avoid hurting and not to give too much pleasure.

first. The nephew has become an independent individual, and yet the old love remains if he will still accept it. As this example shows, combinations of the three kinds of touching enable us to say very precise things to people with whom we have a relationship.

Touching can vary according to its *frequency*, *duration* and *intensity*. Frequency means how often a touch-sequence is repeated. Duration means how long a particular kind of touching lasts. Intensity refers to the amount of strength used and the strength of feeling experienced by one or both of the people involved. Let us consider the example of the uncle and his nephew again. When the uncle touches his nephew, he may be repeating a sequence which he has used many times before; he may have used it only on very special occasions; or he may never have done this before. The frequency of the sequence within their relationship will add to the meaning of the contact and help the nephew to make sense of it. It may have become a meaningless habit; it might signal a pattern of behaviour the nephew knows very well and has come either to dread or to gain reassurance from (for example, it might be the uncle's usual way of leading up to leaving, or asking for money); or it might be the very first time he has produced the sequence, so that the nephew takes it as a signal of a change in their relationship and is puzzled by it. The duration of the whole sequence, or of any of its parts, will also be important. The caress may be shorter than usual. Or, if the act is being produced for the first time, the caress may be the shortest – or the longest – part of the sequence. Whatever happens, each variation in duration will express a subtle difference of meaning

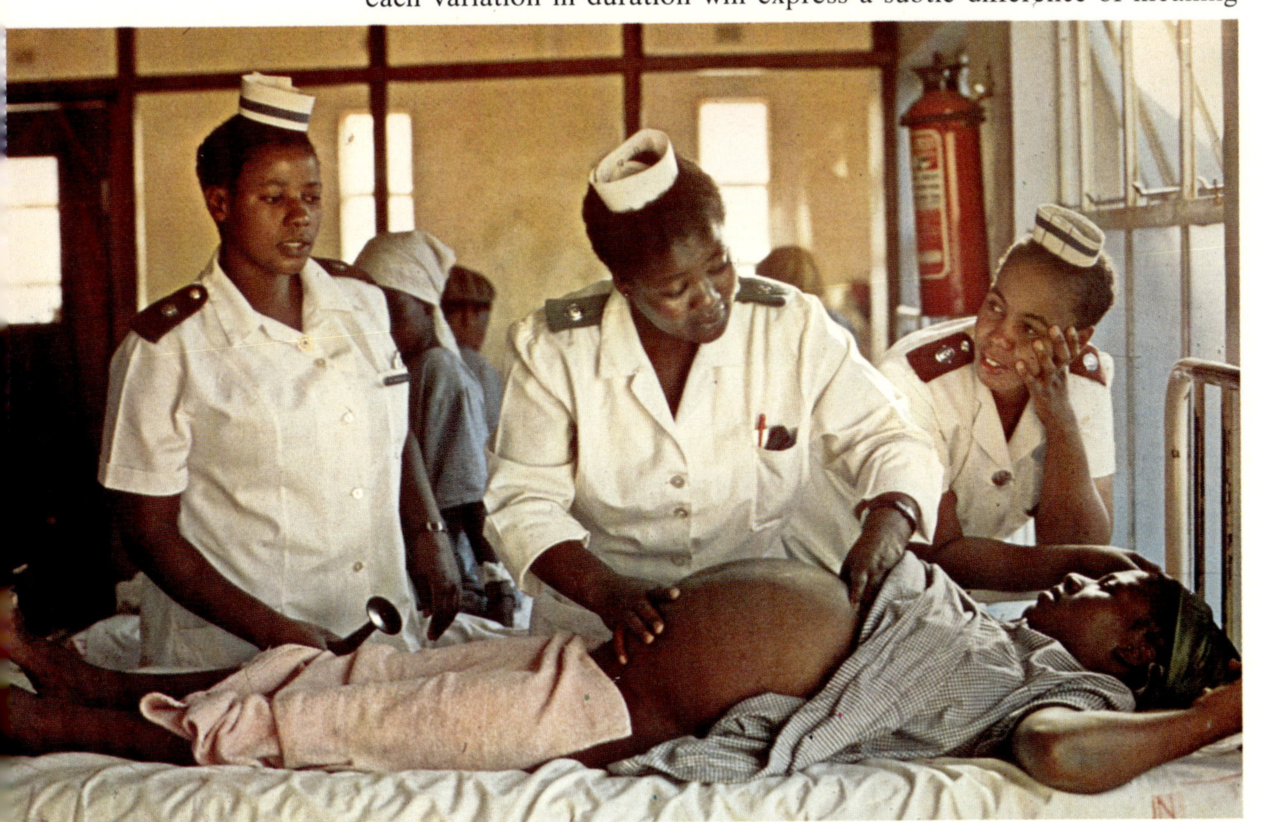

because it will produce a subtly different feeling. Finally, the intensity can vary. The important question is whether the sequence, or any part of it, was pleasant or unpleasant. If it hurt, was it intended to hurt? If it was very light, was it so light that it tickled, and was this intentional or not? Of course, the level of intensity can vary during the touch, or be constant. Where the behaviour has been used before, the nephew may notice some important differences in the intensities used this time.

This is only one example of the way subtle feelings can be expressed by variations in the frequency, duration and intensity of touching. The touching will either be accepted or rejected, and the extent of this rejection or acceptance will vary according to how long the touch-sequence lasts (duration); how often it is rejected or accepted, or has been in the past (frequency); and the strength of the acceptance or rejection (intensity).

The levels of stimulation at which we feel touching as either pleasure or pain vary from person to person, and from time to time within the same person. Our feelings when being touched will depend on who is doing the touching and which part of his body this person is using; which part of our body is being touched; whether the touching is done in public or in private; the intensity and duration of the touch; the pattern of changes in intensity and duration; the frequency of the touching, and so on. These factors all help us decide what the touch means and how we wish to respond. But some things are not so easy to control! For example, a gentle caress which we like in some moods may feel quite different in others. Our mood changes when we are tired or very excited and according to the time of day, the day of the week and (most noticeably in women because of the menstrual cycle) the time of the month. A caress may feel so heavy that it hurts or so light that it tickles. Yet before the mood changed, the caress was pleasant. Medicines and drugs (such as alcohol) alter our 'touch thresholds'. They are also altered by illnesses such as colds and flu, which affect our ability to absorb stimulation from outside the body.

Touching is probably the most important of all forms of non-verbal behaviour, since it can be used to convey subtle variations of reward and punishment, acceptance and rejection; different degrees of intimacy; and differences in status. Even when people do not actually touch, they can use other forms of non-verbal behaviour instead, such as the way they look at each other, how close they stand, how they approach each other and the way they speak. These topics are considered in more detail in the next few chapters.

Variations in the intensity of touch: a playful use of harmless pain (left) and a punch about to lead to a serious fight (below).

25 Eye-contact and Looking

The eyes have a particular emotional significance in person-to-person contact

Two people can easily make contact by looking into each other's eyes. This phenomenon is known as mutual eye-contact. It is quite different from having your eyes looked at as interesting objects by, say, an optician. During mutual eye-contact, each person can see that he is the complete focus of the other person's attention. This is an exclusive type of behaviour; it is not possible to engage in mutual eye-contact with more than one person at a time.

The direction of gaze can indicate that a person is paying attention to something important. This often stimulates somebody else to look in the same direction to see if the object of the gaze is important to him, too. For example, if someone appears to be interested in something going on behind the back of the person he is talking to, the person being spoken to is likely to turn round to look as well. The direction of gaze also shows what is more important at that particular moment, the relationship or whatever else has the looker's attention.

During conversation, the eyes are often used to signal whose turn it is to speak. When he has finished talking, the speaker is likely to look at the listener to show that he has finished and that the listener may reply without interrupting. One study found that if the speaker fails to

Directions of gaze are co-ordinated in a crowd. A carnival incident provides the focus of attention.

The waiting area at John F. Kennedy airport is designed so that passengers look at public rather than private behaviour and can avoid eye-contact.

look in this way, the listener either does not answer at all or delays longer than usual before doing so.

Where, and how intently, someone looks shows what is important to him. People not only point with their fingers; they also 'point' with their eyes. Looking at somebody to get him to speak is rather like 'prodding' him with a finger. Indeed, there are ways of looking at another person which correspond to each of the three main kinds of touching, in other words, impact, pressure and caress. For example, 'staring somebody down' depends on pressure, while lovers often appear to 'caress' each other with their eyes. If someone uses a 'caressing' look with a stranger of the opposite sex, he is making an obvious sexual suggestion. Although many people are unaware of the similarities between touching and looking, with practice they can often extend their 'looking repertoire' until it is as subtle as their touch behaviour.

The emotional significance of the eyes has long been recognized. In 1960 a remarkable discovery by Professor Hess of Chicago University enabled scientists to investigate this phenomenon mathematically. Hess noticed that the size of the pupils changed (regardless of the amount of light in the room) when a person was particularly interested in the object he was looking at. For example, the pupils of a hungry person dilate, or become wider, when he is presented with the sight of appetizing food. Yet pupil size is beyond conscious control. When Hess's students were asked to pick out the most attractive people from a group of photographs, one particular set was consistently chosen more often than the others. This set contained photographs which had been expertly retouched so as to artificially widen the pupils.

By photographing the size of a person's pupils while he is looking at a series of objects, a scientist can obtain an exact measure of variations in pupil size. In one experiment, people were shown a set of patterns, each consisting of two, three or four circles which looked like eyes. When these circles looked most like real eyes – two circles arranged in a horizontal row – dilation was greatest. This suggests that there is a visual preference for eyes which is either inborn, or learnt at a very early stage of the baby's development.

The eyes are the main focus of a person's attention while he is engaged in conversation. Through mutual eye-contact, he can connect his own attention system to that of someone else so that a mutual system is formed. During this contact, each person's eyes focus *into* one of the eyes of the other person. Mutual eye-contact is another form of body motion synchrony; it is impossible unless both partners co-operate. When a person's eyes become tired, he can still maintain contact if he switches his point of focus from one of his partner's eyes to the other. Pseudo-contact is possible when two people are more than a short distance apart. It is made by looking at a point near the eyes, such as the bridge of the nose or the eyelashes.

The emotional significance of the eyes is probably related to a person's very early visual experiences, particularly while he is being fed as a baby. The mutual connection between mother and baby during feeding can include simultaneously very close eye-contact, cuddling, caressing and mouth-to-nipple contact. This combination is a very powerful emotional formula and is repeated by both men and women during love-making.

Mutual eye-contact is a sign of mutuality in other things. For this reason, it is often used sparingly between strangers, who may spend more time not-looking than looking. Friends, and particularly lovers, share mutual eye-contact more often than any other group.

Over greater distances than usual, people can still make eye-contact by exaggerating their signals.

26 The Use of Space

All communication involves the structured use of space

People control their communication with others through the use of space. When two people begin a conversation, they select a certain distance from each other, and orientate their bodies so as to achieve a level of comfort or discomfort which suits their purpose. Two friends, for example, will sit face-to-face for some conversations and side-by-side for others. An employee who is being admonished by an angry manager will be expected to stand or sit in a respectful posture while his superior towers over him or paces backwards and forwards. Two strangers who are meeting for the first time will tend to sit at right angles to each other's line of vision; the position of least effort will be one in which neither is looking at the other directly. In this way, neither will be offended if the other looks away, while the energy required to exchange eye-contact can be clearly seen and appreciated. People use space as their natural medium, just as fish swim in water. Human awareness of space shows in the way men design their environment, allocate territory, and express and describe their feelings.

Proximity

The distance chosen by two people for conversation varies according to culture; people from Latin and Arab countries tend to prefer more proximity during personal communication than Northern Europeans do. It also depends on the immediate surroundings. In a crowded public place, such as a rush-hour train, a person may be forced to stand or sit closer to strangers than he would prefer. Consequently, he will adopt a defensive posture, withdrawing into a small personal space and staying there, so that movements of the hands, for example, will not be misinterpreted as an attack upon one of the other travellers. People in a crowded space also tend to avoid eye-contact. Conversation is limited, or carefully obscured, so that casual listeners will not overhear personal matters.

Body orientation

The head is most comfortable when facing forwards. Any sustained deviation from this position costs effort and the most extreme deviations, such as looking behind, cannot be sustained for long. A person can show how much effort he is making in order to pay attention to someone else by adopting either a comfortable or an uncomfortable position. For example, two people who are sitting face-to-face would need to make an extra effort in order to turn away. If they did so, it would indicate that they wanted to do something more important than look at each other. Many public environments such as waiting rooms have chairs placed side-by-side, so that strangers who wish to talk will have to make an effort to do so.

Looking up at an object requires more effort than gazing straight ahead. Looking down, on the other hand, is relatively easy. A person who is sitting down is forced to use energy just to look up at someone who is standing over him. The extra 'cost' involved in communicating can be emphasized when, for example, a person of high status looks up from his desk at a lower status person, but is careful not to alter any other part of his posture. The body message says, 'I shall make the effort of sparing you a few moments.' Sometimes the person of higher status looks down on the low status person, and makes it quite clear that looking down is costing more effort than he would normally spend in talking to his subordinate. This time the message says, 'In your case, even looking down requires an effort.'

Territory

Space in buildings is often allocated to people as their personal territory. At home, a person may have a room of his own, or a special corner marked by objects he values. This emphasizes ownership and control. Children develop the ability to control and structure space for their personal use during the years from early infancy to adolescence. Some husbands expect all the toys to be tidied away before they arrive home, thus emphasizing their ownership and control of all the resources of the household, including the people who live there. There are often battles between untidy adolescents, exerting their right to control a space of their own, and parents who demand equal rights over what they see as *their* space – not given to the child, but only granted as a privilege in

In a public queue people define their own private space.

People at a committee meeting show which part of the table is theirs by marking the space with their property.

return for certain duties. These power struggles are similar to those which take place at work, where office space, for example, is used to reflect status: the larger the office someone controls, the higher his status.

Symbolic space

We sometimes feel that a person is too close; at other times, a loved one is too far away. This can be true both in the literal and the metaphorical sense. In most European languages, verbal descriptions of feelings depend upon the idea of a symbolic space within which a person experiences his reactions to others. The human attention system regards perceived characteristics of an object as *belonging* to that object. Similarly, relationships are often characterized by a symbolic reference to conditions of communication which are either typical or desired.

For example, a 'distant' relationship suggests two people who are too far apart for a significant amount of mutuality to occur. To 'look up to' or to 'look down on' somebody both indicate a form of relationship which would typically involve communication restricted by these postures. 'Closeness' suggests holding someone close in a hug or embrace, but it can also give the impression of trespassing. This would suggest that the other person is too close for comfort. Communication operates in a symbolic space, which has its counterpart in the real space surrounding the human body.

27 Varied Speech

The human voice can be used in a variety of ways to keep the listener interested

The human voice has a remarkable musical range. Even during ordinary conversation, people use high and low notes and constantly alter their tone of voice. There are wide differences in the tonal qualities of individual voices, for a person's voice is unique, just as his finger prints are. When someone is nervous, however, his voice is more difficult to control and breathing becomes more erratic, leading to embarrassing squeaks and booms. The best way to control these tonal irregularities is to breathe more deeply and start again, while trying not to become more embarrassed.

In addition to varying the musical pitch of the voice, a person can

The power of the voice: at a football game in Ann Arbor, Michigan, the crowd shout with one voice to urge on their team.

Three kinds of speech: the harsh voice of criticism, the soft whisper of a shared secret and the snarl of defiance.

produce a wide range of volume, from the loudest shout to the quietest whisper. Actors, teachers, and others whose work requires them to address large audiences without a microphone, often use a loud form of speech which is more effective than shouting. This is known as 'diaphragm speech'. The diaphragm is a large muscle below the ribs which relaxes to let air into the lungs and contracts to push air out. Diaphragm speech is achieved by keeping the lungs fairly full and tightening the diaphragm very slightly. The throat and mouth are opened wide, and constriction is avoided by keeping the head well up. A loud voice can then be obtained without the effort of shouting, although this takes considerable practice. When using a microphone, however, ordinary speech is more effective, provided that the speaker remembers to move away from the instrument when speaking loudly, and towards it when whispering.

The rate of speech and the number and length of pauses must also be included in the list of speech variables. Some people are naturally fast talkers, others slow, but nearly everybody tends to speak faster when excited, and the meaning is easily lost. A fast speaker who is listening to a slower one is often tempted to finish off the other person's sentences for him. Slow talkers find this irritating but they seldom have the chance to say so! Many people find reading aloud a problem. At meetings, for example, they tend to read too quickly. The listeners may be too polite to point this out, and bad communication results. Long pauses are also a feature of some individual styles of speech. These tend to occur most frequently when someone is thinking aloud, particularly about his feelings. In face-to-face conversation, pauses are usually acknowledged by the listener with a nod or an 'mm' noise, to show that he is still paying attention. But when pauses which would be of normal length for close contact occur over the telephone, the listener often wonders if the speaker is still there.

Some telephone speakers can achieve better communication by nodding less over the phone and using more 'mm's' and 'uh-huh's'. These noises (known as 'pause fillers') serve a very useful purpose in conversation. Not only do they show the speaker that he is still being listened to and that his words therefore have some value; they also imply that the speaker himself is valued within the relationship. Timing is very important here, for pause fillers are the vocal equivalents of incidental body movements, and any lack of co-ordination shows the speaker that he is not getting his message across. Most of us have probably at some time or other listened with only half an ear, simply saying 'yes' or 'no' in the right places, and then startled the other conversationalist by saying the wrong one at the wrong time.

There are vocal equivalents of impact, pressure and caress touching. Short, sharp, staccato words and phrases emphasize dominance and anger. The steady buildup of pressure through increased volume is often used to display power, as when a parent is scolding a naughty child. The voice can also be used as a caress, and many people are attracted just as much by someone's voice as by his physical appearance or by a soft touch from sensitive fingers. In firms which make most client contact on the telephone, the receptionist's voice will be far more important than her looks. A frustrated consumer who complains by telephone can often achieve more with a soft, sexy voice than by being angry or strident. In one company studied by a psychologist, it was found that the office girls who got most dates from company salesmen were not the prettiest, but those with the most pleasant voices.

The amount of speech is another important factor. Almost all of us feel that we talk either too much or too little when we are with other people. The origin of this self-judgement can often be traced back to the parental discipline imposed in childhood. Chattering is part of the natural development of speech in childhood, and good parents listen carefully and patiently. Yet not long ago, children were expected to be 'seen and not heard', and there are still many families today where parents discourage chattering. Children who are told too often to 'shut up' and not talk nonsense can very easily feel restricted in conversation in later life; they become reticent and are easily hurt. Too much parental insistence on 'correct' speech may also act as a contributory factor in stuttering, although some people who stutter are reacting to a need to listen to their words too carefully. Modern treatment for stuttering builds up confidence by using a device which prevents the sufferer from listening to his own voice.

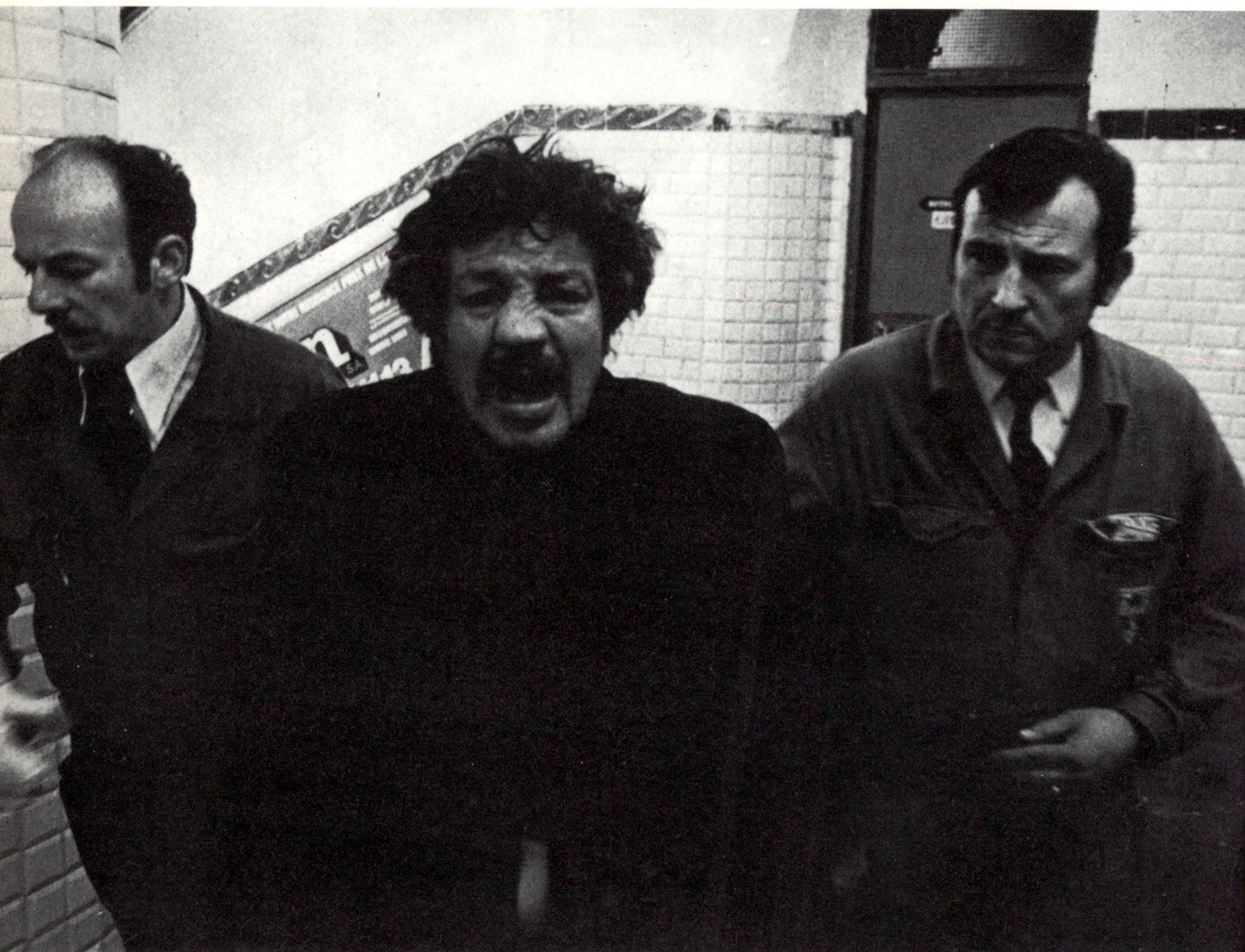

A man arrested on the Paris Metro allows himself to be led away but uses his voice to air his opposition.

28 Better Talking

What can you do to become a better talker?

Some people do not enjoy conversation under any circumstances; others dislike particular situations, such as arguments or party small talk. You may feel that you talk too much or too little, or that you are tactless or too aggressive, or even that you always sound silly. Whatever the problem, anxiety as a result of poor speaking skills deserves to be taken seriously. Although many sufferers bottle up their agony for years on end, unable to admit the sickening fear which grips them whenever they have to make conversation, their difficulties can be overcome with practice.

The first step is to understand what causes the problem. All difficulties with communication stem from relationships with other people. Sometimes the difficulty only shows in a particular situation, such as talking to somebody important, or to a person who is extremely attractive, or perhaps aggressive. Whatever the problem, you are probably responding to hurtful criticism from somebody close, perhaps a parent, a partner or a friend. Maybe the criticism occurred a long time ago, in childhood or adolescence, and it still hurts. Alternatively, you could be experiencing it now in an important relationship. Improving your ability to enjoy talking begins from the moment you realize that you are responding to criticism from somebody else – criticism which was, or still is, part of a relationship that matters to you.

The next step is to decide whether you want to accept the criticism. Whenever other people say you have a problem, there are at least two reasons why they take the trouble to tell you; one is for your good and one is for theirs. For example, a husband who leads his wife to believe she always says something silly in public is not only trying to stop her making a fool of herself; he also fears she will make *him* look stupid. This is because he is afraid he will do something silly himself. His own insecurity and lack of confidence are at least half the problem. A man who is afraid to chat easily and informally with his boss might be reacting to criticism from his father a long time ago. People who criticize your ability to speak should encourage you instead. Try to find out why they choose criticism instead of encouragement. In other words, discover what *their* problem is and see if you still accept their criticism of you.

The next question is why you listen to the criticism. A communication problem grows out of a relationship, but it needs fertile soil to grow in. If you are bottling up anger, you will have trouble coping with aggressive people; if you are afraid you are unattractive, you will resent the ease with which an attractive man or a beautiful woman gets other people to do exactly what he or she wants. Some of us are afraid of people who use words with great skill because we are unsure about our own ability with words. A person who feels at ease with himself does not have to worry about communication problems; he can handle the relationships he gets himself into, and knows how to trust his inner feelings so as to avoid relationships he cannot handle. He is not neces-

Two versions of non-verbal boasting. A man shows off expansively to an appreciative audience (above). Two punks show off to the camera but their already exaggerated dress means that extra effort is required to exaggerate still further (below).

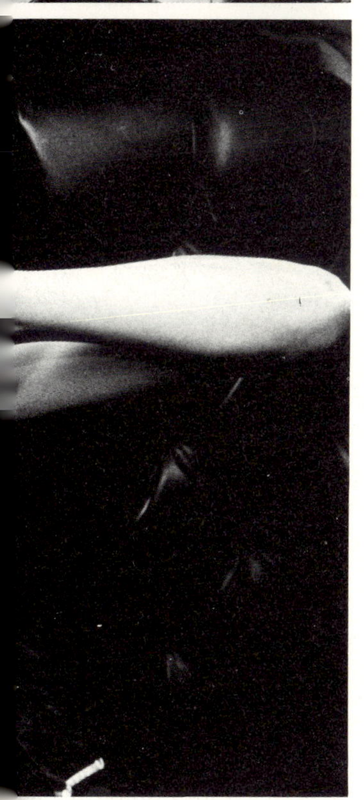

sarily a better talker or a better listener than other people, but he is less self-conscious and recovers more quickly from his mistakes. Everybody makes mistakes from time to time. When it happens to you, try not to feel that you need to reorganize your whole personality, but simply accept yourself as you are.

Suppose you know what you are doing wrong, but still go on doing it. Some hints on dealing with the most common problems might help, although this is no substitute for tackling the problem at its roots.

Some people tend to exaggerate or boast when holding a conversation. They cannot help giving the impression that their lives are more important or valuable than everybody else's. This behaviour takes two forms, verbal and non-verbal. Non-verbal boasting shows in speech that is too loud or too fast, or uses affectations, such as a false, 'educated' accent. Verbal boasting tends always to go one better than the last speaker: 'That's nothing, you should have seen me last Tuesday . . .', and so on. If you catch yourself indulging in verbal or non-verbal boasting, it is because you have begun to feel threatened; your response is a defence against being devalued by others. To overcome non-verbal boasting, try to build up someone else's ego for a change by asking simple questions and using your own behaviour as a reward system. The more rewards you give out, the more you will receive. Stop trying to talk, and learn to become a good listener until you find common ground with your audience. Make eye-contact, and touch the other person lightly to help you calm down. Watch your breathing and your drinking; both should be slow. If you suffer from verbal boasting, stick to what you know, even at the risk of being undervalued.

Small talk at parties is a problem for many people. The simplest advice is to avoid it altogether and try to chat for the sake of learning something worth knowing. Most people prefer to talk about their special knowledge – their work, their families, their home towns, and so on – rather than about the weather or the previous night's television programme. If you admit that you find small talk uncomfortable, you can often get someone else to agree with you.

Debates and arguments on current affairs cease to be fun as soon as you get out of your depth. A useful tactic is to ask someone *how* he came to hold his views, rather than *why* he holds them. This will switch the emphasis away from matters of principle and the detailed analysis of recent political history, and make the discussion more human. There are often interesting personal histories behind the beliefs people hold, and the two of you can compare notes on equal terms. If you like argument, you are more likely to keep the other person's interest if you agree at least half the time than if you always disagree.

Try to avoid clichés and stop yourself telling someone else what he thinks or feels. If you ask for advice, beware of the game of 'Yes, but . . .', in which you merely reject each suggestion the other person offers. Asking questions to which you already know the answer is another common conversation-stopper. It often takes the form, 'You aren't . . ., are you?'

What matters most is the relationship you build up with your audience, whether it is one person or a group. If you show that you trust other people, they will overlook your mistakes. In order to show that you like other people and trust them, you need to be a good listener.

29 Better Listening

However good a listener you think you are, there is always room for improvement

An elderly lady doctor was once asked to describe the case she had enjoyed most. 'Many years ago,' she said, 'a woman swept into my office and began to tell me about her husband's infidelity. She talked non-stop, pouring out the story of her life. I tried to interrupt, but she would not let me speak. I gave up trying, and just nodded and smiled while she described her feelings and went on and on. At the end, without pausing, she thanked me for all the valuable advice I had given her, said she would certainly take it, and swept out. Six months later, she came in beaming with happiness and carrying flowers to thank me again. I hadn't said a word. But that was my most successful case.' The doctor had trained to be a talker, but from then on she strove to become a better listener.

The art of listening depends upon sensitivity to the needs of the speaker. These needs are broadcast the whole time through non-verbal communication. A good listener recognizes that if he listens to his own needs, rather than those of the speaker, he will miss most of what is being said to him. His own broadcasting will act as 'interference', blotting out messages and turning the conversation into a competition as to who is the person with the most needs. At times, everyone needs to be listened to, but to be a good listener, you also need to know when to talk. You cannot be a perfect listener all the time without suppressing some of your own needs. These needs should be met rather than bottled up.

Conversation meets some of our most basic needs. When a new conversation begins, the paramount need is to have one's own identity and purpose acknowledged. Two strangers get along better if they know each other's names, even though they may forget them soon afterwards. Identity is also established by sharing information about jobs and asking why each person happens to be there at that particular time. People who have met before usually need to re-establish contact at the point where they left off when their last meeting ended; the feelings they had about each other at the close of the last encounter will almost certainly influence the start of the next.

Both people will also want to feel secure. The greater their need for security, the harder they will work to make time and space available for their conversation. A good listener gives the impression that there is all the time in the world to talk, even if there is not. If he can only spare five minutes, he says so, but he makes the time feel much longer by putting everything else to one side and giving his whole attention to the other person. Helping someone feel secure and relaxed is repaid because the time is used effectively.

This then means that the next set of needs can be met. This is the need to feel that you belong, that you feel relaxed and at ease with the other person. Touching meets this need very clearly, for it shows ac-

Dr David Owen, British Foreign Secretary, and Mr Cyrus Vance, US Secretary of State. At an important international conference the listening skills of these two professional communicators are stretched to the maximum.

ceptance of the other person's body. It can be expressed in a handshake, a light touch on the arm or under the elbow, an arm round the shoulder for a moment, or simply by standing in a relaxed way close enough to touch. Eye-contact is nearly as effective as touch in showing acceptance. A good listener takes the risk of being misunderstood, and trusts the other person. If he cannot do this, it is only because his own needs intrude, thus lessening his effectiveness as a listener.

By accepting a person, we make him feel special; he knows he is valued for who he is, not what he is. Nothing is more uncomfortable than trying to talk with someone who cannot accept you as you really are. Some people are not able to listen because they impose a status on their audience and refuse to accept a person's own view of himself. Common examples are the boss who seems to think your whole life is spent at work, being subservient to him, or the man who talks to women not as people but as sexually attractive objects. Good listening depends on honesty of purpose. If this cannot be established, it is better to extricate yourself politely and move on to somebody else.

We talk because it helps us to increase the value of our resources. Through talking, we can unload negative feelings, find solutions to problems, receive permission to be ourselves, or simply fill in time so it will not be wasted. Without communication, we can only guess what we are worth to others. Yet we each have parts of our inner world of which we do not know the value. Conversation helps us discover and make use of them.

Fidel Castro is called out of a meeting to listen to the problems of one of his former schoolteachers. His deliberately informal posture makes him approachable to the average citizen.

Good listeners learn to recognize when someone is making statements about his own value to himself. For example, 'It's not important' often means '*I'm* not important.' The phrase 'Not really' means 'Yes, to some extent'. For example, 'I'm not really angry' means 'I'm angry, but I don't think I should be.' The role of the listener at such times is not to reject the feelings of the speaker, but to help him clarify them. Conversation is much more valuable if it helps a person realize some of his own worth.

Better listening and better speaking both contribute to more rewarding relationships. They are skills which can be improved at any time of life by observation and practice, and by accepting other people as you wish to be accepted yourself.

30 Counselling

What is the best way to help when people ask for advice?

When someone turns to you for advice, you may feel flattered or insulted. In either case, you should avoid certain temptations. You may feel insulted because the person seeking advice has often received it in the past and never followed it; he seems to be using you as a convenient prop to support his own ineptitude. Or you may feel flattered because being asked for advice increases the sense of your own importance. Whenever someone needs you, he is vulnerable and you have power. It can go to your head like wine. Even trained doctors, teachers, lawyers, nurses and counsellors are often unaware of the extent to which they have become dependent upon the power they wield over others.

The best way to help someone who asks for advice is to use counselling skills. Counselling is a way of listening to and talking with another person to enable him to arrive at the decision which, under the circumstances, he can live with longest. This may not be the decision you would make, or even one which you would advise someone to make. Counselling skills are not given to everybody. The best counsellors not only spend a great deal of time on training and study; they continue to make mistakes and to learn from them long after their period of training. However, there is no mystery about counselling; it is better to know what counsellors do, and to try to be good at counselling, then to let down a friend or hurt a loved one simply because you have not been trained.

What does a person want when he asks for advice? First, he is looking for someone he can talk to freely and without embarrassment and who will treat what he says in confidence. Usually this has to be somebody who is not involved in the problem. Secondly, he wishes to be more certain of how he feels. He wants to work things out for himself and make sense of what is happening in his own way. A person in trouble is beset by doubts about his ability to cope, partly because of his confused feelings at the time. Talking about the problem helps him clarify his feelings about all the alternatives available to him and then choose one of them. Thirdly, a person facing difficulties looks for support. This may mean that he needs reassuring that he is doing the right thing. But reassurance is best if it comes from within, rather than from a friend or counsellor. The most durable kind of reassurance is renewed self-confidence. The need for support can also mean sharing pain and anger with someone who is uninvolved. For example, many problems arise from broken relationships under circumstances which prevent a person showing the anger or grief he really feels. A supportive counsellor is able to share these feelings without being so hurt or frightened by them that he is forced to protect himself. Counselling means facing pain and living through it by sharing, not by running away, being shocked or driving the feelings underground.

There are some things the person asking for advice does *not* want.

Above all, he does not want a solution which has no chance of success. Advice based on the formula 'If I were you . . .' is not going to work. He would have to learn how to be you before he could act on your advice! Nor does he want to be told to pull himself together, behave like an adult or act his age. He is trying to do all these things in any case and this may partly explain why the problem exists in the first place. A person usually wants to solve his problems for himself; he does not want you to do it for him, only to help him do it. He may give the impression of wanting you to wave a magic wand so that all his troubles go away, but beware! You may be imagining this because, deep down, you wish he would go away and burden somebody else. It is important to avoid reassuring him by saying it will all blow over and some day he will look back on the crisis and find it funny. This makes it look as though you cannot face the problem which exists now. A person worries because he needs to, not because he wants to. He is asking for help in order to worry more effectively.

It should be emphasized here that the person asking for help is not doing so in order to find a new sexual partner. A person often turns to a member of the opposite sex for help and support, and finds that this is the first time for months that someone has really listened to him. Counselling brings people into a very close relationship and much of the talk is highly intimate and emotional. As a counsellor, you cannot stay detached all the time and your own needs are bound to surface. Touch and cuddle by all means if this gives comfort and is a sincere expression of the way you feel. But watch out for what psychiatrists call 'transference', the loving affection a helped person gives the helper. It looks very like a sexual invitation, but if accepted by the counsellor, would add yet one more complication to the other person's life. If you feel sexy, this is your body being greedy, and your own need to be loved getting the better of your ability to listen to the other person's needs.

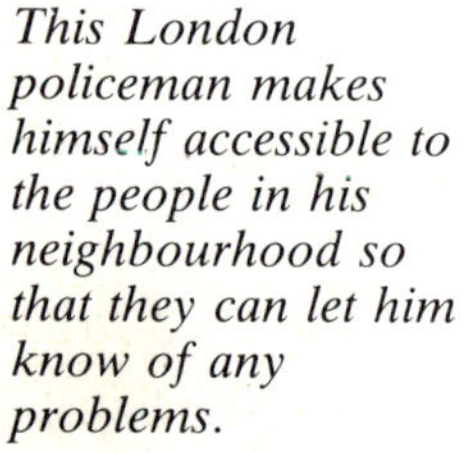

This London policeman makes himself accessible to the people in his neighbourhood so that they can let him know of any problems.

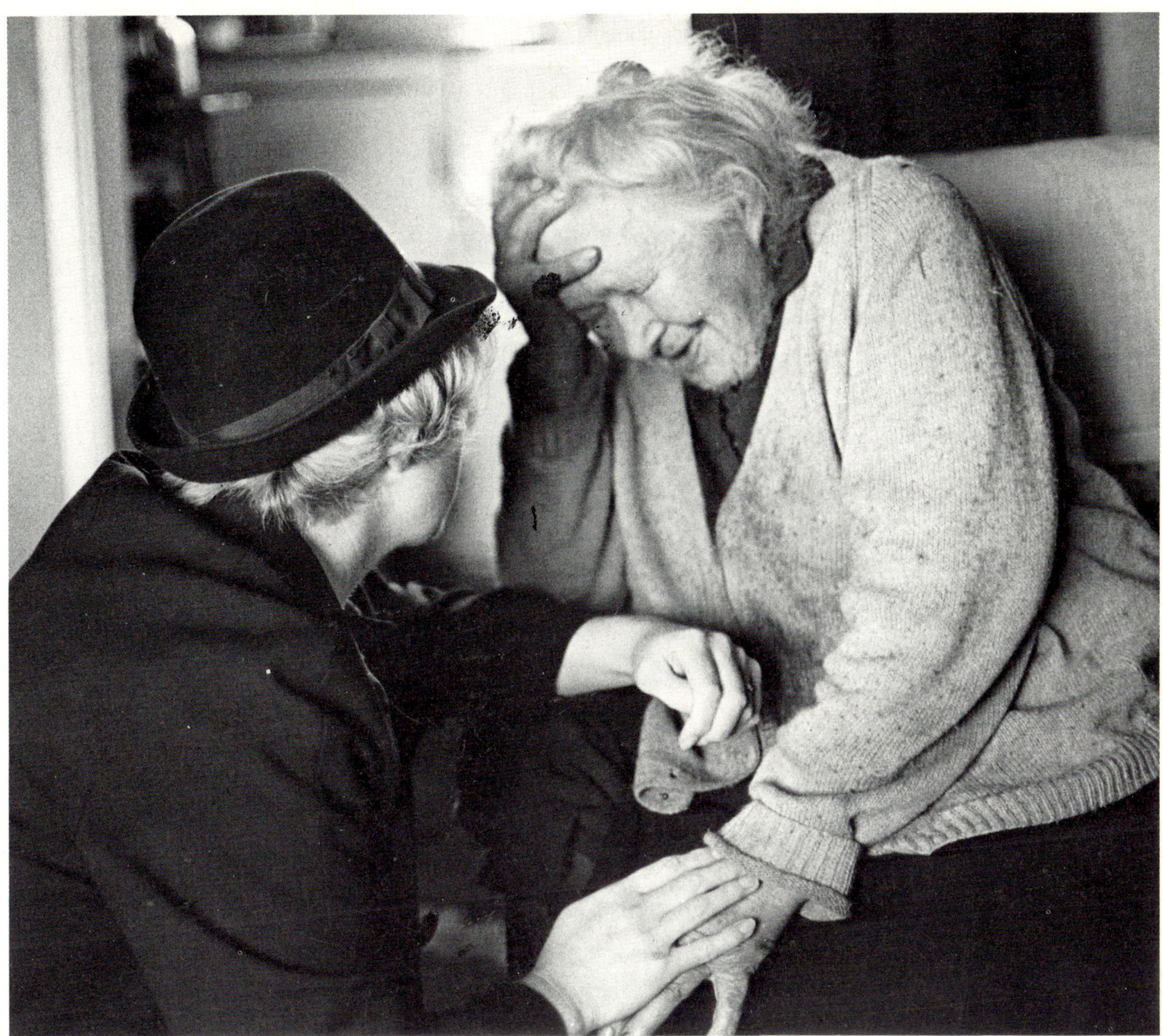

Sharing feelings is a vital part of a counselling relationship.

You may be tempted to tell someone what he feels, particularly during the long and painful pauses when his fear, anger or pain takes over. But 'I know how you feel' is simply not true. As Solzhenitsyn once said, a man who is warm cannot understand a man who is cold. It is also better to avoid the temptation to tell someone what he must or ought to do. This will only make it more difficult for him to take charge of his own life. The realization that there is a solution must come, not from you, but from the person being counselled. If you can stay in touch with his feelings and simply be present as a warm human being, you will be helping. If you feel cut off from him, ask him how he feels and wait to be told.

Not everyone makes a good counsellor. You may not feel sufficiently at ease with your own feelings. Someone who has achieved the full peace of self-acceptance through his own crises is often better suited for counselling than the rest of us. But if you use counselling in your work, or think you could become a counsellor, there are training courses and books which will help you. The more people who have these skills, the better off we will all be.

31 Sympathy and Empathy

Understanding your feelings and sharing them with somebody else

Feelings are the body's way of drawing attention to increases and decreases in need. A good feeling shows that a need is being met, while a bad feeling shows that a need is getting stronger. Being able to understand your own feelings means knowing what your needs are. This is not a simple question. Because we have many needs throughout life, and cannot always be certain of satisfying them all, we have to suppress some of them from time to time. We tolerate discomfort when we cannot meet some of our needs, or when we think it will pay us to accept a short-term loss in order to make a long-term gain. Whenever a need is suppressed, feelings are bottled up inside us. This may be done for good reasons at the time. For example, we may suppress our delight when we gain the upper hand over a rival because it would show us in a bad light, or suppress anger with a child because he would not understand and anger would only make the situation worse.

As a result, we all have needs hidden away inside ourselves and feelings which we cannot use. Relationships enable us to put these hidden feelings and needs to work, thus making better use of our whole personality. Two of the most important ways in which we can use our hidden feelings and meet previously suppressed needs are through the expression of sympathy and empathy. Sympathy enables us to show concern for others in such a way that we feel better ourselves. Empathy takes this process a step further and allows us to take our own needs into another person's inner world to be shared and met.

Let us look first at how sympathy works. Suppose that Clare is a widow and today is the anniversary of her husband's death. Some people will have no sympathy for her. They will be individuals who have never experienced loss and grief, or who have suppressed the feelings because they have stronger needs of a different sort. Clare's boss is such a man. 'Get on with your work,' he tells her. 'You should be over all that by now. We have to get those letters out by five and it's already half past three.' He is alarmed by Clare's grief and by the look of desolation on her face because it awakens his own distant memories and draws attention to needs he has suppressed. Unable to tolerate his own discomfort, he issues his orders and then retreats to his office and keeps himself busy. June, the youngest typist, wonders what all the fuss is about. She says to herself, 'It's been five years now, the silly woman. Why can't she cheer up? She's making everyone feel miserable!' She hopes she will never be like Clare, old and unattractive, just like June's own mother. But deep inside, she is afraid she will be just the same one day. Karen, the other girl in the office, puts her arm around Clare and soothes her. The feeling of misery in the office has upset her and comforting Clare helps her feel better. Besides, she does not like her boss, and showing sympathy to one of his victims helps her cope with the anger she dare not show him directly.

Sympathy depends on people sharing similar feelings in order to meet

Empathy and sympathy. Mary Barnes was an 'incurable' schizophrenic, but after treatment from R. D. Laing she became a successful artist. Mary has just seen the major crisis in her life re-enacted on stage. Here Mary and the actress who played her openly share their feelings.

their own individual needs. There is nothing immoral about this; we all have needs which only we can meet. When we sympathize with someone, this may give us the opportunity to express feelings which circumstances would normally prevent us from showing. By showing sadness or pleasure on behalf of someone else, we can express part of our hidden feelings without having to admit the real basis for them.

Sometimes a door can be opened into the inner world of feelings to let someone else in. This is how empathy feels. It is like being at home inside somebody else, and it comes about by allowing another person to enter your own inner world. Sometimes it happens without a word being said. If Clare's boss understood and accepted his own feelings, he would recognize that grief and the fear of pain are just as much a part of his life as of Clare's. He too is lonely, and there are people he misses in his own way. All he has to do is to sit beside Clare for a moment and show that he has heard what her body is saying through the drooping head, the sad face and the way she sits lifelessly on her chair. He need not try to drive her feelings away or encourage her to get them over and done with; he can simply feel his own suppressed grief alongside hers and let her into his world in the hope that she will let him into hers. They need only stay a few moments, but the opening of the door will help them both to be whole people.

It is never easy to share feelings which have been hidden inside a person for a long time. Even in the closest relationship, there are often needs which are kept secret. People who are very good at talking to each other, and who think they know one another very well, are sometimes afraid to open up the part of the mind where frightening thoughts and negative experiences are tucked away. 'If he really knew me, he might not like me' is the thought which people use to defend themselves against their own suppressed rage and fear. 'It happened before I met her and has nothing to do with her' is another common excuse.

Is it better to let sleeping dogs lie, not to stir up past miseries and to put such things behind us? This is what Clare's boss thought he had done, and what millions of people think they have accomplished. Small bouts of unaccountable cruelty are often the result – cruelty to oneself, as well as to others. Sympathy is desirable, but it is only second-best. Good communication depends on knowing your needs and accepting even negative feelings. It also depends on the ability to share these feelings and to trust people to like you, not in spite of them, but because of them. This is where sympathy ends and empathy begins.

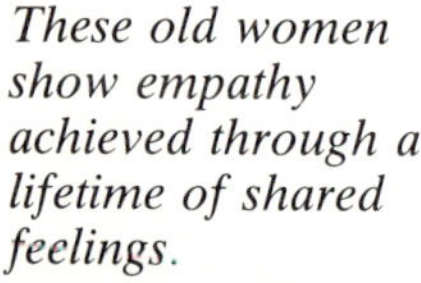

These old women show empathy achieved through a lifetime of shared feelings.

SECTION THREE ACQUAINTANCE

Acquaintance can be seen either as something which happens in one encounter or as a long-term process lasting several meetings. Section Three looks first at why we get to know some people better than others and then explains how we reveal our identity, personality and objectives, both consciously and unconsciously, together with some of the risks involved.

The next few chapters examine single meetings: how we can deliberately set out to get to know one particular individual, how we can make the right first impression, and the short cuts we take in acquaintance by 'labelling' others. Some specific problems are dealt with next – the difficulties posed by shyness, loneliness and getting to know children and adolescents.

The final part of the section deals with the way acquaintance can grow into friendship; and how our hidden needs can be met positively, or used against us in manipulative relationships.

32 The Importance of Acquaintance

Acquaintance skills can help us change the nature of a relationship or keep it stable

Relationships differ in the extent to which people know each other. At one extreme, strangers may be meeting for the first time, forming only the most temporary of relationships, perhaps as salesperson and customer. At the opposite end of the scale, we may find an elderly married couple whose lives have centred round each other for many years and who are familiar with almost every detail of each other's personality and experience. Within the set of relationships which surrounds us, there will usually be some people we have known a long time and others we have only recently met.

Yet this is not always so. For example, somebody who has just arrived in a new district might have cut all previous ties and not had time to form new ones. All his relationships will be with people who are strangers. Alternatively, an elderly person, or someone who is lonely or shy, may have a set of relationships which consists entirely of acquaintances he knows equally well and has known for a long time.

These examples point to two important facts about acquaintance. First, it can act as a stabilizing influence on a relationship. When two people meet for the first time, their relationship could, in theory at least, develop into a friendship or love affair which lasts for the rest of their lives. If this happened, they would spend their lives getting to know each other in all their different moods and in varied situations. Usually, however, most of the people we know stay at around the same level of acquaintance. The relationship develops fairly rapidly up to the point where we know them well enough for our purposes and theirs, and then remains stable.

Secondly, acquaintance helps us change our relationships. This may be necessary because our personal set of relationships is unsatisfactory. For example, somebody who is lonely or shy may feel depressed because he cannot widen his circle of friends and fully meet his emotional, intellectual, social or sexual needs. Or perhaps a particular relationship is causing distress, as when a married couple have drifted apart and can only be happy once more by getting to know each other better. Sometimes we try to increase acquaintance with somebody, not because our present relationship with him is obviously unsatisfactory, but because new opportunities have arisen for us to work together more closely and knowing him better will help.

Some people prefer a dynamic set of relationships, in which there is constant change as old acquaintances disappear and are replaced by new ones; they seem constantly to be meeting people, making new friends and getting to know a wide circle of old friends even better than before. Not everybody is as extrovert as this. Many people are happier to have a small group of close friends and to avoid change in their relationships. Such people are introverts; they see no advantage or excitement in making new friends just for the sake of it. Many of us seem to become particularly extroverted or introverted at certain times of our lives, such as adolescence.

Both extroverts and introverts can benefit from a better understanding of the process of acquaintance. For example, someone who dislikes change may be forced to make new friends as his valued relationships end, when people move away from the neighbourhood, children grow up and leave home or old friends die. Alternatively, someone who normally enjoys getting to know people may need to resist advances from an unattractive but insistent stranger. We need skills to stabilize or change our relationships, and a knowledge of acquaintance theory and techniques forms the keystone of such skills.

The simplest way to understand acquaintance is to see it as one of the products of communication. Basically, people get to know about other people by hearing about them, watching them, or meeting them and talking with them. However, mutual acquaintance is best achieved through face-to-face conversation. This is borne out by many laboratory experiments and long-term studies conducted by social scientists. The people we get to know best are likely to be those who live near us or

In theory, any two people in a crowd could meet and build a relationship, but in practice they tend to be suspicious of strangers and, in any case, may already be in the company of friends.

work at the same place. We are most likely to marry someone from our own neighbourhood, and almost certainly from the same social class. We also get to know someone better if we are attracted to him, and this usually happens when we have similar attitudes and opinions.

Because communication and acquaintance are linked, every time people come into contact, they can learn something new about each other. Through non-verbal communication we become familiar with someone's appearance and style. By talking to him or listening to him in conversation with a third party, we can collect information about who he is, what he does and what his attitudes and opinions are. Part of the skill of acquaintance lies in collecting information which enables us to get to know somebody rapidly. If we like him we can then enjoy more of his company; if we do not, we know what to say in order to protect our own interests against any attack he may direct against us. By understanding how somebody consciously sets out to project a certain image, and how he unwittingly reveals his unconscious objectives, we widen the scope of what we can learn about him.

A neighbourly chat on a derelict street. A relationship which began because of the neighbourhood has survived the destruction of the area.

33 The Process of Acquaintance

Why do we get to know some people better than others?

Although frequency of meetings, attraction, and length of acquaintance are all important factors, none alone explains why we get to know some people better than others. For example, nearly all of us have acquaintances we have met many times yet hardly know, and friends we have seen less often but know better. Similarly, many people we know very well are unattractive to us, while others are very attractive but we deliberately avoid them or cannot get to know them. Also, the people we know best are not always those we have known longest – not even necessarily those who are the most attractive and the most often encountered of the ones we have known longest!

Each individual is the centre of a set of relationships designed as far as possible to meet all his needs. For example, he may be able to find enough companionship and employment by having half a dozen friends and one employer. If someone comes along who would potentially make an excellent friend or boss, there may be no 'vacancy', and so the relationship does not develop further. If a particular need is already met, the relationship which meets it can be considered 'exclusive', because its existence excludes the need for duplication. Marriage is the most obvious example of an exclusive relationship, but it is not the only one; all close relationships are to some degree exclusive.

People have a limited amount of time for their relationships. However sociable someone is, there are simply not enough hours in the day to keep an infinite number of close friendships flourishing. Space also limits some kinds of relationships. We can only have a certain number of next-door neighbours, for example, or colleagues in an office. Individual resources also vary greatly. Some people can spare more energy than others for meeting people and relating to them. We choose as friends the people who suit us best, but in order to meet our need for security, we tend not to drop friends immediately when new ones come along who would suit us better.

We sometimes forget that each of us is just one out of many people in the life of somebody else. The reasons why we do not get to know

One-way acquaintance: fans get to know all about their hero, but the object of their affection knows them only as a group.

The student chefs will be well-acquainted with one side of their instructor's personality, but his private life will remain a mystery to them. The potential for further acquaintance is limited by the instructor's need to make objective judgements about their work.

Equal colleagues: their acquaintance is designed to enable them to work easily in close proximity, but no real friendship need follow. They share eye-contact but still defend their personal space.

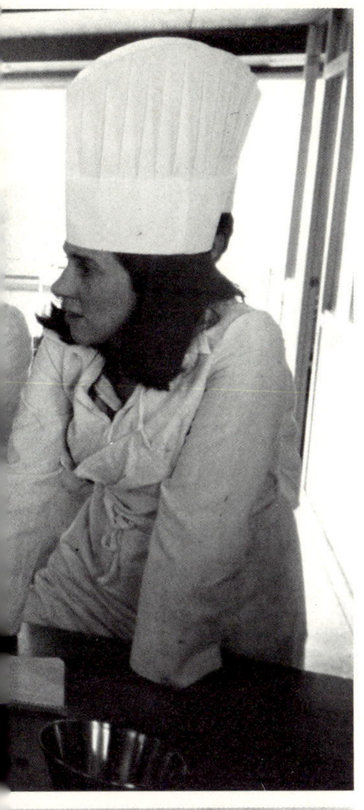

that person better, despite his attractiveness, his availability and the fact we have known him for a long time, may lie in other relationships of his about which we know nothing.

For a personal relationship to develop between two people, each partner has needs which must be met. However, acquaintance, attraction and communication are not always equal on both sides. One-sided acquaintance occurs when two people do not know each other equally. For example, a mother may know her son very well, but never be seen by him as a person in her own right, only in terms of the part she plays in his life, cooking his meals, washing his clothes, and so on. A manager may be known in all his moods by his staff, but he may not even know their names. Attraction, too, is often one-sided. This does not only apply to sexual attraction, as in cases of unrequited love. Someone may be admired for his work and never realize that other people have noticed, or he may be liked by people he does not like in return.

Communication is often a one-way process. Through a person's non-verbal communication in particular, we can get to know many aspects of his personality without him noticing. We each have an individual style – a way of walking, moving, speaking, choosing clothes, reacting to events, and so on – with which people can become familiar if they see us often enough. We know many people by sight but not by name, and know a great deal about others but hardly ever talk to them.

One-way acquaintance can meet many needs, but for two-way, mutual acquaintance to occur, the needs of both people must be met. Many of our most important adult roles would be impossible without a measure of mutual acquaintance. This is particularly true of roles such as husband or wife, best friend, trusted assistant, and so on, which depend on personal qualities of a highly individual nature.

The people who get to know each other best are those who love each other most. In determining the level of acquaintance, love is more important than intimacy. It is perfectly possible for two people to have an intimate or sexual relationship without wanting to get to know each other. The doctor and his patient and the prostitute and her client are extreme examples. All societies accord special status to people who love each other mutually and exclusively; the family is the most universal of all social institutions. Societies are organized to allow or encourage those who love each other to stay together.

The people who get to know each other least, and whose acquaintance is most one-sided, are those whose relationships are based on power. In any group, the people who are the best, and most widely, known are those with the highest status, but this degree of acquaintance is mutual only between the high status person and a few colleagues or cronies of similar status. Sometimes a leader is loved by his followers, or an entertainer by his fans, but this is not a unique, exclusive mutual love between individuals such as that between two people who are 'in love'. 'Stars' are worshipped from afar; the love between soldiers and their commander is kept hidden.

How often people meet, the way they communicate, how long they have known each other and how attractive they find each other are only important when there is a need for the relationship. If the value of one person to the other is already fully exploited, further development is unnecessary and tends not to take place.

34 Self-disclosure

Revealing ourselves intentionally

During conversation a person frequently reveals who he is, what he is doing and why, and how he feels. These statements are known as 'self-disclosures'. Psychological studies of this phenomenon show that a person talks about himself and his true feelings most with the people he knows best. If one partner in a conversation self-discloses, this encourages the other to do the same; if you say more intimate things about yourself, the other person will do likewise. Each individual has a characteristic level of intimate self-disclosure. If forced above this level too quickly, he will often decide he does not like his partner.

Verbal self-disclosure between strangers usually begins by establishing identity. If the two people concerned feel safe as a result of these first exchanges, they will then say more about their general intentions in the situation and their feelings about other people, and begin to talk more intimately about themselves. Important elements in establishing identity are learning the other person's name, hearing about his social connection with the other people present, why he is there, where he lives, and so on. Each person will usually also talk about his job, and say whether or not he is married. Sometimes this information is given indirectly, such as, 'I was telling my chief accountant the other day . . .' or 'My daughter said that . . .'. In many cases, the information given first has frequently been presented before to strangers. Certain items will look prepackaged for easy consumption, whereas health problems, a 'failed' marriage, a bereavement, and so on, will probably be touched upon only briefly. This may indicate that the speaker does not wish to be seen as the kind of person who discusses his problems with strangers or burdens others with them.

Friends also begin most of their encounters by using identification self-disclosures. They may mention names (in some cases, to show they have not forgotten them) and will often check systematically through things they remember about each other to see which of the other person's needs have been met since their last meeting, asking about family, friends, work, health, and so on. These preliminaries establish the identity of the *relationship* in much the same way as strangers establish their individual identities. Laboratory experiments have revealed interesting differences in the way pairs of friends and pairs of strangers converse. In either case, both people make an equal contribution to the conversation over a twenty-minute period. However, strangers will tend to ask each other long questions and receive long replies, whereas friends tend to ask short questions and receive long replies.

In the identification phase, people appear to be looking for similarities, such as mutual friends or acquaintances, similar work or home circumstances, or places they both grew up in or have visited. They are also looking for differences, partly to see if they are addressing someone of higher status. They tend to display attitudes and opinions later, and will only do so if they feel safe because they are speaking to somebody like themselves. In the early stages of acquaintance, people tend to avoid disagreements. If one person expresses strong opinions, the other may make a mental note to avoid him in future (or to avoid the topic if he cannot avoid the person). As people get to know each other, they establish enough common ground for them to disagree without seriously threatening the relationship.

Verbal statements of intention are often phrased so as to show an acceptable or appropriate image. For example, 'tough' language may show determination, or stressing that what you say is only an opinion may show caution. During early acquaintance these displays are often produced in order to be admired: you are expected to be impressed by the other person's image. Similarly, a person may display his status by 'name-dropping' or by revealing confidential information which only somebody 'in the know' would have.

Much of this intentional self-disclosure is non-verbal. For example, a woman may reveal the kind of person she is by her choice of clothes, jewellery, make-up and accessories. Expensive clothes draw attention

In a formal situation people may be reluctant to self-disclose. Alcohol can help them to relax.

to wealth and their absence shows the reverse; wedding or engagement rings indicate marital status. (The absence of a wedding ring may also be revealing. It might signify that somebody is open to a sexual relationship, even though he has said he is married.) Fashionable items may be used in an attempt to indicate a youthful outlook; clothes which are simple, practical, yet decorative, are often chosen to indicate an efficient person with a capacity for enjoyment. One of the most revealing elements in dress is the way a person shows how much care he has taken over his choice of clothes. On formal occasions, this is often deliberately emphasized in elaborate hair-styles, ties, fasteners which take a long time (such as 'hooks and eyes'), or even clothes which look uncomfortable. Sometimes, however, dress for formal gatherings is exaggeratedly simple but totally impractical for everyday use, such as the backless gown or the white tuxedo. In many primitive societies elaborate tattoos stress the identity of the individual by showing off his tribal and religious loyalties.

Intentional self-disclosure through body language is often designed to reveal the kind of relationship somebody has. A stable, exclusive sexual relationship is indicated by 'tie signs', such as holding hands, linking arms or standing close, which show that each person will be loyal to the other. You are forced to regard both people as if they were one person.

Unintentional self-disclosure: how we reveal our 'hidden agenda'

We are not always fully aware of our intentions. We may suppress parts of them because we are 'not that sort of person'. For example, if somebody describes himself as patient, this may be because he had a bad temper when young, but has learned to hide the anger which builds up when he is frustrated. Or someone who is easily aroused sexually may see himself as the kind of person who would never have a casual affair with a stranger, even though the suppressed urge to be promiscuous is still strong. Suppressed desires often form the basis of a 'hidden agenda', a set of unconscious needs which someone cannot satisfy because he is 'not that kind of person'.

Someone's public image draws attention to the kind of person he thinks he is. However, in order to get to know him, we often need to see the hidden reasons for his choice of image. Someone with more than average patience has his reasons for not displaying normal anger. It is possible that he truly never feels angry; but it is more often because he has been taught, or has taught himself, not to display anger. If we understand why this was necessary, it will tell us a great deal about him and enable us to make contact at a deeper level. Similarly, a person who appears sexually unresponsive may have a very low sex drive. But exactly the same behaviour may indicate someone who is suppressing unconscious fears of being extremely sexy and who is hiding an unconscious desire to lose control of his sexual urges.

Casual acquaintances, and formal relationships with colleagues and neighbours, seldom require us to analyse a person's hidden agenda. We only need to do this when we are trying to find someone who will accept us as similar in order to build a more intimate relationship. When we come into conflict with someone who is not aware of his motives, exploring his hidden agenda is equally counter-productive. There is no point in telling him what he is 'really' doing unless he can see this for himself, for it would merely strengthen the defences which forced his motives underground in the first place.

Because unintentional self-disclosures are based on unconscious needs, the person concerned is secretly trying not to be aware of them. You should therefore be extremely careful before you accept someone's unintentional self-disclosures as evidence of his character. First, you should try to guess what they indicate – for example, anger suppressed in childhood by an authoritarian father in the case of the over-patient person, or sexuality suppressed in adolescence by over-cautious parents in the case of the sexually unresponsive. Secondly, you should try to know more about the person's early experience. For example, you can ask a very patient person if he had a bad temper when he was young

The public image of the street urchin draws attention to who he would like to be rather than who he is.

or what his father was like, while somebody who is sexually restrained might tell you about his adolescence and discuss his relationship with his parents. To encourage the other person to self-disclose, make similar disclosures about yourself. But avoid sounding as though you have already made up your mind and are merely looking for evidence to show how clever you are. The system outlined above only works if you really like the other person, want to get to know him and want him to get to know you equally.

Common verbal indicators of a hidden agenda are self-discipline statements ('I must, ought, should; I must not, ought not, should not'), statements of self-deprecation ('I'm not very good at . . .') and self-control statements ('I always' or 'I never'). Self-discipline statements may seem trivial, but they often help to reveal the kind of person somebody is afraid of being. For example, 'I ought to stop saying that about him' after over-elaborate praise or condemnation shows a suppressed desire to lose self-control in a relationship. Self-deprecation is also common. 'I'm not very good at talking to strangers' is often a request for reassurance which should be met immediately if you want the person to feel safe so that the relationship can progress. The things a person is 'not very good at' are often those he really thinks he is good at, but he has decided (or been trained) not to show off. Self-deprecation statements are always worth checking, either by a direct question, or by guessing what the person's skills are and then questioning him indirectly, so that you can enjoy talking about them together.

Self-control statements reveal much about the way the person's parents related to him. 'I always try to . . .' and 'I never manage to . . .' often enter the self-image very early in childhood, taken over from parents who grumble about their child's 'bad' behaviour. These complaints from parents are known as 'injunctions'. The child usually complies with the letter, but not the spirit, of an injunction. ('Don't you dare come and tell me you're pregnant' is an example: if the girl gets pregnant, she does not dare tell her mother.) People who 'always' or 'never' do things are often obeying injunctions. For example, 'I always talk too much' may indicate that someone's parents often made that accusation because they were too busy to listen. 'I never tell lies' may betray the influence of a parent who demanded the truth more often than necessary because he saw the child as not to be trusted. Most of the time, 'always' and 'never' are untrue. None of us are that consistent; we simply wish we were.

Self-control between adults and between children. (left) The man goes through the motions of dancing rather than offend his partner by expressing unwillingness. (below left) Self-control is learned in childhood; here a baby learns to accept an unwarranted gesture of friendship rather than cause offence by rejecting intimacy.

Whenever a body movement is exaggerated or suppressed deliberately, it indicates that someone is trying to avoid being the sort of person who would *not* behave in that way. We often notice these traits first in someone when we find we are imitating them. Since we prefer people who are like us, we all tend to take up postures similar to those adopted by people we wish to impress or whose good opinion is important to us. For example, when talking to someone who stands very stiffly, we tend to adopt a similar way of standing; if we showed tendencies which he is unconsciously suppressing, he would be more likely to reject us. When getting to know somebody who has a distinct style of movement – for example, a very rigid stance or a characteristically undisciplined sprawl – it is difficult to know whether to continue imitating him once we are aware of doing so, or whether simply to be ourselves. Once somebody has accepted us as similar enough not to be a threat, we can usually relax. On the other hand, our willingness to mimic can be *self*-revealing. We usually copy someone who controls the same kinds of behaviour as we do. Long after we have grown up, we still behave in ways which would have pleased our parents.

Letting people get to know us involves taking risks

Nearly all of us keep parts of ourselves hidden away for use only with special people, and some of us hide more than others. There are usually good reasons for these defences, since we have learned from experience (particularly in childhood) that we would be open to attack or exploitation without them. But we cannot let someone get to know us without taking the risk of lowering our defences, at least temporarily. A case history will help to illustrate these risks.

Jean had been married twice when she met Bill. Her first marriage ended in divorce when her three daughters were nearly grown up. She then met and married Philip, but he died a year after their son was born. Six years later she joined a voluntary organization of which Bill was the secretary. She liked him immediately. He was a widower, looking for a new wife to be a mother to his two sons. Jean had decided never to remarry, but at her second meeting with Bill she felt her resolve weakening. He was obviously attracted to her and keen to get to know her better. How much should she tell him? In effect, she had to decide between becoming lover, friend or wife.

(facing page) Passive self-disclosure. In one-to-one conversation at a party, small talk can keep self-disclosure to a minimum (top). A family unconsciously displays its unity by the use of space. An outsider would be unable to approach one member without recognizing the group as a whole (right). A young man is protected from self-disclosure by his dark glasses (far right).

First, she knew that there was a strong sexual attraction between them. Should she admit this? If she did, it might frighten him off and she might lose him both as a lover and as a friend. On the other hand, if they became lovers, she was likely to lose control over her emotions, which were only now becoming stable after the loss of her second husband. She would go down in her own estimation if she let matters get out of hand.

Bill had made no secret of the fact that he wanted to find a new wife. Jean wondered whether to tell him about her marriages and her young son. Once he knew she was a widow, there was every likelihood that he would want to get to know her with a view to marriage. She had decided never to remarry, but she knew she would enjoy being courted. On the other hand, it would be cruel to lead him on if she had no intention of taking him seriously. Jean could start to enjoy herself again, end her loneliness and perhaps even remarry if she played her cards right. Should she keep herself controlled and calculating in order to gain a new chance for herself, or should she take the bigger risk, open herself to Bill, take down her defences, but possibly start an adventure that would end in heartbreak?

How well Bill and Jean would get to know one another depended on the extent of Jean's self-disclosure. As in all such cases, Jean had to decide what she really wanted. In the event, she took the greater risk, told Bill about her previous marriages, made it clear that she liked him, and a courtship followed, ending in marriage. Jean had had to understand her own agenda in order to resolve the dilemma.

Not all self-disclosure problems are as dramatic as this example. Dr

Jones and Dr Brown met at a conference. Dr Jones wore a name tag, but Dr Brown did not. 'My name's Edward,' said Dr Brown, holding out his hand. Dr Jones shook hands limply. 'I'm Dr Jones. Are you a doctor, too?' 'Yes,' came the reply. 'Then you'd better call me Tom,' said Dr Jones, tightening his grip. (It was safe to let out his first name since the two men were of equal status.) Then he realized that he had also accidentally revealed his own love of status and some of the sense of insecurity on which it was based. 'Sorry about that,' he added, 'but I've been so busy lately I forget my own name.'

Unintentional self-disclosure may give someone an advantage he can exploit if he does not like you or if you are meeting as competitors. A person who is insecure often protects himself by keeping the conver-

Flirtation: a cat and mouse game until one person is prepared to disclose his or her sexual intentions.

sation as formal as possible. Alternatively, he may avoid conversation altogether, in case he should reveal the true value he has placed on himself. These tactics are self-defeating, for lack of friends is one of the causes of insecurity, and protecting yourself by not making friends will only make your sense of insecurity worse. If this is your problem, you should take the risk, admit to feeling ill at ease and show the anger you feel if somebody tries to make you feel insecure.

Self-disclosure works rather like the children's game of 'I'll tell you if you tell me.' First one person reveals something, then the other makes a self-disclosure of equal value. If the value of the disclosures stays equal on both sides, acquaintance will progress but the two people will not increase their level of intimacy. However, an increase in intimacy may be desired so that a new kind of relationship can develop. In this case, one partner in the relationship must go out on a limb and disclose more personal information than the other, then wait to see if this will be matched by the other person. People who desire friendship can only build up mutual trust by revealing and exploiting parts of their personalities which they have never used in this way before.

There is an interesting exception. Strangers who meet on trains and planes and are unlikely to meet again are often willing to talk at great length, giving very intimate details, and expecting no equal self-disclosure in return. They feel safe enough to do this because they can see no risk that their disclosures will ever be used against them.

35 Planned Acquaintance

How can you deliberately get to know someone better?

Laboratory studies have shown that, at a single meeting, people get to know each other best through relaxed, one-to-one conversation under conditions of safety where they meet as equals. The ideal way to improve your acquaintance with someone is to arrange a meeting at which everything helps both of you relax and talk, where interruptions from other people are unlikely and where neither of you is seen to start with an advantage over the other. There are various ways of organizing this, according to whom you have in mind. It might be a stranger you are meeting for the first time and wish to know better, or perhaps somebody you have often encountered before, such as a colleague, a

The shared umbrella creates a relaxed and cosy space for two people to get to know one another.

neighbour or the friend of a friend. There are also occasions when you will deliberately want to improve your acquaintance with somebody you already know well because your relationship with him has changed and you need to reassess your attitude to him.

People cannot relax if they feel threatened by hidden motives, so it helps if you make your intentions clear from the start. If you have a motive which you cannot admit, such as sex or using somebody in a power struggle, it is best to separate the two parts of your strategy and try to improve acquaintance first. Acquaintance for the sake of sex is fun, but the sex will be better if the two of you really enjoy each other's company. Acquaintance for the sake of power can be useful, but the better you know somebody the more success you are likely to have with your strategy.

Tension, interruptions, the pressure of other people who might join in, and differences in status between the two people holding a conversation all slow down mutual acquaintance. Shy people in particular need extra time. Laboratory experiments have shown that even short ten-minute periods spent in conversation affect subsequent performance in tasks which require co-operation. Where people are only asked to get to know each other and are given no subsequent task, structure changes appear in their speech after about eight or ten minutes indicating that they have started to relax. The pauses become longer between their bursts of speech, or 'utterances', and on both sides more variation appears in the length of these utterances. Over trial twenty-minute conversations, the pairs who subsequently reported that they liked each other were likely to relax earlier than those who were unsure about each other. In one experiment, people who liked each other very much were producing speech patterns by the end of twenty minutes which were indistinguishable from those produced by pairs of long-established friends.

It is worth noting here that a room full of strangers chatting to each other usually takes between ten and fifteen minutes to 'warm up'. This is indicated by a staccato characteristic in the general hubbub which appears at about that time due to the coincidental overlapping of longer pauses in the conversations.

All this evidence suggests that if you arrange specially to get to know somebody, you would be well advised to allow at least twenty minutes. If the person is shy, there are likely to be interruptions or there is a status difference between you, you should allow even longer. These factors should also influence your choice of where to meet. With somebody who is a stranger, meeting at your home or place of work may slow down acquaintance because you are familiar with the surroundings and the other person is not. If you meet in a public place which neither of you knows well, you are more likely to behave as equals from the start of the conversation. On the other hand, when improving acquaintance with somebody who is already familiar, it often pays to meet on his territory. Giving him the advantage in this way helps to offset any suspicion that you have a motive other than wanting to know him better. But because you will have less control over potential interruptions, it is best to begin the conversation knowing how long you are likely to be undisturbed.

Strangers talk to each other by exchanging 'utterances' of about the same length, not interrupting each other and taking turns at introducing new topics of conversation. From time to time, there may be reasons why you wish to get to know a stranger faster than would be normal, such as in an emergency or if you meet an attractive stranger you might not see again. Experiments show that when people know they are likely to meet again, each listens more carefully to what the other has to say. If you wish to get to know somebody better, the sooner you tell him that you would like to meet again, the quicker your acquaintance will develop.

When you want to get to know somebody rapidly, the most effective technique is to control the range of topics dealt with, rather than alter your speech patterns. This is easiest if you both make a 'contract'. For example, you can quite swiftly exchange information about where you live, and your job, marital status and main interests, while staying relaxed and friendly, simply by saying that you regard these as preliminaries which must be got out of the way before the 'main' conversation starts.

With a person you know well but wish to know better, it is difficult to converse as if you were still strangers. The better you know somebody, the harder it may be to persuade him to see you in a new light. But by keeping the conversation equal at all times and always giving as much information as you receive, you can encourage your partner to tell you things from his point of view which you might have taken for granted or misunderstood. Because you know each other already, you are both likely to hear only what you are used to hearing and think you understand. If you try to ask questions as if you were a stranger, and listen carefully to the answers, you can often discover the gaps in your understanding which will enable you to alter the relationship.

A problem cannot be talked through without mutual acquaintance. At this advice centre in Belfast, Northern Ireland, the man in the doorway is made highly suspicious by the presence of an unknown photographer. This suspicion is extended to the others in the room so that, although he is probably not usually shy, he now behaves as though he were.

36 First Impressions

How to control the first impression you make

Social psychologists believe that, in any meeting with a stranger, the first four or five minutes are crucial. The impression you create at this stage, right or wrong, will get harder to change as time goes by. Four minutes may not seem very long, but it is enough for a good athlete to run the best part of a mile. When a first meeting really matters, such as an interview for a job, it is worth taking the trouble to understand first impressions and to know how to influence them.

Whoever you are meeting for the first time, what happens during the early minutes is always more or less the same. You will be looked at and judged on your general appearance, the way you move and the clothes you wear. If you wish to be accepted by the people you are meeting, the way you dress should be appropriate, so that they feel at ease with you. This will help to convince them that they were right to see you. At an interview, your clothes should show that you have taken the trouble to prepare for the occasion, and did not simply put on the first things you happened to find that morning. Clothes similar to those

This woman displays complete self-assurance in conversation. She encourages acquaintance, widening her eyes to improve eye-contact, and tilting her head to emphasize the fact that eye-contact is maintained.

An ambivalent pose makes acquaintance difficult. This man's smile is strained, he tries to make eye-contact through half-closed eyes, and even his posture is not a clear statement that he wants to get to know you.

of your prospective colleagues will suggest that you can fit into an established team. If you are applying for a highly paid job, wear the sort of clothes you will be able to afford if appointed. If this makes you feel self-conscious, simply wear clothes in which you feel comfortable.

You can control how long people spend looking at you by the way you make eye-contact. This should be the friendly, confident kind of looking which shows you feel at home already. But if you like being looked at and have enough self-confidence to know that your appearance will help you, delay this first eye-contact or make it brief. This is how someone 'makes an entrance': he walks boldly into the space provided, waits until all eyes are upon him, then holds this attention by slow and deliberate movements until he feels ready to look at one person in particular, usually the most important person present. However, this may cause resentment, so if you try it, do not pause too long after you have attracted attention, but move to eye-contact almost at once. It often helps if you make eye-contact as soon as you enter the room, particularly if you want to show you enjoy meeting people.

There will also be a test of touching. By now people will be starting to decide whether they like you or not, so take the initiative and show that you like them. If a handshake is in order, move to touching distance and relax. Keeping eye-contact, offer the handshake. This can cause problems. If you are too close, the handshake will be cramped; if you are too far away, you will find yourself bowing or losing your balance. A common mistake is to produce a one-sided handshake, by not responding to the subtle variations in touch – impact, pressure and caress – produced by the other person. A good handshake is a touch dialogue, not a monologue. (See chapter 24.) The pleasure of this meeting through touch should also show in your tone of voice and in the way you smile. Use your non-verbal behaviour to help others relax.

You will also need to establish conversation. It is easier to spell out what not to do for 'openers' than to say what to do. Try to avoid negative statements, intimidating questions, or questions to which you already know the answer. The latter can turn your first meeting into a general knowledge quiz which looks designed for you to win and the people you are meeting to lose. Questions with a single-word answer – yes or no – are awkward, because you will need another question immediately after the first one. At an interview, the first question will come from the interviewers and will usually be designed to help you feel at ease. If you are asked about your present job (the standard opener), answer briefly. Say a little about how long you have been doing the job, how you feel about it, and what you have achieved. For example, 'I've been doing my present job for six years and I enjoy it, but I want something more challenging. Lately, my job has been to introduce word processors into the company.' The subject you end with is very likely to be what you are asked about next. For example, if you end with how you feel, you will probably have to talk more about your feelings, although you may not be prepared for this yet. You may be asked straight away why you have applied for the post. Use a similar formula in your reply. For example, 'I know I can do the job and that I shall like working here. I am also fairly certain that my recent experience will be of some use to you.' This will help the interviewers to ask you about your experience.

By this time, people will be forming their opinions of you on the basis of what you say, rather than how you look or use touch. You will need to show you are sufficiently at ease with the people interviewing you to behave as part of their group. For example, if you are seated at the same table, you can take charge of the space allocated to you by placing your papers there and relaxing in your seat. If you suffer from nerves, breathe deeply before you start and visit the lavatory ten minutes before the meeting. If you feel nervous, try to maintain eye-contact, and remember that other people are probably just as anxious as you are that you will prove to be acceptable. They will probably not notice some of your anxiety because their own is just as evident. After the first few minutes most of the uncertainty will have been resolved, either in your favour or against you, and the worst will be over.

37 Stereotypes – Appearance and Role

Labelling people by how they look and the jobs they do prevents acquaintance

There is a subtle difference between getting to know somebody and getting to know *about* him. You are beginning to get to know someone when you exchange confidences which would not have been swapped with anybody else. Frequently, however, people only pretend to get to know each other, and assume that they have learned a great deal about someone just by looking at him or knowing what he does for a living. Such assumptions are called 'stereotypes'. They are rather like the labels on paintings in an art gallery: you imagine that because you have read the label, you have looked at the painting. Stereotypes prevent acquaintance because they satisfy our curiosity through providing us with misleading 'short cuts' in the way we see people. Although most of us object to being stereotyped by other people, we forget how often we rely on such short cuts ourselves.

Stereotypes are based on a false logic, which works as in the following example. 'This woman is blonde. All blondes are promiscuous. Therefore she is promiscuous.' The key to the false logic lies in the middle section of the assumption, where all people of a certain type are believed to share particular characteristics which are more important than any of their other traits. In fact, there is no reason to suppose that the

Two elderly women on a park bench in London: their self-stereotypes will enable them to refuse the advances of anyone who does not accept them as they wish to be seen.

A 'Darby and Joan' stereotype. It enables the couple to identify themselves completely with each other and their environment.

most important characteristic of a blonde woman is the colour of her hair. Nor is it logical to suppose that all blonde women are promiscuous. Most people who use stereotypes are unaware of this false logic. They miss out the middle sentence altogether and jump to the final conclusion: 'This woman must be promiscuous because she is blonde.'

A person's appearance is often used as the basis on which to label him. The hardest stereotypes to combat are racial and sexual labels. For example, in many white, Western democracies, different expectations are attached to being black and white. A young black man may seem threatening to a white female teacher or a prospective employer. When a black girl leaves school, she often finds it easier to obtain work in a shop or an office than an equally educated, intelligent black male of the same age does. On the other hand, an intelligent black woman who reaches the ranks of middle management may often find her next promotion more difficult to obtain than her male contemporaries (black or white) do. This is not a simple matter of prejudice, but a complicated mixing of stereotype expectations. All intelligent women have this problem in a world dominated by men, but to be black can be an additional burden. If a woman also happens to be sexually attractive, it is even more difficult to get the men in charge to judge her work on its merits.

Psychologists have demonstrated that attractiveness is often thought to give someone an unfair advantage. In one famous series of experiments, students were asked to read an account of a crime and then say how long the offender should be imprisoned. A third of the students were shown a photograph of the 'offender' made up to appear very attractive; to another third the same 'offender' was presented as highly unattractive. The other students had no photograph. The sentences suggested for the 'unattractive' woman were much the same as those where no picture was shown, but the attractive offender received very different treatment. If she was being sentenced for burglary, she was let off more lightly; but for swindling a middle-aged bachelor she was seen as deserving much heavier punishment, presumably because she used her attractiveness unfairly.

Stereotyping according to physique is common: an overweight man is seen as jolly and a large woman is expected to be motherly. People who are taller than average often seem intimidating to smaller people. Many of these responses are produced unconsciously and unthinkingly. It often helps if you are aware of the effects of your physical appearance upon others. You can then decide consciously when and when not to use it to your advantage. For example, if you are very much fatter than

A West Indian carnival in London. A deliberate breach of a stereotype.

Two contrasting stereotypes of royalty: the Queen of England and the King of Tonga.

someone you want to get to know, you will need to allow him extra space; at the average distance for conversation, you may easily seem to swamp him. If you are very much taller than someone, it is easy to forget that he will be forced to look upwards to see you, so sit down more often. Beware of the tendency to stereotype people who are physically small as mentally and socially 'small', or inferior, too. If you look the 'motherly' type, you will receive more than your fair share of people wanting advice and a shoulder to cry on. There are two solutions: either accept the compliment and learn more about counselling, or alter your appearance! It is no solution simply to drive people away when they need you. 'Motherly' types often resent the fact that when it is their turn to seek comfort, they are rejected because no one believes them. Very tall people often wonder why others expect so much of them and 'look up to them'. Tall people can gain consolation from the fact that in every US presidential election since at least 1900, the taller candidate has won.

Many people stereotype themselves. They try to look the part they play by the emphasis they place upon certain aspects of their appearance. Self-stereotyping is a form of self-disclosure – a way of letting other people get to know you by your role in life and your status. It tends to draw attention away from questions about who you are which you may not have resolved for yourself. Self-stereotyping is often a sign of shyness and insecurity; but it may also indicate that someone who is confident in his role is showing his intention not to get involved with anybody outside this role at that particular moment.

38 Stereotypes of Personality

'Labelling' someone may blind us to his true personality

If a way of interpreting someone's attitude happens to suit our needs at the time, we are likely to adopt it, whether it is right or wrong, because it appears to save time and effort. This is the basis of 'labelling', or fitting people into personality stereotypes. These stereotypes can become self-fulfilling prophecies.

Suppose that twelve-year-old Paul goes to school after a fight with his mother. She has constantly told him that, since he is only a child, he must obey orders. For example, he must keep his room tidy and not leave his dirty sports clothes all over the house. Paul has not the power to stand up to his mother and express all his anger, so he takes the anger to school with him. His fists are constantly clenched and he is prepared to fight anybody else who treats him as a child. For the rest of the morning he is spoiling for a fight and he feels that all the teachers are trying to make him feel small. His perception of the teachers is a response to his need to work through his anger.

Paul will probably be calm by the end of the school day, but by then he may have become labelled by the teachers as 'aggressive' or 'difficult'. Because of the way our system of perception works, we easily confuse fact and opinion. When we perceive an object as having certain

In the comradeship of a London street-market people can act out their personality stereotypes: the bold blonde, the gossip in curlers and the shrewd stallholder.

characteristics, we mentally attach the characteristics to the object. For example, if a person behaves foolishly we tend to think of him as a fool. If somebody is caught being lazy we see him as a lazy person. If twelve-year-old Paul is angry at school too often (in response, perhaps, to his mother's inability to cope with a regular job and three children), he is labelled 'bad-tempered' or 'moody'. If he tries to do better and occasionally succeeds, he will be called 'inconsistent'.

Personality stereotyping often makes the disturbing aspects of someone's personality easier to ignore. We have probably all met someone like George. Everybody likes him; he always seems to have time to listen to any problem, even after work. He nods, puffs at his pipe and peers through his spectacles in a kindly way. He is seen as good old dependable George, the salt of the earth, with thousands of friends. But does anyone notice that he has so much time to give because, once work is over, he has nobody to talk to until he arrives at the office the following day? He is lonely and this could easily make others aware of

Two familiar stereotypes: a jolly country lady and a boisterous beer-drinker.

their own loneliness. People stereotype George in order to see him they way they need to see him – as sociable and predictable. As the cannibal said to the missionary, 'Well, if God didn't mean you to be eaten, why did he make you out of meat?'

Personality stereotypes can influence personality development, too, because a person may be forced to grow more like the 'labels' imposed on him by others. Paul may give up the unequal struggle against the labels imposed on him at home and at school and accept himself as moody and inconsistent. George may develop the dependable, sociable side of his nature, but be forced to avoid deeper relationships in which his own selfish needs might surface and damage his public image.

The interplay of personality in a relationship often reflects the stereotypes people have of each other. Over the period of getting to know somebody, we become expert at meeting our own needs through appearing to become what the other person expects.

When we feel we already know somebody, we often stop trying to get to know him further. However, personality stereotyping leads many people into the trap of stopping too soon. When we receive evidence which conflicts with our view of someone we think we know, we treat it with cautious scepticism, rather than change our minds. For example, a person who is labelled honest, but is caught lying, is excused as having had a temporary lapse. A person who is known as a liar and tells the truth is treated with great suspicion. (This explains why, in a British court of law, the previous convictions of the accused are not read out unless he is found guilty.)

So many of our active attempts to get to know other people are reactions to our own needs that we often forget how easily we take short cuts. Stereotyping is simpler than getting to know someone; it saves time and energy. However, we should be aware of its dangers.

39 Getting to Know Children

Because a child is also a person,
he has the right not to like you

Our early conditioning has left many of us with contradictory feelings about children. As a result, we often find it difficult to get to know a child. Childhood may be idealized as a time of innocence and simplicity, when the child is entitled to special care and understanding. Seen from this perspective, a child can be naughty but he is never 'evil'; his bad behaviour is merely the result of deprivation or a lack of parental guidance and so can be dealt with leniently. However, behaviour which is acceptable in children is often rejected when it comes from adults. The terms 'babyish', 'childish' and 'infantile' all imply criticism. An adult is often expected to 'put away childish things' and to cut himself off from his own childhood experience as soon as possible. Our culture tends to make 'growing up' into a moral duty and to see childhood and adulthood as two separate parts of life. Yet in many of our most delightful and creative moments as adults (and when we are very angry) we are still the children we have always been.

Some people find it very difficult to see a child as a person in his own right. For example, some men feel awkward holding a baby, and even more uncomfortable talking to one. They prefer the child to be able to hold a conversation which consists of words, rather than gurgles, cries, and facial, hand and body movements. Some men are even afraid of being thought feminine if they appear too comfortable with babies. This is often because they have deliberately cut themselves off from their own early experiences, as a result of the cultural demands made upon them to be 'grown up' and 'manly'.

Communication with a child who is too young for speech is nevertheless as full of fascinating possibilities as communication with any stranger. A baby will often indicate by its wriggling exactly how it wishes to be held, and what it wishes to look at and grasp. A wide awake, energetic baby likes to change position often, as long as it feels safe. It constantly seeks stimulation – interesting things to look at, different noises to listen to, and various ways of being held, such as swinging and swaying, either upright or lying down. Play which depends on imitation, particularly through repeated patterns of movement or noise, often delights a baby. The baby learns through exploration and will usually enjoy what it learns. Most babies who are held confidently will respond by trusting the stranger, although there are times when every baby wants only its mother and nobody else will be acceptable.

Because we were all once babies, somewhere inside most of us are babyhood responses which have survived into adult life. If you want to get to know a baby, you should use these same responses and thus share with the baby the things it enjoys. Discovering what these are can become a joint adventure. There are different colours and shapes to look at, and the different textures and weights of objects to be sampled. The baby will usually want to be talked to; you can use many different tones of voice and vary the volume from a whisper to a soft shout. A baby can often be engaged in dialogue; the adult imitates the baby's own noises and is imitated back. Stimulation should be as varied as possible, but since most babies are easily frightened, the intensity of sound and touch should be kept within the bounds which the individual baby can tolerate without fear. Getting to know a baby always entails recognizing its limits of tolerance, by finding out when its cries and movements indicate hunger, anger, fear, irritation or tiredness. Even very young babies show the same range of individual differences as that found in adults.

Conversation with a toddler, as with a baby, is best achieved through play. Again, this can present difficulties for the adult who has not allowed himself to retain his own childhood instinct for play, or who was conditioned to repress this instinct early in life. A child who can crawl and walk, but has only a limited vocabulary, lives at floor level. He will often enjoy the company of an adult who is prepared to go down on all fours to join in. Favourite games at this stage are building piles of objects and knocking them down, hiding and finding things and the game of 'fetch and carry', in which the child repeatedly hands an object to an adult, takes it back and hands it on to someone else.

The universal game of 'peep-bo' helps to illustrate the principles which lie behind these games. In 'peep-bo' the adult makes eye-contact with the toddler, holds his attention by showing 'surprise', and then hides behind a convenient object, such as a book, a newspaper or a piece of furniture. The child watches for a moment and the adult reappears, surprising the child. The Swiss psychologist Piaget has explained that this is one of the many ways in which a toddler learns about the properties of objects. For example, he discovers that just because he cannot see something, it has not ceased to exist. Like 'peep-bo', games of building up and knocking down, hiding and finding, and 'fetch and carry' help the child to learn (over many hundreds of similar experiences) that objects retain their main characteristics whatever we do to them. Even if they do not stay in the same place, as when a ball

A mock-serious conversation between an adult and a child: although the man grips the boy's arm he is meeting him on his own level.

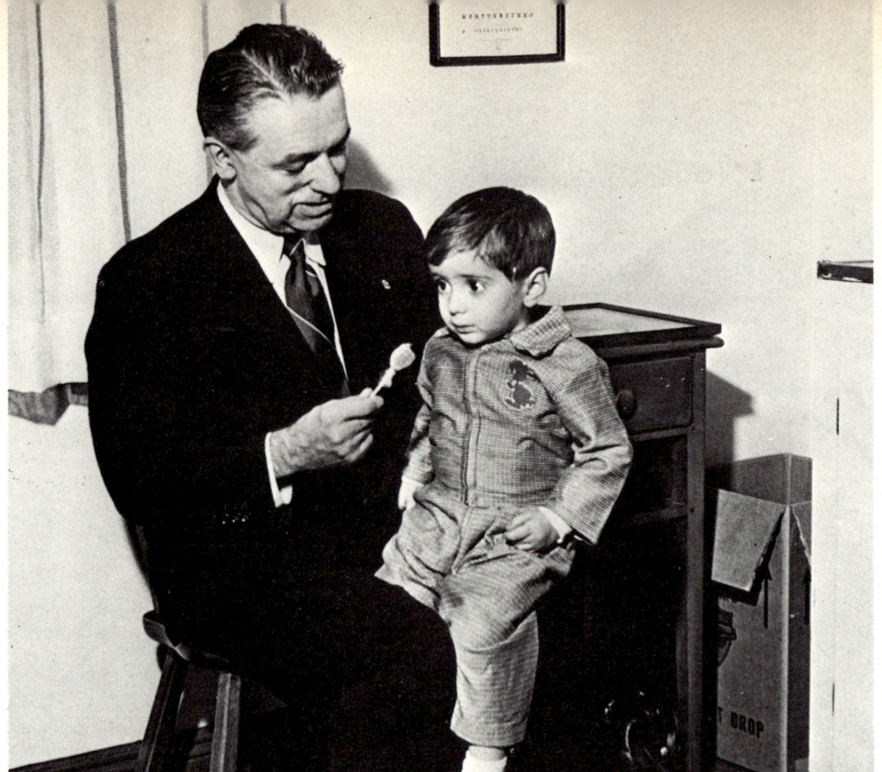

The doctor's well-tried formula to facilitate his consultation. There is no real contact, as the boy's awkward posture shows.

rolls away, they have a way of behaving which will tell us where to look for them. Objects retain their size and shape and are just as hard or soft each time we touch them. The play of a toddler is often a long series of experiments designed to help him work out how objects and people behave.

A toddler will also enjoy naming objects and looking at pictures. If he becomes anxious or tries to reach things which may hurt him, try to distract him with something else and, above all, avoid showing anger or anxiety yourself. During the stage of development when he is learning to talk, a child will often imitate words inaccurately, or even use swear-words which adults would prefer him not to use. All imitative behaviour should be understood. It should never be punished because it is inaccurate or embarrassing, but only if it actually hurts somebody, as when a toddler smacks a younger child. Encouraging imitation in general helps a child to improve his skill at learning anything new. Getting to know a pre-school child requires patience in dealing with his lack of self-control, since at this stage of development he is often learning to come to terms with his own aggressive and antisocial impulses.

Conversation with a young child is most successful if the adult does not talk down to him, either physically or metaphorically. Listening is equally important. Perhaps this is an obvious point to make, but it is one which is often forgotten. If the adult feels awkward and asks a child silly questions, he is just as likely to be thought silly and awkward as if he was talking to an adult. Touch contact is particularly important to a young child, but it should never be imposed on him by a strange adult. Whether or not the child will accept touch on the hand and face, or allow a stranger to pick him up or hold him, is the main test of whether the new adult is liked or disliked. Because a child is a person, he has the right to reject other people. How well you get to know a child depends on how far he – not you – is prepared to go.

40 Getting to Know Adolescents

An adult often finds it hard to treat an adolescent as his equal

Adolescents can seem particularly irritating to an adult, perhaps because adolescence is a time of uncertain change from child to grown-up. The teenager often wishes to be a child one moment and an adult the next. The adult may feel threatened when he sees young people 'getting away with' precisely the kinds of behaviour his own parents rigorously controlled when he was an adolescent. Getting to know an adolescent often involves understanding the restrictions imposed during our own childhood. It also means that we must respect the individuality of the young person, even when the 'child' is uppermost, and however much he tries to shock or alarm. There is nothing morally wrong in childlike, or even childish, behaviour. An adult controls his own childish impulses because he was conditioned to see them as socially inconvenient in his family of origin. He often imposes his internal system of self-control on someone else just because this person is young.

Freudian psychologists see adolescence as an elaborate replay of the main childhood tasks. The child who once learned to walk must now learn to 'stand on his own feet', 'go his own way', but not 'go too far'.

A non-conformist adolescent often has a history of poor communication in the family. This has separated him from the older generation, and also from conformists of his own age.

Adolescence can become a cult. All adolescents need to combat feelings of inferiority and may take refuge in an exaggeration of the virtues of being young, as shown by the mass of posters on this girl's bedroom wall.

The infant who once explored his sexuality by competing with his father to gain his mother's undivided attention and by masturbating openly now begins to masturbate for his own private pleasure. In seeking sexual attention from people of his own age, he stirs up forgotten rivalries with his own parents in arguments over suitable partners for him. The infant explores the physical properties of objects. The adolescent explores the characteristics of his world with similar vigour, through ideas and idealism. He alternates between periods of rebellion and times of conformity, just as the child did, but now that he is stronger and more independent, the impact of these changes in mood can be more disturbing and bewildering – particularly to a middle-aged adult who is himself struggling with conflicts whose origin lies in decisions he took during his own adolescence, and which may have produced a marriage or career which now seems unsatisfactory.

Communication between a middle-aged person and an adolescent is frequently competitive rather than co-operative. This is particularly obvious within the family. The adolescent may test his developing strength in contests over property, such as using his parents' things without permission. Territorial disputes are common. In some households there are regular fights over the cleaning and tidying of an adolescent's room, or over objects left lying around in the bathroom, kitchen or sitting room. There are frequent conflicts over staying out late. The adolescent still has to ask his parents' permission before going to parties which might involve sex or coming home late. These battles are tests of the young adult's strength against that of his parents. If the parents treat him as a child, the adolescent may rebel openly or merely pretend to conform, unless he has already developed with his parents a relationship based on mutual love, understanding and respect. An adolescent seldom understands why his parents worry about him: he sees it as a lack of trust. An elderly person often copes better with these conflicts than a middle-aged person does, since the older person has resolved more doubts about his own limitations, or perhaps is more apathetic about the probable outcome.

Getting to know an adolescent is no different from getting to know any stranger. The most common mistakes arise from the illusion that it is easier just because the adolescent is younger than you are. To some adults this suggests that the adolescent will want to learn from a wiser, more experienced person; to others it suggests that he should and must learn, and ought to be grateful. An adolescent often sees these assumptions for what they are: attempts to underline a superiority based on age alone. When you are young you see no virtue in being twenty years older; indeed, you see the drawbacks more clearly than you will ever do later. Advice is not something for which you are grateful. You want to make your own mistakes. If you are patronized by somebody older, it shows his inability to accept you as a person in your own right.

Mutual acquaintance works best when there is no prior assumption of inequality, so an adolescent usually gets to know other adolescents better than he gets to know adults. This is, first, because even the physical differences between an adult and an adolescent are a constant reminder of inequality. Physical growth is accelerated in puberty, and a tall young man may seem gawky and clumsy because he needs time to get used to his new size. A girl who is suddenly a sexy shape or taller than her parents may not at first understand the social significance of her new figure; even if she does, only experience will teach her how to use her adult sexuality. A voice which has just broken and fluctuates in pitch emphasizes immaturity whenever it is used. Thus the young person's social, intellectual, sexual and emotional immaturity is all too obvious when an adolescent and an adult try to get to know each other.

If you want to get to know an adolescent, let him make the first moves. Show that you accept him as an individual who may, like other people, have problems, instead of seeing him as a problem individual, or one who is going through a problem phase. Above all, try to avoid being stereotyped as the critical parent.

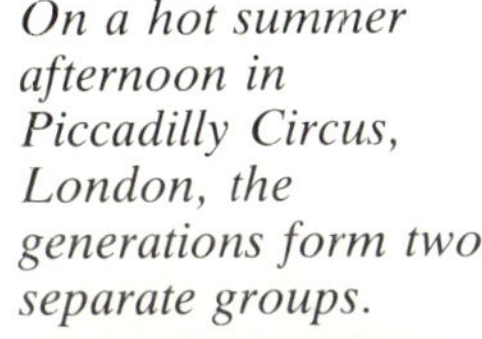

On a hot summer afternoon in Piccadilly Circus, London, the generations form two separate groups.

41 Strangers

When a new member joins an established group he takes on the special role of 'stranger'

'Strangership' is the point of zero acquaintance. In this chapter we examine some of the problems of the newcomer to a group. A stranger is marked out by his ignorance of the group he has joined. Everybody else is more familiar than he is with the elements which give the group its identity and status – the names and faces of the members and their special skills, as well as the group's purposes, territory and recent history, and the extent and limitations of its power. The new member gains acceptance by the progressive destruction of his own ignorance as he adds to the power of the group to achieve its purposes.

At the start, however welcome the new member may be, he is the most difficult person for the other members to talk to. A person feels he belongs to a group because so many things can be left unsaid. A stranger requires explanations which cost extra time and effort; he can only offer attention in return. During the early stages of his acquaintance, he will often have to stand by while other members hold rapid conversations or mysterious consultations from which he is excluded by his ignorance. The way a group treats its strangers during such moments reveals a great deal about the kind of group it is. It will also help the stranger decide how committed he feels to achieving full membership.

Some examples will help to illustrate the ways in which a group may respond to a new member. Mark joined a company which produced films for the advertising industry. After a brief welcome from the managing director, he was handed over to an assistant to be shown round. The assistant was not properly introduced, and before Mark could ask his name he was handed over to yet another person. This man began the tour, but in every office there were people who were already very busy and who wanted his advice immediately. He was soon tied up in the details of one such consultation and a third person was deputed to show Mark round. At the end of the morning, Mark felt like a battered parcel which had been passed from hand to hand and never opened. His impression of the firm made him doubt whether he had been right to join. He had no way of judging whether this was a typical day or not.

There are ways in which a new member can become integrated into the group, as the following example shows. When Graham joined an evening class in carpentry, he found that all the other members had been on the previous course and liked it so much that they had signed up for another year. On the first evening, Graham felt left out of their private conversations as they exchanged family news and asked each other about their holidays. Although they virtually ignored him, he was so impressed by the fact that they had all returned for a second year that he persisted and tried not to feel excluded. As soon as he could, he mentioned his feelings to the teacher, who then went out of his way to make Graham feel welcome. During the first few sessions, Graham traded on his ignorance of carpentry, using it as an excuse to ask other members questions and get them talking. Soon he felt accepted.

An established group often has its own jokes, or 'in' jokes, which are based on an agreed opinion of people whom the stranger has never heard of before. One man's new colleagues on the sales team kept making fun of a man on a rival team. The jokes sounded cruel, but helped to illustrate for the new member the philosophy which he must accept as part of the team. Although he was unable to see the funny side of the remarks, he felt obliged to join in by smiling broadly. If a stranger does not identify with the group's ethos, he will be seen as rejecting full membership.

Because of his ignorance, a stranger has to ask many questions about things the established members take for granted. He may easily forget people's names, particularly if all the members of a large group are introduced at once, and it may not immediately be clear to him who is important in the group. In an unhappy group, the members may take advantage of the stranger's ignorance, sometimes making fun of him

Princess Anne surrounded by a group of orphans on her visit to Kenya. Courtesy is shown by the way in which the group treats the stranger as an equal, in spite of her being older, white and a princess.

for their own amusement. The newcomer's arrival will have automatically 'promoted' the previous newcomer, who is then licensed to be patronizing or vindictive. An unhappy group uses its strangers to relieve its own unhappiness; a newcomer will often be neglected by the members if they themselves feel neglected. In a happy group, by contrast, a stranger is treated with patience and encouragement. The newcomer's questions are welcomed and answered and his opinion is sought early.

In general, a group is happiest if it feels it is achieving its official purpose, but has time to build informal relationships as well. The established members of any group feel a stronger sense of their own group identity when they are in the presence of a newcomer. They often use such moments to display their true feelings about their membership. Thus a close group which is proud of its sense of purpose will boast in the presence of a new member, but one which feels anxious and threatened will complain more loudly when a stranger can hear. During the early encounters with a group, particularly in informal situations, a stranger will often see amplified both the worst and the best characteristics of the members as they 'show off'. He would be wise to make allowances for these exaggerations.

Strangers sit close together on a bus, but actively avoid contact. While the couple on the right talk discreetly the others turn away and try to ignore the conversation.

A stranger is often tempted to cover up his ignorance when he feels uncertain of how secure he is in the group, but this is usually a mistake. In an unhappy group it will make him more vulnerable, and in a happy group it will offend people who would have been prepared to help if they had been asked. If a stranger tries too hard to label his own contribution as valuable and special, he may be rejected by the other members. He often has to earn the right to be treated as an individual by his new colleagues, not through making an individual contribution, but by taking a back seat and knowing his place. By the time he knows enough about the group to be able to contribute on equal terms to its mutuality, he has ceased to be a stranger. In other words, when a new member has helped to further any of the group's purposes in such a way that his contribution is so involved with that of other members that it does not stand out as his own, he has been accepted.

42 Shyness

How can you help yourself to overcome shyness?

Perhaps the most important thing to remember about shyness is how many people suffer, or have suffered, from it. According to surveys in many countries, around 80 per cent of us have felt shy at some time or other. Shyness is found in all cultures and among people of all ages. However, many people who were once very shy have now overcome their shyness or grown out of it. It is not unusual to find people whose work involves meeting strangers every day or performing in public (actors, journalists, broadcasters and politicians, for example) who were once painfully shy, and still are under certain circumstances. However, the evidence shows that people whose lives are totally dominated by shyness form only 4 to 5 per cent of the population, although this varies from culture to culture.

Studies of shyness show that, for most people, the worst situation is to be faced with a great deal of attention in circumstances where they feel they are being judged by people they do not know. The least threatening times for shy people are when they are with parents, children, friends, elderly people or relatives. These people have the least need to subject the shy person to cold, calculating, objective scrutiny. Nearly all of us are shy when other people are concentrating particular attention on us, or on those aspects of our personality or our body which we feel unsure about and usually keep to ourselves. We become self-conscious and begin to panic because we dare not show our feelings. Instead of responding to the other person or to the larger audience and forgetting ourselves, we become acutely aware of our own behaviour and begin to concentrate on controlling it, while at the same time fighting the rising tide of fear that threatens to swamp us. But in cutting ourselves off from the unwanted attention, we reject the other person and make the situation worse.

A shy person often thinks of himself as unattractive and not very friendly. By remaining shy he can avoid any challenge to this view of himself, and thus avoid coming into conflict with his need to see himself as someone who is not worth getting to know. The more unattractive he feels, the more conflict there will be when somebody treats him as attractive. Each time the shy person suggests that he is unworthy of this attention, the other person can either dispute the suggestion or accept it and go away. Thus a shy person has to drive others away, or simply clam up, in order to maintain his view of himself and avoid an argument he cannot win. Yet someone who is shy is frequently wrong about his own attractiveness. Many very shy people have attractive faces, voices which are easy to listen to, and a highly individual and lively intelligence which makes them a pleasure to be with. On the other hand, someone who sees himself as very attractive tends to be the opposite of shy. When he meets strangers who want to get to know him, treat him as an equal or talk to him in a more personal way, there is no conflict; he already believes he is worthy of attention and when

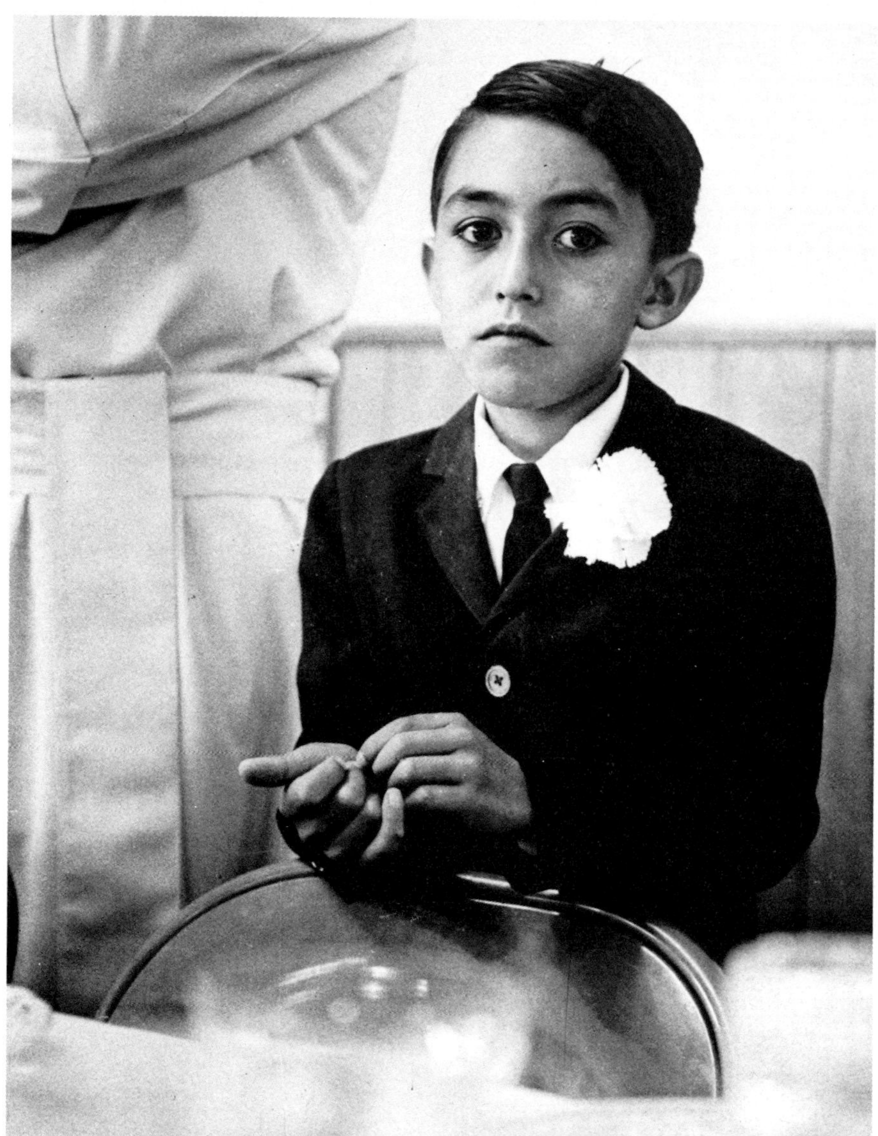

All of us are shy under some circumstances, particularly on a formal occasion when we do not know what is expected of us. The little boy is made self-conscious by being dressed up and photographed so that he must behave like an adult.

he obtains it, this merely confirms his view of himself.

Some shy people may be helped by a better understanding of their non-verbal behaviour. A shy person talks very quietly or not at all. He avoids eye-contact, touching, changes in tone of voice, movements which increase proximity, and any kind of high-intensity behaviour which will draw attention to himself. A non-shy person produces similar low-intensity behaviour from time to time, but he achieves it in a different way, by relaxing. A shy person tries to lower the intensity of his signals by an effort of self-control which uses up more, not less, energy. As a result, when he wants to act in a more friendly way, all his body movements and ways of talking seem very tense, so they either look too fearful or too angry. This makes it very difficult for him to judge the effects of his own behaviour. He cannot tell, for example, whether his smile was too cold or too friendly and whether his voice is too loud or too soft.

Many people cope with their shyness by only accepting encounters where they will be in charge. This enables them to reduce their internal conflict by directing attention at the other person. For example, a journalist asks questions as part of his work, and thus has an excuse for not making an equal contribution to the conversation. An actor speaks someone else's words and is not held responsible for how he behaves on stage. There are many shy politicians whose work gives them the opportunity to divert attention from their intimate thoughts to arguments about policy or concern for other people. Many people who are able to control a conversation because of their high status become awkward and shy when their status is unknown or irrelevant.

Most human skills improve with practice, and the ability to feel at ease with strangers is no exception. Some people who have overcome their shyness seemed to make very little progress at first and were easily discouraged. Once they had learned not to be impatient with themselves, they found it easier to relax.

However, some shy people are responding to lessons which, although learned long ago in childhood, are still important to their adult behaviour. Parents who think they are hiding their emotions from their children often fail to do so. An intelligent child picks up the suppressed signals and knows when the parent is angry or afraid, but to say so would only make matters worse. Shy people often learned in childhood how to read the subtle signs of rejection and to avoid aggravating the conflict, without even admitting that it existed. They reject themselves first, before others can reject them, and deep inside still feel very angry with their parents. They often need the help and encouragement of a therapist before they can come to terms with the feelings which have made them into shy people.

The modesty of the bride represents the traditional shyness expected of a virgin at her wedding, although here both partners are getting married for the second time.

43 Loneliness

Loneliness is the progressive destruction of the ability to communicate

Sometimes a person's relationship set is not sufficient to meet his needs. The result is loneliness. The feeling of loneliness arises from an inability to communicate and to receive the normal benefits which communication brings. This may be the result of separation from loved ones, either temporary, because they have moved away for some reason, or permanent, as when a valued relationship comes to an end through divorce or bereavement. Or it may be because the lonely person is unable to make or keep friends or to benefit from friendship. Loneliness is not just a feeling of being alone. The person who suffers from it often has a large number of acquaintances and appears to have some friends; he frequently has a husband or wife and children, and perhaps a close parent.

Loneliness is the numbing conviction that nobody in the world really knows or cares about you, and that if you were to die tomorrow it would make not the slightest difference to anybody. With 'acute' loneliness the feeling is short-lived but intense – a condition which most people have experienced and come to dread. 'Chronic' loneliness is far more serious; it can end in the premature death of the victim through self-neglect or suicide. The chronic sufferer receives permanent and irreversible damage to his ability to make relationships and fails to derive any emotional benefit from human contact.

Acute loneliness often affects someone who has close friends and a loving partner, but is separated from them. When you are lonely as a result of a short-term separation, it is often difficult to get other people to understand how you feel. It is no consolation to be told that the person you miss will be back soon, or that you can always write or telephone. A week may feel interminable. However, you can help yourself if you try to understand why you feel like this. One common cause stems from early childhood experience. When we are very young we have no sense of time. This develops at the earliest around eight years old, and often not until the child is ten or eleven. When a child's mother leaves him alone, even for a short period, he finds it very worrying. Although the mother has said she will return, the child has no sense of time unless she is there. The same fears return in an adult who is separated from his loved ones. Yet adults reject these fears as 'childish', instead of accepting them as childlike and as a natural part of being human. When you miss someone you love, there is a childlike part of you which grieves and is full of fear. This may be fear of desertion, death or accident, or the fear that comes from unreasonable jealousy. You may feel silly if you tell people, because your fears sound so childish. But it is better to take this risk and admit your loneliness to a friend.

Acute loneliness is harder to cope with if you do not know when it will end. A deserted wife or husband, or a parent who is missing a child

We cannot always tell whether somebody is lonely or simply wants to be left alone.

who has left home intending never to come back, has the extra problem of having to decide whether the relationship is over for good. This kind of loneliness may turn you into a prisoner of the past, trapped inside the memory of a relationship.

In order to overcome your loneliness, you should deliberately set out to make new relationships. If the person you miss eventually returns, you will be better able to build a new relationship with him. The old relationship may not have worked as well as you wanted it to, and in any case, the other person will have changed. If he never comes back to you, there are other people who can learn to value your unique qualities if you give them the chance. The most constructive preparation for a new relationship is the death of an old one. You will need time to grieve and you may also need to come to terms with guilty feelings about things you have done, as well as angry feelings about things which were done to you. All this is a normal part of grief. But remember that there will never again be somebody exactly like you. Your unique qualities will be wasted unless you use them, and you alone can do this. It means you can start afresh as a stranger, uncluttered by past commitments, alone and in charge of your life once more.

The lonelier you get, the less attractive you feel. Many lonely people look in the mirror and wonder who they are.

Loneliness makes you doubt your own value because you have no way of checking the reality of your worth. For example, loneliness may make you feel unattractive, simply because you know nobody who finds you attractive and can convince you that you are. It may make you feel stupid, because you do not know anyone well enough to tell you that you are not. But the feeling of being unattractive or stupid is caused by your lack of friends. It is not the cause of loneliness, but one of the symptoms. Loneliness makes you afraid of being yourself.

One result of this fear is that you will find it harder than ever to face the most important reality of all – the fact that only you can decide whether to live or die. A lonely person often finds that he does not want to go on living, but cannot bring himself deliberately to end his life. He ends up being not quite dead and not quite alive. If you feel like this, admit to yourself that you have already chosen life. You are not afraid of dying, but living. Loneliness is something you have to cure for yourself. Pills can help a little at first, but in the end you have to fight back to life without them. Perhaps you need to break some of the old rules which governed your life and make new ones for yourself. You may disappoint or hurt a few people, and surprise others who thought they knew you. Defeating loneliness means learning how to be alone and increasing your ability to love. You alone can decide whether the damage this illness does to you will be permanent or temporary.

44 Friendship

For two people to become friends, acquaintance is not enough

Social scientists see friendship as the end-product of a complex selection process, of which acquaintance is only one part. In theory everyone we meet can become a friend. In practice the process of selection 'filters out' many of the people we get to know, so that only a few become close friends.

First, however, the two people have to be able to get to know each other. Some factors prevent this; others merely make it less likely. Obviously people cannot get to know each other if they never make contact. Of all forms of contact, direct communication – and particularly face-to-face conversation – is the most likely to lead to friendship. People can become acquainted at one meeting, but friendship is more likely the more often they meet.

Secondly, friendship between people who meet and converse frequently is most likely when they want equally to get to know each other. Several factors may interfere with this. There may be insufficient time because of other commitments. There may be no 'vacancy' for a friend within one or both sets of relationships at the time the two happen to meet. (A vacancy which occurs suddenly may cause a panic reaction and lead to a new relationship 'on the rebound'.) The two people may not like each other equally, and this is more likely if they

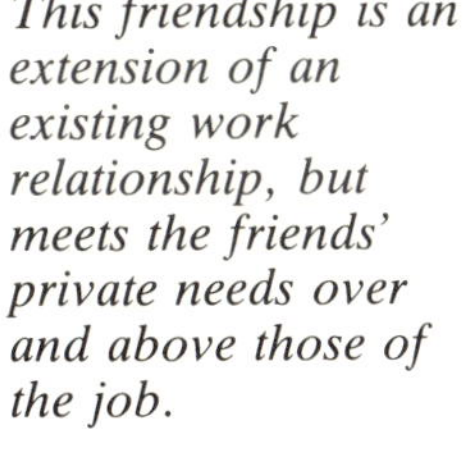

This friendship is an extension of an existing work relationship, but meets the friends' private needs over and above those of the job.

disagree about important matters or have opposing attitudes on general issues. They may be attracted equally but for reasons which are incompatible, as, for example, when a married man is sexually attracted to a colleague who admires his work but does not wish to become his lover. Status differences may also prevent people from getting to know each other equally, or from wanting to. The most important factors in determining whether or not two people become friends are opportunity, mutual attraction, equality and coincidental need.

Even if two people are willing and able to become friends, this does not automatically mean that friendship will follow. They need to tell each other that they are friends, or at least form a contract of some kind to go on behaving as such. Other people usually learn about the friendship, either because they are told or because they assume that a friendship exists from the way the friends behave. This is known as 'legitimation'. Not all friendships are legitimated, but those which are not are less likely to last. Being known as friends within a larger group means that the couple can help each other even when one of the partners is absent – by clearing up misunderstandings with colleagues, for example, or by doing favours for the absent partner like passing on information or completing tasks for him. Public acts of friendship show other people that the friendship exists; their approval or disapproval will make the friendship easier or harder to sustain. Doing public favours for a friend can also strengthen or weaken the friendship,

These two Parisian street musicians share their common interest in a friendly way.

This is the ideal position for a friendly chat: close but not too close, at right angles rather than face-to-face, and as a part of a wider shared activity.

depending on the expectations friends have of each other. For example, somebody might not want his friend to deny a rumour and be annoyed if he does.

Friendship can exist as the only form of relationship between two people. However, most friendships are extensions of an existing relationship. The pair get to know each other in the first place because they belong to the same group, such as the family, neighbourhood or leisure organization, or work group. Their friendship develops first within the context of that group. Some relationships are designed primarily to meet the needs of a group and the individual benefits at second hand through his membership of the group as a whole. These are called 'formal' relationships. By contrast, a close friendship is designed to meet personal needs directly, and is one of a group of 'informal', or 'private', relationships. Formal relationships are mainly to do with power; private relationships are more concerned with sexuality than with power.

45 Being Friendly

The first step in making a friend is to be friendly yourself

Each time you meet somebody you can either be friendly or unfriendly. Friendliness shows that you like being with him and that you find him attractive in some way, perhaps because you admire and respect him or because you are sexually attracted. Friendliness also suggests that you both have similar attitudes and opinions. Showing somebody that you like him implies that you want to go on seeing him in the future. Friendliness is indicated by communicating warmth – using less impact or pressure in your non-verbal behaviour and more caress. For example, you can look at the other person in a relaxed way, instead of staring or using very brief, sharp glances. You can use a tone of voice which indicates interest, encouraging him to express his own feelings and accepting them yourself, rather than contradicting him or pressing him to say only what you want to hear. When you are being unfriendly, you refuse to reward the attention somebody gives you and show no enthusiasm for continuing the conversation unless you are being rewarded and the other person is not.

Friendliness is not always reciprocated. In general, if two people are to become friends, they need to show warmth towards each other, indicating that there is two-way attraction and that both are enjoying the encounter and would like to develop a closer relationship. Once a friendship is established, however, one partner can often behave in an unfriendly way towards the other without destroying their relationship.

If we examine any conversation in detail, we see that friendliness may vary from moment to moment. Each fragment of non-verbal behaviour will either indicate an increase or decrease in warmth or confirm that the level has not altered. Each partner watches the other to see what effect his words are having. He notices two kinds of reactions: one is to the words and comes across as agreement or disagreement; the other is more personal and is perceived as like or dislike. At the start of a relationship, disagreement tends to imply personal dislike. Only when people are secure in a relationship can they disagree about personal matters without implying that they dislike each other.

Over a series of encounters with someone, you tend to show how you feel about him in general. If you wish to become more friendly, you will probably increase the warmth of your non-verbal behaviour over successive conversations. You may also suggest increasing the length of your meetings and the frequency with which you meet. You will probably also discover more attitudes and opinions upon which you agree. This is partly because you will tend to modify your views to accord with the other person's, and partly because he will alter his views to take account of yours. These shifts in attitude towards agreement are not insincere; they are the long-term verbal equivalents of co-ordinated body movements. Whenever two people wish to increase co-operation, they not only synchronize their actions but also co-ordinate their way of looking at things.

The friendly way in which one woman touches the other helps to combat the status differences between them.

As a friendship lasts longer, it may also grow in width and depth. That is to say, the range of shared activities increases, as does the intensity of the experiences. Sharing a wider range of activities means that the friends meet more of their needs when they are together. For example, intellectual, physical and emotional needs can be met in addition to social needs. Within each set of activities a greater depth or intensity of sharing grows as the friendship progresses. Friends feel safe enough to reveal anger or childlike delight; from increasingly intimate self-disclosure, each can learn about the other's suppressed emotions. The partners see each other more often in unguarded moments, share more secrets and trust each other more.

This development also enables friends to begin to reassess their own resources with each other's help. They can say things to each other which are new; because each has learned to be a good listener to the other, they can express and put into words thoughts, experiences and emotions which were previously only half understood or entirely unexplored. The hidden agenda can now be revealed, and perhaps altered. This is possible because a need cannot be satisfied as long as it remains unconscious. When somebody becomes aware of his real wishes, he can satisfy them and stop wasting energy suppressing them.

A British police sergeant accepts a friendly gesture from a member of the public. The barriers between them are lowered in the carnival atmosphere.

If you are friendly, you show the other person that all these developments are possible if he is willing and able to get to know you better. It opens the door to increased friendship in case your partner wishes to come in. Obviously there will be people to whom you cannot open this door, sometimes because you are not sufficiently attracted to them or they to you, and sometimes because power or status differences keep you apart.

Nevertheless it is a sound policy to open the door as far as you can to everyone. The people with whom we find it hardest to develop friendships are those who appear most threatening to us. We are afraid of the unfair advantages they might take if we appear too friendly. We tend to label such people, and then react to the stereotype we have adopted rather than to the realities of their personalities. But their reactions to us often arise because we seem threatening to them. By getting to know them better, we can learn why this happens and reduce the threat. Friendliness is above all the use of verbal and non-verbal communication as a way of reducing threats.

46 Manipulation and Aggressive Criticism

The influence of the 'hidden agenda'

When there is a lack of friendship in a long-term relationship, this is often because a person's hidden agenda has not been changed. He can therefore be manipulated into feeling guilty and this places him at a disadvantage so that he can be controlled. In effect, the manipulator 'plugs into' the controls placed there by the victim's own parents and reactivates these mechanisms. The victim usually does most of the work; all the manipulator has to do is press the right buttons.

A skilled manipulator can make you feel guilty without saying a word. His reluctance to come near you may do it, or a stiffness in the way he moves or looks at you. He might place an object on the table with a slightly louder noise than usual, or ignore you for a few extra seconds although he normally stops what he is doing and takes notice of you. You are supposed to know what you have done wrong, and to feel guilty about it. The manipulator usually issues several such signals and watches you to make sure you have picked them up. Your discomfort shows plainly, either because you indicate that you are ready for a fight or because you seem at such pains to ignore the message.

A case study will help to show what happens. Although this study is an example of manipulation in a private relationship, a similar effect is often achieved in more formal groups.

When Peter arrived home late from work, he knew that his wife Diane would be angry. Even while he was taking off his coat, he was pretending not to care. Diane usually met him and made a fuss of him when he arrived home. This time he could hear her in the kitchen, rattling pots and pans. He prepared a few sentences about missing the train and going for a drink while he waited. Then he went into the dining room.

'Your supper's spoilt,' she said. He looked at it and could see that she was right.

'That's all right,' he replied and began to eat.

'You're late again,' she said. He did not reply.

'That's twice this week. You know how I worry. And your mother telephoned. You weren't here.' He nodded, pretending to like the dry meat. Diane ignored this and carried on.

'I tried to keep the food nice for you. It's your favourite. I had it ready for you exactly on half past. Your mother's feeling ill again. It was you she wanted to talk to, not me. You always seem to be out when she calls. Then I have to deal with her. You know I get my headaches when she complains.'

'I missed the train,' said Peter apologetically.

'The doctor told me I had to avoid stress. And now you've been drinking.'

Diane's manipulative behaviour consisted of a series of statements of fact. It was true that the supper was spoilt, that Peter was late, that it was the second time he had been late that week, and so on. Diane's

Manipulation is a common feature of many relationships, although it may not always be apparent to the outside observer. Is this woman making her partner feel obliged to buy her a present? He seems to be more concerned with what she might decide than with helping her choose.

whining tone of voice showed Peter that he was being treated like a naughty little boy who ought to be ashamed of himself. Her timing was also important, since he had to listen and eat at the same time. She walked behind him while she spoke, so that he would have to look up at her and twist round into an uncomfortable position to see her. If he did, he would have to stop eating and then she would ask if he liked the food, suggesting that he did not. It would also give her a chance of telling him he was talking with his mouth full, not looking at her while he spoke or not speaking clearly.

Peter's parents had trained him to feel guilty if he did not conform to certain standards of behaviour. He had been taught to be punctual, not to repeat his mistakes, to be grateful for his food (and particularly grateful when given his favourite meals), not to be a worry to people, not to make excuses, to respect his parents (particularly his mother), to be available when somebody needed him, to value a doctor's opinion and not to drink. He had also been taught not to talk with his mouth full and to look at people when he was being spoken to. He was expected to feel guilty if he broke any of these rules. Each of Diane's statements was carefully designed to trigger his guilt.

The short-term way of dealing with this kind of manipulation is to agree with the facts and ignore the implications. When Diane told Peter that his supper was spoilt, he could have replied, 'Yes it is, isn't it?' When she told him he was late again, this too was something he could have acknowledged. He knew she was upset, but that she was not going to say so. He could therefore have said, 'You look unhappy. Is it because I'm late again?' They might then have been able to deal with her feelings together, instead of working themselves into a situation where all the responsibility fell on Peter. Acknowledging the facts stated by an angry manipulator requires a special skill, that of ignoring the tone of voice and other non-verbal clues and hints, and simply replying to the words. The long-term answer is not to feel guilty for matters which are beyond your control, including other people's feelings.

This situation looks manipulative. The man seems to be ignoring the woman's restive look. Is he forcing her to say she is dissatisfied, thus manipulating her into being responsible for their moving on?

A potentially manipulative situation (right). The man is in an ideal body position to be critical without saying a word – too far away for co-operative contact, his hands in his pockets showing a determination not to help, and a slightly aggressive posture, his head jutting forward, his shoulders hunched.

Parental control may be used as the basis of manipulative criticism when the child grows up (right).

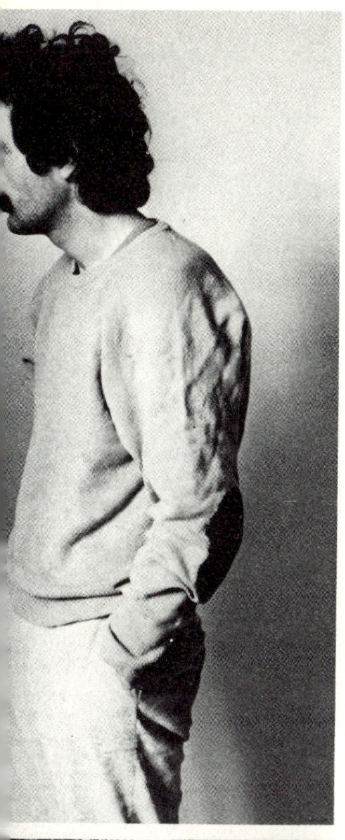

Sometimes, however, the manipulator finds that his carefully chosen facts are not enough to trigger the intended victim's sense of guilt. When the victim fails to respond, the manipulator is forced to use aggressive criticism. Like manipulation, aggressive criticism harnesses the victim's unconscious desire to be a more acceptable person. It works best with someone who has a low opinion of himself and has been trained in childhood to try harder, do his best, and respect people more powerful than himself, particularly his parents. Most people like this have also been taught not to show anger and that if they do something wrong they should expect to be punished.

Let us return to the example of Peter and Diane. Although Diane was probably not fully aware of her motives, she wanted to make Peter feel guilty so that she could control his behaviour in future. When he failed to respond to her manipulation, she felt anxious and angry. She decided to use aggressive criticism instead.

'Can you hear me, Peter?' she demanded. The question was designed to force a response which she could then criticize.

'Yes,' replied Peter. 'I can hear you.'

'Then haven't you got anything to say for yourself?' This question implied the criticism that, like a naughty little boy, he was too ashamed of his crime to defend himself. If he said he was sorry, he would be admitting his guilt. If he said he had nothing to say 'for himself', she could still criticize him by rejecting his answers as unsatisfactory. Peter felt uncomfortable in the trap, but could see no way out, so he said nothing at all. Diane then increased the intensity of her anger.

'Talking to you is like talking to a brick wall. You never listen; you don't even try to understand my point of view. You always put your own selfish interests first. There's no excuse. You could have telephoned, but no! You're a stupid, selfish person, without even the good manners to apologize.'

Her criticism was aimed at Peter's opinion of himself, in the hope that she could thus destroy his self-control. As Peter pushed aside his half-eaten supper, the plate crashed to the floor.

'Now look what you've done! Look at the mess! Don't you come near me. Control yourself,' said Diane. The broken plate could now be used as evidence of Peter's loss of self-control. If this did not have the desired effect and he hit her, she could also make him feel sorry for this, since he had been trained to feel guilty about losing his temper.

Aggressive criticism is always designed to make the victim so angry that he loses control. There are two aspects of our internal control system. One part is designed to make us into a certain type of person; the other is to prevent us becoming a certain type of person. When the victim of aggressive criticism loses control, he becomes the kind of person he has been taught not to be. For example, someone who thinks of himself as reasonable may suddenly realize that he is behaving in an unreasonable way. A victim who is not usually violent suddenly finds that he is ready to hit somebody. Someone who does not usually bear a grudge becomes malevolent and spiteful, and is surprised that this can happen to him.

As with manipulation, the best way of dealing with aggressive criticism is to agree with it. When somebody says you are stupid, say that you have often thought so yourself. If you are told you are clumsy, admit it. There is no need to feel guilty about being stupid or clumsy. The aggressor's criticism will be aimed at turning you into the kind of person you fear you might be, but have unconsciously tried not to be. Since you are already this type of person, you have less to lose by admitting it than by trying to cover it up.

The long-term solution, both to manipulation and to aggressive criticism, lies in developing better friendships. These enable us safely to explore the things which make us feel guilty and to replace unconscious controls with better self-management. We cannot achieve this by ourselves, but only by getting to know other people and, through them, ourselves.

Anticipating a partner's needs. In a long-term, stable relationship this is done honestly, but dishonest anticipation would be manipulative.

SECTION FOUR
RELATIONSHIPS IN GROUPS

Most relationships take place as part of the activities of four kinds of group: the family, the employing organization, the neighbourhood and the friendship group. Section Four looks at the way in which a group controls communication and acquaintance as part of its organization, and we consider why this is necessary. We also look at the needs of a group and how the groups to which we belong help us meet our own needs.

The economic and psycho-economic structure of a group is examined next, to show the nature of power struggles and how they are won or lost. The final chapters deal with the principles of good leadership and the importance of status.

47 The Importance of Groups

Groups influence how you relate and to whom

Our way of life depends on organized groups to such an extent that it is difficult to look at them objectively, yet it is important to do so if we are to see relationships clearly. A relationship cannot take place in a vacuum; the way two people communicate with, and get to know, one another must reflect the nature of the organized groups to which they belong.

One such group is the family. However loving a family might be, its powerful members insist that certain purposes are accomplished, certain values and attitudes are respected and adopted and certain controls are imposed. Your personal style in relating to other people is just as much a product of the control which was imposed on you as it is of the love you received as a child. If you have children of your own, you will no doubt control them in addition to loving them and caring for them.

To understand yourself and your relationships thoroughly, and, more particularly, to understand other people and their ways of relating, it is not enough to take for granted that your family has influenced you, nor even to recognize some of the differences between your upbringing and that of other people. What is required is a more fundamental understanding of the nature of the family as an organized group held together by the power of its dominant members.

The family into which you are born influences you more than any other organized group to which you can belong because, even after you have grown up, it continues to affect the way you relate to people. But other groups play a major part in determining this, too. One is the company or organization for which you work, or which employs the people on whom you are dependent. A business organization brings people together as part of a system, so that they cannot easily relate to other people in ways which might destroy that system. It influences whom you meet and how you deal with them. You are not only paid to help your employer stay in business; it also pays you to do so, and your relationships reflect this fact.

There are two other important groups: the neighbourhood, and any group of friends with whom you may enjoy your leisure or to whom you turn for support and advice when things go wrong. Such groups also depend for their existence on organization, and therefore on the power and influence of their dominant members.

Three friends in County Kerry, Eire. In some societies, a man's friendships with other men may be more important than the relationship with his wife and children. Such men may turn to the group of friends rather than the family for approval, support and advice.

These four groups – the family, the employing organization, the neighbourhood and groups of friends – probably provide you with nearly all your relationships. Each one acts as the focus for a part of your life. You depend on organized groups to provide the resources you need to maintain an acceptable standard of life: earning and spending power, goods and services, support and protection, respect and love, and so on. You could survive without these groups, but with a quality of life you would probably find unacceptable. Equally, the groups to which you belong depend on you to some degree for their

At the races. Each group can be distinguished by its use of territory and style of organization. The family in the foreground indicates its territorial boundaries by the way it spreads objects around; other groups create boundaries by avoiding communication with strangers.

own survival. The more a group needs you the more power you can have within that group; but the more you depend on a group, the more power it can have over you.

You need relationships to protect and improve your chosen quality of life. Similarly, groups themselves need to guarantee their survival and success by relating to other groups. You play your part in this by representing the interests of your own groups in the economic, political or social structure of society. You have no choice about this, even if you are not particularly interested in economics, politics or society. The clothes you wear, the shops you go to, the kinds of people you count as friends, the accent you use when you speak and the place where you live are only a few of the ways in which, unwittingly perhaps, you advertise which groups you belong to, which ones you are pleased not to belong to and which you would like to belong to next.

A distinction was made earlier between loving, trading and power relationships. Whilst all three types can occur inside a group, the next few chapters will focus on the internal power structure. Social scientists see a group as being held together by the power of its dominant members, exercised through active control of the ways in which the members communicate and the extent to which they are allowed to become acquainted.

48 The Nature of a Group

The main features of an organized group

Imagine arriving late at a meeting of a discussion group to which you belong. You will probably sit down quietly and look around to see who else is there, exchanging a smile with any members you recognize. Your arrival interrupts the proceedings briefly, and the person in charge welcomes you with a few words before the meeting continues. You start to relax and listen to the discussion. During this period you are being absorbed into the group, connecting up with its communication system and becoming further acquainted with the other people present. By analysing what happens in this situation we can identify all the main features of an organized group.

First, a group distinguishes between members and non-members. Had you been an outsider it is unlikely that you would have relaxed or been welcomed in exactly the same way. Secondly, a group exists for a purpose – in this case, discussion. If you had wandered into the wrong group, not only would you have failed to recognize other members, but you would also have found that they were not carrying out the purpose for which you had come. These two features of a group depend on acquaintance and communication. The identification of members and non-members depends on acquaintance; and a group cannot advertise its purpose, decide on a policy for achieving it or put this policy into practice without communicating.

Let us suppose that, after you have listened to some of the other members speaking, the group leader asks you to state your views on a particular point. Several members turn to look at you. This helps to illustrate further important features of a group. First, it has leaders or co-ordinators who assist the group to achieve its purpose by sharing out the work. To do this efficiently, a leader must be a good communicator; he also needs to know the members and be recognized by them as leader. We can also see that communication within the group works in several different ways. You can communicate on a one-to-one basis, as when the leader addressed you in the above example. You can talk to a section of the membership, such as those members who turned to look at you. Or you can communicate with the group as a whole. If at that moment another group entered the room, thinking they had hired it to play basketball, this would illustrate yet another level of communication – that which may occur between two or more groups. Everybody might shout at once, but it is more likely that the two leaders would settle the problem by talking on behalf of their groups.

Each of the ways of communicating outlined above can, of course, apply to acquaintance, too. People can get to know each other on a one-to-one basis, as a result of communication with a section or sub-group, or by addressing the whole of a group; or they can get to know other groups or their members on behalf of the group they represent. Each combination can lead to a different kind of relationship: individual, partial, collective or representative.

The relationships within a group, however, cannot be left to chance. A group would be disorganized and ineffective unless it controlled the communication and acquaintance of its members. The discussion group helps to illustrate this point. Suppose that you and the person next to you (and other pairs of members) decided to become better acquainted by holding private, one-to-one conversations during the discussion. This would prevent the group from carrying out its purpose. Alternatively, suppose all the members talked at once, each of them addressing the whole group or separate sub-groups. This, too, would disrupt the discussion.

Communication and acquaintance in a group are controlled in order to serve the interests of the group. To ensure that this happens, somebody with power shares out the work and enforces the rules. Members support this when they know that it is in their own interests to do so. The result is a system of relationships between members, designed to achieve common purposes. These relationships are not free to develop if they might threaten the success of the group.

The next step is to see how this analysis applies to other important groups. Before doing so, however, it would be useful to gather the threads together and sum up the main features of a group. These are as follows. A group has membership, purpose, leadership and organi-

A therapy group acknowledges the value of a member. An understanding of the way groups work is used to set up therapy sessions like this one, where young offenders get to know each other and learn to communicate better by forming a more positive idea of their own value.

First day at school: the little girl is joining an established group with its own system of communication and acquaintance. Here she is taught how to use this system.

zation. To carry out its purpose it must agree policies, put them into practice and be seen to do so by other groups. All this depends on communication and acquaintance. To remain organized it must distinguish between members and non-members, and have some form of leadership. These processes also depend on how the people concerned communicate and get to know one another. A group is therefore a system of controlled and organized relationships, in which the way you communicate with people and get to know them is restricted in the interests of your fellow-members.

49 Restrictions on Relating

The control of communication and acquaintance

Communication is always controlled to prevent or to encourage the development of an equal relationship. (below) These young men indicate a readiness to get to know each other as equals. (right) The huntsman's position encourages those on the ground to address him as a superior.

The ideal way to develop a relationship is through face-to-face, two-person conversation, meeting as equals with no pressure on the time spent together. If a family or any other organization wishes to control a member's relationships, therefore, there are several ways in which it can interfere. One is to prevent face-to-face conversation. Another is to prevent people meeting as equals. A third is to restrict the time allowed for communication. In this chapter we look at how communication and acquaintance are controlled in a group, using the family as an example.

In a family, certain controls apply to the way the child speaks to his parents. When a child is being disciplined, for example, he is not allowed to talk back to the parent as an equal. If he does so he may be punished further, because an assumption on his part that he is equal will sound like insubordination. The time spent arguing the rights and wrongs of the matter is strictly limited. The child is often not allowed

to argue at all, and if he tries to do so, the parent shows impatience and says he is not going to waste time discussing the issue. In a normal, face-to-face conversation, each person would be equally interested in the other's feelings; but in the case of the child and his parent, each is mainly concerned with his own feelings. The parent prevents long replies, even to long questions; he uses a tone of voice and ways of looking which are dominated by pressure and impact. Caress is limited or does not appear at all.

In many families, the children are not allowed to get 'too close' to their parents. In other words, it is considered acceptable for the children to talk to the parents, but not for the parents to self-disclose equally. In some families (within what is known in England as the 'Victorian' tradition) children are expected to be 'seen and not heard'. Where this happens, the child is not allowed to initiate conversation with the parent, but is nevertheless expected to know him. He can only speak when spoken to. True communication is not approved of, but one-way, limited acquaintance is.

The control of communication and acquaintance can also be seen in the way children are allowed to develop some relationships outside the family, but not others. Something similar happens in all organized groups. Non-members fall into four categories: equals, inferiors, superiors and outcasts. A few examples will illustrate the differences.

An 'equal' is somebody it is 'acceptable' to talk to and to get to know. For example, families control the kinds of friends their children can make. If the child is mixing with equals this process is left to develop with a minimum of interference. The children are allowed as much time together as possible, and parents facilitate communication by being friendly towards the parents of their child's friends. In some families children meet most of their out-of-school friends through the social life of their parents; while the adults talk and play, their children are put together to do the same. This also helps to lower the risk of their children mixing with non-equals.

An 'inferior' is somebody it is 'acceptable' to talk to, but not to get to know as an equal. Families often have very clear ideas about who is an inferior, such as a member of a minority group. In a liberal community, a family may consider it acceptable for their children to talk to members of other races or religions, but not to get to know them 'too well' in case the family loses control over the values and beliefs of its own children. (It may try to prevent them becoming biased or sectarian, for example.) An inferior may also be someone who belongs to a different social class or has a lower standard of education. People tend not to marry outside their social class. A recent British survey showed that, out of 5,000 couples, more than 80 per cent had married people with a similar class or educational background.

A 'superior' is somebody it is not 'acceptable' to talk to, but it is 'acceptable' to get to know. A child is taught to recognize his superiors and not to be presumptuous by taking the initiative in acquaintance, as, for example, with a strict teacher. Spouses also control one another in this way. For example, if a husband meets a 'superior' while out shopping with his wife, he will not expect her to act boldly or treat the person as an equal. If she does so, the husband may be embarrassed, partly because he does not feel able to treat the person as an equal himself. However, if he is addressed by his superior as if he were an equal, he will be proud of this, and flattered that this person wants to get to know him.

An 'outcast' is a person whom it is not 'acceptable' to talk to or to get to know. For example, a clean child may be prevented from playing with a dirty child. In many neighbourhoods, mixing is carefully controlled to reinforce the social differences between families, thus protecting the standard of life approved by the parents. It would be a mistake to assume that this is always rich families preventing social mixing with poorer families, for the process works both ways.

50 Approval and Popularity

Approval shows that your value to somebody has increased

When you belong to a group you are not completely free to choose how you relate to people. Sometimes this is because other members intervene to prevent you following a certain course of action. Most of the time, however, you exercise self-control, and deliberately avoid doing things which you know will make you unpopular.

Studies show that the members of a group are usually accurate judges of their own popularity. Somebody becomes more popular when people approve of what he does, and less popular when they disapprove. It can be seen, therefore, that popularity and approval are connected. Both can constitute an important form of control by a group over its members, providing feedback which encourages certain actions and discourages others.

People show approval by being more willing to communicate with someone and to get to know him. This is shown by a pleasurable increase in the intensity of non-verbal behaviour – more smiling and mutual eye-contact, for example, together with a more caressing tone of voice and more relaxed behaviour at close proximity. Acquaintance levels are raised by an increase in self-disclosure on the part of the person showing approval. This can be embarrassing, as when somebody who sees himself as very inferior is suddenly allowed to share in the personal feelings of a superior. Disapproval is indicated by a withdrawal from contact, producing a suspension of acquaintance and difficulties in communication. For example, self-disclosures may not be answered equally by somebody who disapproves: one person shows his feelings but the other hides his. Requests for help may be ignored, or the unpopular person may be asked for lengthy explanations as to why he wants help. Non-verbal behaviour is less co-ordinated: body motion synchrony, for example, is avoided or disrupted by the person showing disapproval. He may stand still as if rigid with anger or fear, ignore attempts at eye-contact, tense himself even more when the other person comes close, refuse to be touched and try to break contact when spoken to.

Popularity and approval are not always effective controls. In an informal group, they are designed to limit choice rather than physically prevent somebody doing something. There are times when you may be pleased to be unpopular, either because you will not lose the approval of those you respect or because you do not respect the people who show disapproval. At other times you may be forced to follow procedures of which you disapprove: you may have to accept a majority decision or be forced to carry out instructions from a superior, for example. Approval can be shown by an individual, a sub-group or the entire group, or be expressed on behalf of a group by a representative. Its effectiveness as a control depends on the status of the people who show it, or refuse to show it.

We saw earlier that non-members of a group can be separated into

Meeting as equals: each little girl gives approval to the other.

superiors, inferiors, equals and outcasts. This often applies inside a group, too. The category into which a person is placed shows his value compared to that of somebody else. Thus the people whom you treat as your inferiors are of low value compared with you, those you see as equals have similar value to yourself and your superiors have more value than you or your equals. An outcast is somebody with negative value: he can do positive harm to your chances of maintaining the quality of life you regard as right for you. In achieving your own desired standard you usually wish to avoid being like your inferiors, want to stay at a similar level to your equals or aim to become more like your superiors.

Approval shows that your value to somebody is increasing, while disapproval shows it is decreasing. For example, if a superior shows you more approval than usual, you know your value to him has risen because he treats you more like his equal. However, this in turn may affect your position with *your* equals. Suppose they disapprove. In this case, they may accuse you of behaving in a superior manner and try to redress the balance by 'taking you down a peg or two'. In other words, they treat you as their inferior. Or they may tease you by showing exaggerated 'approval' – addressing you as 'your highness', for example, or pretending to bow and curtsy. If they approve, however, they will begin to accept you as someone who will eventually be a superior, and show pleasure because this brings credit to the group as a whole.

Similarly, in work groups, there is less risk attached to being unpopular with subordinates if you have the approval of a superior. Some managers show a lack of confidence when they have just been promoted: they 'trade down', or try to treat their subordinates as equals, thus losing the respect of their subordinates as well as that of their superiors.

Jon Voight and Jane Fonda received Academy Awards for Best Film Actor and Best Film Actress in 1979. These awards are highly regarded because they show the approval of colleagues in the film industry.

Disapproval shows a loss of value. This can be illustrated by looking at how a child may be punished in a family. If the child does something wrong and wastes expensive materials or damages equipment, he is reducing the value of the family's resources. The greater the loss of value, the more severely he will usually be punished. He becomes temporarily an outcast, but is allowed to return to his former position when the family has accepted the loss.

However, an extremely unpopular adult, whose actions threaten the viability of the whole group, may be treated as a permanent outcast. For example, a doctor, lawyer or priest found guilty of serious malpractice may be expelled, so that he becomes a non-member. Unlike other non-members, however, he is deprived of the right to join the group in the future; this shows his *negative* value. Sometimes a member who is guilty of serious misconduct cannot be expelled and becomes an outcast within the group, as when a worker is 'sent to Coventry' or a prisoner who commits an offence in prison is rejected by the other prisoners. In the same way that a group shows its extreme disapproval of a member by treating him as an outcast, you may feel you disapprove of a group to such an extent that you reject all the members, by walking out or resigning.

A display of approval. Such marks of popularity within a group help to establish the relative value of each member.

51 Organization

Organization limits the harmful effects of competition

A group is not only a system of relationships; it is also a system of resources. Every group owns resources, in much the same way as an individual does. It has the physical resources of its members when they are present in the group; it uses their behavioural resources, such as their skills and intelligence; it owns property, such as territory and money; and it has social resources – the support and help its members receive privately from their own families and friends outside the group, in addition to the group's own relationships with other groups. Control is necessary to ensure that these resources are used to the best advantage. We have already seen that all groups are organized. The next step is to examine in more detail why and how they are organized, and to understand the principal reasons for organization.

The main reason why groups have to be organized is that their resources are limited. Indeed, groups do not form, and organization does not appear, in situations where people have everything they could possibly need. This is illustrated by a remarkable observation made over fifty years ago by the anthropologist Margaret Mead on the island of Manus, New Guinea. She found that the children there had everything they could wish for. Her previous studies had led her to expect

Organized play. These Corsican children will act out a fantasy in their play, but first their leader gets the group to agree the outline of the story.

that children everywhere were naturally organized and competitive in their play, but this was not so on Manus because there was no competition over resources and so the children had no need to control one another.

When resources are in short supply, people have to compete for them. We can illustrate this point by looking at some of the things groups own. Organization is designed to limit competition and thus to save the group from wasting the value of its resources.

Competition inside a group

Two of the most important resources a group owns are space and time, because without them we can do nothing. A family, for example, owns the space it calls home. Members may compete for this space in several ways: one person may wish to use a room for conversation, but be prevented from doing so by another member of the family listening to

School uniforms seen in Hyde Park, London. Within each group the same uniform stresses equality of membership, but between the two groups uniforms emphasize competition.

Drought victims in Ethiopia. Their lives depend on their organized behaviour; if they competed for the water, the result would be chaos and few would benefit.

loud music or watching television; or the members may compete for the use of the bathroom. An organized family routine helps to limit the potentially harmful effects of such competition. A daughter and her mother-in-law may compete territorially for the use of the kitchen, and only by organizing separate parts of it to suit both of them can they avoid destructive conflict.

In the same way, a large group using a small kitchen has to be very well organized and good-tempered if everyone is to be fed. Once they all have what they need, however, they can relax.

Being present in a group also takes time, and the group owns and controls the time its members contribute. This is so vital to a business organization that it is frequently said that 'time is money'. The time of the most important people in a group is the most limited, and there is often competition to make appointments with them. This could increase the pressure on them if they did not have assistance. Most executives have a secretary who, amongst other duties, organizes an appointments diary. In all voluntary organizations, if you are absent too often from meetings, family gatherings, the neighbourhood, reunions of old friends, and so on, this weakens your claim to be a member. The other members feel that you are valuing them less because other groups or activities are evidently competing more successfully for your time, and

therefore must be seen by you as more important.

A group owns resources other than space and time, notably money. Competition for money is always strictly organized within a group. We are generally so accustomed to this that we tend to take it for granted, but imagine what it would be like if employees were paid by being told to help themselves to as much money as they wanted. Most would probably not take more than was due to them, but there would be no certainty of this, and if somebody took too much, the members to suffer would be those who were honest or weak.

A group of friends also helps to illustrate how competition for money is restricted by a group. Friends share money by taking turns to pay for things, or by buying one another gifts of roughly equal value. One friend might compete with the others by insisting upon buying all the drinks every time, or showing that he had more money than the others. If he did so he would cease to be an equal and become a superior, and this would be resented. Another way of competing would be by saving money and expecting the other friends always to pay. Too much generosity and too frequent meanness are controlled by the way in which friends take turns to ensure equality.

A group also owns resources such as property, equipment and the skills of its members. The more valuable these resources, the more damage would be done by members competing selfishly for them. The community might lose not only the resource, but also the time and energy of the members who competed. Organized team sports illustrate this point. The members of a football team (or the partners in a card game) would not be breaking the rules if they competed against one another instead of against their opponents; but they would considerably lower their chances of winning. A selfish player prevents his team-mate from exercising what might be his superior skill. The side loses the value of this skill, and also loses the benefit it might have gained from the wasted energy.

Competition between groups

A group owns its resources as a result of successful competition with other groups. To continue to own them it must continue to compete successfully. Alternatively, it must end competition completely. All groups use both methods.

A group prevents competition from other groups by making certain that these groups and their members know which resources it owns: those it owns are inside its boundaries, and those it does not are outside. Spatial boundaries mark where one group's territory ends and another's begins. This can be seen in the way a group of friends encloses the space across which the members communicate and stop talking if an intruder occupies this space. Similarly, a family's home is its preserve, and interference from outsiders is prevented. A visitor may be accorded certain privileges in the house, but he has no rights unless he is related to the family. This shows in the way a stranger who enters the home is expected to wait until asked before sitting down or eating. A business organization protects its space by a variety of means, including the use of guards and security checks; the members may have to show proof of membership.

A group also has temporal boundaries to show which time is theirs.

(above) A family eats in cramped conditions. Each member has to contribute to the organization either by doing some of the work or by limiting competition. (below) Brick Lane, in the East End of London, has become a focus for racialist agitation. Here the local residents react angrily to interference from an anti-racist 'outsider'.

A baton change in a relay race. Perfect communication between team members is essential; the slightest self-consciousness may result in a split second's delay and the loss of the race.

For example, the members of a family deliberately spend time together to emphasize their unity as a group and to strengthen this unity. People have no time for the unpopular families in a neighbourhood, particularly if these families are reducing the neighbourhood's ability to compete successfully with other neighbourhoods, yet people can always 'make time' for a popular family or its members. An employing organization prevents competition from other groups by not allowing employees to work for another company at the same time; 'moonlighting' is always frowned upon.

Territorial competition between groups can be illustrated by the way in which a business organization tends to see its traditional markets almost as its own property. Because it expects less competition here, it begins to take its supremacy for granted, and may become complacent. In an industrial society, most competition between groups concerns money. Neighbourhoods compete in this way: a 'superior' district has higher house prices than an 'inferior' one. In many districts, families with economic or financial aspirations compete with one another in displays of wealth, such as owning bigger houses or cars or wearing more expensive clothes than their neighbours.

Groups also compete for skills: a football team may buy the most skilful players, a college may attract Nobel prize winners and a family may show off the talents of its children. Attempts by other groups to take away the value of such resources (by offering the 'star' more money and better facilities, for example) are regarded as unfair competition.

Competition between groups can become violent. This may result in urban warfare, as when a minority believes that it is being deprived of its rights by the majority, for religious, racial or class reasons, and it begins an armed struggle. Attacks on the group strengthen its unity. The members need to compete successfully with other groups if their way of life is to survive. They therefore organize their lines of communication. 'Freedom fighters' are protected by a wall of silence, to

The start of a carefully planned move in an American football game. Each player knows what he and his team-mates must do to complete the move. In this way, competition between members of the same side is limited in the interests of more effective competition with the opposing side.

Women in Belfast, Northern Ireland, play their part in defending their community. By beating the tin lids on the ground, they are taunting the security forces and warning the neighbourhood of the army's presence.

guarantee their anonymity. When the group is threatened, warning of the threat is broadcast swiftly throughout the group.

Representational competition

Competition between groups may take the form of representational competition. This occurs when a group supports one of its members to act on its behalf against an opposing group, or against this group's representative. Examples of this can be found in sport, where a champion is seen as competing on behalf of his club, district or nation. The support the competitor receives is invested with the hopes, fears and ambitions of the group he represents. Similarly, wartime heroes are seen as displaying their courage not for themselves but on behalf of the whole group they represent. The leaders of a group which demands representational sacrifice have a special role to play and are always at the forefront in honouring the hero, thus acknowledging publicly the representational act.

In urban warfare, the army or police have to intervene to represent the whole community. If they try to separate the two sides in the dispute, they may come to be seen as the enemy by both sides. In trying to lower tension and reduce the harmful effects of the conflict, they may thus make the conflict worse. Less violent representational competition can be seen in the way we all represent the values and purposes of the groups to which we belong, not only when we are present with other members of the group, but also when we are not. The groups to which we belong are part of our identity, for our ability to maintain the standard of life we wish to keep depends on the survival and comparative supremacy of these groups.

We defend our interests by displaying our status socially, economically and politically. We want our group to succeed, and groups with aims and objectives which conflict with our own to fail. As a result, one of the first tasks facing us when we meet someone else is to identify the groups to which he belongs, whether or not these are groups we support, and discover how much power he has. If we feel strongly about his groups – particularly if we oppose them – we will tend to treat him as a representative of his 'kind' rather than as a person in his own right. In other words, we compete with him on behalf of our own 'kind'. The higher his status in his groups, the more likely we are to see him as

Formal representation at the Lord Mayor's Show, held annually in London. The Lord Mayor is the elected representative of the Corporation of the City of London. The ceremonies surrounding his election display the traditional wealth and status of the Corporation.

Symbols of high status and their owners, gathered in the car park at Royal Ascot races, England. Dress and posture enable those present to recognize instantly people who are equal in status. It is assumed that all who dress alike share the same social values.

responsible for their policies and the less likely we are to treat him as an ordinary human being who is interesting for his own sake. Equally, if we strongly support the activities of a group to which we know he belongs, we treat him as an ally in a battle and assume that he is interested in winning the same fights as we are.

There are therefore very few, if any, relationships which are not affected by the groups to which we belong and by their need to compete successfully for the limited resources available in our society.

52 Contributing

All groups have the same kinds of needs

Advice is more readily accepted if it is seen as a contribution from another member of the same group, and not as interference from outside. The London health visitor (right) dresses casually so she will be accepted by her clients. In fact, she is a highly qualified nurse of senior status.

Whenever you join a group, you have to put something in, in order to take anything out. In other words, you have to make a contribution towards the needs of the group before you can use the resources or share in the profits. Part of your contribution will be the time you spend being physically present in the group. You may also contribute the strength and health of your body, as when you work for your family or for a company, or help a neighbour by carrying something for him. You may contribute your attractiveness, as when a person is popular at parties not because he says anything important but simply because he looks good. Next, you might contribute the skill you have as a thinker, organizer, craftsman or artist, or resources such as money or equipment. The child who joins a game because he owns the ball is doing something very similar to the shareholder who puts money into an enterprise and expects to get a return on his investment.

All groups have similar needs. They therefore collect the resources they require to meet them. As a member, you are expected to contribute to all the group's needs. We will examine each of them in detail.

A group needs identity. Unless it has identity, other groups will not recognize its existence and might take away its resources; trade would also be impossible. For example, unless a family is seen to have its own identity, there is nothing to stop other families from interfering in its affairs. Similarly, a firm cannot sell its goods without a trade mark or label which identifies the product and the company. Without this, it could not build up a name for excellence and publicity would be meaningless. In a give-and-take situation, both sides need identity. If a trade union is not recognized, for example, it cannot bargain about wages; and if the members of a local pressure group cannot be identified, the authorities do not need to pay attention to its protests.

Groups meet their need for identity by having titles, names and labels. Many groups such as the police or the armed forces have distinctive uniforms for their members; organized divisions within the force are plainly marked by such things as shoulder flashes or differently shaped hats. Family names indicate identity; moreover, they often show where a person comes from or what his ancestors did for a living (Schmidt, Carter and Thatcher are examples).

The football supporters' group identity is heavily emphasized in an enthusiastic welcome for their triumphant team. Their unity as they celebrate helps to increase the sense of security felt by each member.

Each of the young people pushing the vehicle expects an equal measure of commitment from the others. Any evidence of slacking may be treated as a threat to the security of the group.

A group needs security. In other words, it needs to be able to protect its own resources. If one member of a family is attacked, the others are likely to join in to defend him. A company which feels its reputation has been unfairly attacked may sue for slander or libel. Companies and nations protect themselves by joining associations and federations. The United States is better able to defend itself because it is a federation, but it also belongs to associations such as NATO and SEATO. Without security a group is open to attack and unable to defend itself; it cannot have stable relationships with other groups, trade peacefully or earn their respect.

A group expects its members to be committed. It also tries to show commitment when it deals with other groups. When you join a group, you show your commitment by the value of what you contribute, and of what you forgo in order to participate. If you make a special effort to attend a meeting, even though you are ill or have to travel a long distance, this shows your commitment. A group shows its degree of commitment to its purposes whenever it comes into contact with another group. Commitment may even be the most important feature of a group, as with rival football teams.

A group needs a specialized membership. A meeting proceeds far more efficiently if it has only one chairman, for example, however democratic it is. When the members of a family have an argument, it is often because they are all trying to do the same thing at once, instead

Architects at a planning session. The success of the group as a whole depends on the specialized skills contributed by each of the members.

of taking turns. At work, all jobs tend to become specialities. In a group of friends, one especially valuable resource might be the individual style of a member's sense of humour, such as his gift for witty repartee or sardonic understatement.

A group needs success. First, the purpose of the group has to be clear. The identity of the group will stress the kind of group it is, why it is special and what it is particularly good at. The group will need to secure the means to stay 'special' so that it can achieve its objectives. The support demanded of members is designed to enable the group to succeed, and the specializations within the group are also justified to this end. In other words, all the needs of the group are directed towards its survival, and it cannot survive unless it succeeds. All members are therefore expected to contribute to group security. A member who actually reduces security will incur the severest of penalties; for example, in most countries traitors are executed.

53 Belonging

Membership of a group helps you to meet your needs

Belonging to a group helps you meet some of your needs. First, you have a need for identity. This is partly a private need, the need to know who you are, and to become the sort of person you would like to be through your private relationships. But it is also a public need: unless other people know who you are, they will not know how to relate to you, or, in other words, whether to react as part of a power, trading or loving relationship. Membership of a group helps you to meet this need

A Republican delegate in the US Presidential elections, 1976. His individual identity is less important at this moment than his group identity, indicated by his hat and badges.

Expressions of the need to belong to and be accepted by a group. (right) The clothes worn by the worker on the right show that he belongs to the group, yet his posture and facial expression indicate how far he is prepared to conform. (below) The young people on the beach meet their need to belong to a group by sitting close, adopting very similar body positions, looking in the same direction simultaneously, and unselfconsciously sharing a mutual identity.

for identity. For example, citizenship gives you nationality, which is an internationally recognized status. The work you do also gives you identity. You may not only work as an engineer, for example; you may also be an engineer working for a well-known engineering company or specializing in a specific branch of engineering. You may also have a special status, such as the 'Chief Aeronautical Engineer at Brown's'. Membership of a family identifies you by name. It may also tell people your position in the family, as somebody's son or daughter, husband or wife, father or mother, and so on.

We all gain security by belonging to groups. This may be physical security (the protection of the family home, for example) or behavioural security (when we belong, we know who our friends and enemies are). When we have the same friends and enemies as the group to which we belong, we have less trouble knowing where we stand and we may feel emotionally safer. Our property resources are also more secure as a result of our group membership: having a steady job which we are good at brings security of employment and less worry about where the next meal will come from. At the same time, our social resources are more secure, for group members are often the first to help and support their own fellow-members. Belonging to a group helps you know where to turn to for help.

We not only give commitment to a group; we also receive the benefits of other people's commitment. When you have a bad day at work the commitment of others can keep you going. Should you feel that your family can manage without you and that they no longer care, a few words of encouragement from one of them can make all the difference and help you feel committed to them once more. Commitment is shown by how much you put into a group; in return you usually gain rewards of equal value – but only if the group is succeeding. When you publicly declare which side you are on, therefore, the enthusiasm you show for the people in your group will be repaid in popularity. The people who work hardest for a group may not always be those who get the highest financial rewards, but they will probably receive higher psycho-economic rewards in terms of the respect and love of their fellow-members.

The groups to which you belong treat people differently according to their special qualities. You gain from this, too, first by having your talents recognized, and secondly by knowing whom to approach for specialist help within the group. Many groups have promotion ladders the members can climb as their abilities become known. The public side of specialization is particularly important, for what matters in a group is not whether you feel different or special in some way, but whether the group as a whole recognizes this. For example, you may be the person with the best ideas at a sales conference, but unless you tell other people about them and they accept them, your status will remain the same. In any group, a member's status gives him identity and security, thus encouraging even more commitment: the higher the status he can gain, the more committed he will feel.

A group helps us to be more successful at meeting our needs. There are many things we can only do effectively through our membership of families and neighbourhoods, leisure and work groups. In showing allegiance to the groups to which we belong, we show publicly our own sense of purpose. Each of the group needs listed above assists us in

Belonging to groups helps us to meet many needs. The individuals in the picture gain security from belonging to their families, which in turn are more secure because they belong to a cohesive neighbourhood. Within each group individual differences are recognized and fully valued.

this. For example, clothes show the purpose of our activities, whether it is the white coat of the doctor, the overalls of the engineer or the uniform of the policeman or soldier. When we identify ourselves as belonging to a group whose purpose is known, our own purpose is more evident. Similarly, the security we earn from group membership helps us to feel safer in achieving our purpose, and gives us the confidence to meet people outside while we are working on behalf of the group.

54 The Economics of a Group

Money circulates inside a group

It would be unrealistic to consider relationships without taking money into account. There are two reasons for this. First, the way a group uses its resources is much the same, whether we consider money or any other resource. An understanding of the economy of a group therefore provides a valuable starting-point from which to look at its psycho-economy. Secondly, in an industrialized society, people cannot achieve an acceptable standard of *life* without money. Health, for example, depends on being able to afford to live in clean surroundings, buy enough food of the right kind and not be faced with constant anxiety over money. Similarly, education is less of a struggle for a child whose parents can afford books and who have the leisure to encourage him. As we saw in chapter 43, when discussing loneliness, even having friends may cost somebody more than he can afford.

Poverty and privilege in Britain, 1937. This famous photograph illustrates the difference between economic groups within the same society.

Each group owns and controls money. There are rich and poor families, for example, just as there are rich and poor neighbourhoods. The wealth of a business can be judged by its turnover and the number of employees it can support, as well as by its profits. Groups of friends may also be rich or poor. Money circulates inside a group – in a family, for example, as cash for housekeeping, as pocket money or in the form of goods and services purchased for the members. In a business organ-

ization the money is spent on wages and salaries, equipment, raw materials, advertising, and so on. Groups of friends buy one another gifts, and may also lend one another money. In a neighbourhood the residents spend money at local shops or on leisure activities, and may also finance community projects like a children's playground or a meeting hall. Many have to pay local service charges or taxes.

The money owned and controlled by a group constitutes an 'internal economy'. It is a closed system, in the sense that all the money in this economy at any particular moment has had to be earned outside and brought in. In a family, for example, the parents may pay a child to do a small chore; although the child's earnings rise as a result, the family as a whole is no better off financially. In a neighbourhood a shopkeeper may spend money at another local shop, but this does not increase the amount of money circulating in the area. People who earn high incomes in a poor area tend to live and spend their money elsewhere. The neighbourhood therefore remains poor. When one member of a group of friends lends money to another member, he is only redistributing the wealth of the group, not adding to it.

The family group is a 'closed' economy. Resources are shared in a relaxed moment, but everything made available within the group must be earned outside through economic or psycho-economic activity.

Bargaining in a Tunisian market. The villagers trade their surpluses in the market-place so as to increase the range and quality of the resources available to their families.

The fact that a group's economy is closed means that every group always has only a limited amount of money. It is limited in the first instance by how much its members can earn outside the group. For example, some families have more earning power than others because they have more members able to work for money. This also applies to communities and groups of friends. A business, too, is limited in what it can earn by the size and ability of its salesforce, regardless of the quality of its product. Secondly, however, a group's economy is limited by the prevailing external conditions. Even the best salesforce with the perfect product cannot sell if people outside cannot afford to buy. In other words, the 'external economy' of the group partly determines the value of the resources which group members can use amongst themselves.

There is, however, another factor which determines the amount of money actually circulating in the internal economy of a group. This is whether or not the members who earn the money share it with the group. They will, in any case, share only what they can spare, or a proportion of this surplus. Also, they have the final decision as to what they need for themselves. Those members who have a large surplus are clearly in a very strong position in the group. They can decide how much money circulates in the internal economy, thus giving them control over one major factor which determines the standard of life of the other members. Those members who earn money, but have a smaller surplus, are in a relatively weaker position in the group. They cannot contribute so much; at the same time, if they quarrel with the wealthiest members, they might be left to finance the whole group. The members in the weakest position, however, are clearly those who cannot make any contribution to the group's finances. They are dependent upon the members who earn.

Approval and disapproval circulate inside a group

We saw in Section One how economics helps to explain much about individual relationships; it can also help us understand the relationships within a group. The next step is to see how the psycho-economics of a group affects relationships, and then to apply this analysis to some of the common problems which arise in groups.

The psycho-economy of a group has many features in common with its economy. For example, just as money circulates inside a group, so do approval and disapproval. If one member is out of favour with another, everybody seems to hear of it. If anybody is suddenly more popular, the other members find out, too. There are psycho-economically 'rich' groups which approve of their members often, and 'poor' ones where there is very little approval to go round. This is an important point in practical terms, since 'rich' groups tend to be happy, while to be a member of a psycho-economically 'poor' group can be a miserable experience. If we understand why some groups are 'richer' than others, we can be better equipped to achieve a happier life.

A group's economy is a closed system: so is its psycho-economy. This is because approval and disapproval only really affect members. A group can grumble as much as it likes about a non-member, but it will have little effect because the group cannot do anything to control him. Suppose you have a next-door neighbour who is a nuisance. Nobody in your family likes him; you cannot, however, expel him from your family, because he is not a member of it. To expel him from the neighbourhood is only possible if enough of your other neighbourhood-members feel strongly enough about his misdeeds to want to drive him away. Even then, he will only leave if he feels so much a part of the neighbourhood that being disliked by the other members really hurts him. If he does not see himself as a member, he will simply take no notice.

Approval and disapproval are like money in another respect, too, namely, that the amount within any group varies from time to time. This is partly to do with conditions outside the group, in the other groups to which the members belong. For example, the weekly get-together of a group of friends could be happy one week because a member has had a piece of good fortune, and miserable the next because one of the friends is unhappy (perhaps due to an accident to a member of his family or a problem in his work). People have less approval to spare when they are unhappy, and are far more ready to show that they value somebody else if they feel valued themselves. In other words, just as we can earn money in one group and spend it on another, we can earn approval or disapproval in one group and carry it over to another.

Psycho-economic trading. The senior members of the community admire the new baby, acknowledging their approval of the family in an unconscious but time-honoured ritual.

Obviously, one way to make a group financially richer is for the members to earn money in outside groups and then bring it back to share. Similarly, if a group is unhappy, one solution is for the members to earn approval in another group and then return to share their good feelings. For example, a bad day at work, followed by a good evening at home, makes for a better tomorrow at work. Also, somebody who is unhappy at home, and finds he is not giving approval to the other members of the family, may benefit from successfully winning the approval of his friends outside the family. He can then go home in a better mood, more willing to communicate approval, and all the members will be happier. We can also see that if somebody belongs to a group where what he does is popular, he spreads his happiness into all the groups to which he belongs, gives out more approval and becomes popular everywhere.

Because the psycho-economy of a group is, like its economy, a closed system, there is only a limited amount of approval to go round. This is the amount of approval which those members who are present at the time are able to spare. Suppose that a family is waiting to meet a relative at a railway station. The parents are anxious, perhaps because the train is late; the children misbehave because they are bored. Any family in this situation tightens its control on the children. But the relative's arrival alters the way the group behaves. He brings a new capacity for approval into the group. He is so pleased to see the parents that they feel valued and rewarded. The children are excited and dance around – behaviour which a few moments earlier would have earned a smack. The family uses up this approval and calms down as the relative himself tires and begins to express fewer marks of approval – making fewer self-disclosures, producing quieter non-verbal behaviour, and so on. He has used up his own surplus, but he has also helped the other members of the group to have a surplus.

A moment of conflict among children in Tompkins Square, New York. Those members of the group who depend on others for approval become inferiors and may temporarily be treated as outcasts.

Within the economy of a group, there are some members who depend on others for money. They are, in effect, 'economic inferiors' and the people they depend on are their 'economic superiors'. In the psycho-economy, people also have dependents. Your freedom of action in a group is limited by how much you depend on the approval of other people. As long as you need more approval from somebody than he needs from you, he will remain your superior. He can control how much satisfaction you get from anything you do for him. At the same time, you are less dependent on your equals in the group; if you start to become dependent on their approval, they are becoming superiors, instead of equals. For example, two people who marry may start off as equals, but steadily change into superior and inferior. At first, the husband probably wants his wife to approve of him as much as she wants his approval. If he goes out on his own in the evening he seeks her approval; if she goes out alone, she seeks his. But after a time the husband stops asking, while the wife has no need to ask because she never goes out, and stays at home to look after the children instead. When, finally, she wants to go out alone, she finds that she needs his approval of how, when, where and why; yet he has been going out on his own for years without thinking of asking for hers.

55 Group Stability

How a group remains stable and united

Group stability is threatened when an autocrat puts himself above the level of group approval. Note the array of medals worn by ex-President Amin of Uganda (right) – mostly awarded by himself as an expression of his own approval for himself, not by the community.

A group which is unstable and disunited is usually unhappy. There is confusion as to who is superior, equal or inferior. The members have no way of judging whose approval or disapproval is important. They stop communicating and start talking *at* one another, instead of *with* one another. If they try to disclose their true feelings, either nobody listens or somebody takes advantage. Members quarrel and the whole group is vulnerable to attacks from outside. A disunited, unstable group is characterized by power which is beyond the control of the majority. The rich members force people to obey them, repressively exploiting the advantages of their wealth. Dissension and disunity are encouraged, so that resistance to autocratic power is almost impossible to organize. These features of a group are not confined to a military dictatorship; they are also the conditions under which families of all social classes live in our relatively free society – for example, where battered or intimidated wives and children are trapped, or where the unthinking despotism of an elderly handicapped parent imprisons a single son or daughter.

Threshing in the traditional manner in Finistère, north-west France. The unity and stability of the group are re-emphasized during a moment of relaxation. The status structure of the whole community is maintained while the members work – and play – together.

For a group to remain stable, certain conditions must be met. The first of these is that those members who are equal stay equal and that there are no sudden changes as to who is superior or inferior. The second condition is that the members must be able to voice an opinion on the effects of any changes in status. Thirdly, the members must have the right to leave the group if they want, and to expel any member if they believe this to be in their interests. Finally, it should be noted that the wider society of which the group is a part must operate on similar principles: stability of government; freedom of speech, association and mobility; and a framework of law, justly administered to safeguard these freedoms.

The reasons why these conditions are important to the unity and stability of a group can be explained by an example. Suppose a group member on whom others depend acquires an unexpected financial surplus. Perhaps the father of a young family earns or inherits a large sum. His money can be divided into two parts. First, there is what he needs for himself to maintain his current standard of living. (Technically, this part is known as his 'costs'.) Secondly, there is what is left over, in other words, his surplus (known as his 'reward'). Because the man has a surplus, he has a choice as to how he uses it. One option open to him is to keep the money for himself and thus increase his personal standard of living. His other option is to share his good fortune with his family. Suppose he keeps the money for himself. If he does this openly he will meet with the immediate disapproval of his family, and possibly also of his friends, colleagues and neighbours. They will resent his selfishness, and, provided they are free to show their disapproval, they will try to ensure that he does not enjoy his increased wealth. The sudden change in the differences between the members of the family will unsettle every member, making the family unstable and disunited. Until the father agrees to share, he will be treated as an outcast in the group. But the group cannot express this disapproval unless its members are free to speak, and, in the last resort, to leave or to throw out the offending member. Should he try to prevent this, they depend on justice and the law to guarantee their rights.

An example of a different kind of resource will illustrate how a group retains stability and unity in its psycho-economy. Suppose the same man, instead of having a money bonus, met somebody at work who made him feel very attractive – much more so than his wife and family. Again, he can share his reward or keep it for himself. Naturally, he will spend some of the good feelings on himself, enough to meet his usual need to be seen as an attractive person. But whether or not he tells his wife about the surplus depends on several factors. First, will she approve? She might feel threatened and jealous, and if so he will regret sharing. If his feeling of increased sexual value might be rejected by her, it is likely that he will spend it privately elsewhere. He could, for example, boast to his friends. Or he could start an affair and privately raise his own standard of life. If the family eventually finds out, it will become unstable and disunited.

Even if the members of the family never know, the man will inevitably have to destroy some of his unity with them, because of the lies he will have to tell and the conflict between being happier outside the family than inside. The group therefore controls the power of a person's sexuality; the stability and unity of a family is achieved through a set of rules which make disapproval of adultery acceptable. Outside the family are larger groups which follow the same rules: institutions such as the law, and society as a whole, which will guarantee the family's right to express its disapproval and, in the last resort, enable the partners to obtain a legal separation or divorce.

These examples show that when a member of a group has surplus value he can choose whether to keep it or share it with the other members. However, they will only let him share if they approve of him and value him. Problems arise when a group member feels that he is not sufficiently valued by his fellow-members. His response is to save up a private surplus and spend it on finding people who will value him.

In a stable, united group, it is possible to experience a sense of 'belonging'. This is composed of several feelings. One is the feeling of being recognized, valued and accepted by other people. Also, you feel no conflict with other members. The purposes of the group are yours, too. You feel safe. All the sacrifices you make for such a group will be willing ones, and all your surplus will be shared with the members. Every other member of the group is especially important to you, as you are to him. The sense of belonging is a feeling which comes from knowing that all the resources in your system are valuable to people with whom you can share them. There is therefore no pressure on you to prove your value. You can give without counting the cost, and feel a sense of harmony, freedom and love.

56 The Organization of Power

Whoever has the most power has the highest status in a group

A person's power is greatest when somebody else depends on him for the things he needs most. For example, in a life-or-death situation, one person may have the power to save a life or to end it, as when a surgeon performs a life-saving operation or a gunman threatens to kill you if you do not obey him. These are extreme situations, and one purpose of groups is to organize resources so as to avoid emergencies like these. Nobody can be comfortable for long if he is dependent on somebody to this extent.

Control of resources in a group therefore tends to be carefully organized so that the members have different amounts of responsibility. A leader may delegate power to his subordinates, and they in turn delegate it to theirs. For example, a parent or manager may have to

The US Grand Prix West at Longbeach, California. The drivers, once regarded as of fairly low status, have now asserted their power and threatened to withdraw unless improved safety measures are adopted.

Children acquire resources in play. Each child has the power either to disrupt the skipping game or to help the other members of the group to enjoy themselves. In avoiding disputes they adopt a system of co-operation which becomes an accepted routine.

put somebody else in charge when he is away, thus delegating power from the top downwards. Alternatively, a group may begin with collective ownership of its resources, but develop leadership because this seems to work better. An example of delegation upwards occurs when a commune which started by taking all its decisions in a full assembly of the members finds that it has to appoint trustworthy people to make the day-to-day decisions between meetings. These elected members at first only have power when the whole group meets to approve their actions, but as time goes by the most successful of them become skilled at keeping their power by only doing what they know the group as a whole will support. They also begin to delegate their power downwards, at first by suggesting to the group who should be elected to help, later by making private arrangements about which the members do not know, but to which they will not object, provided they are successful.

When the members of a group have different amounts of power, this has to be organized and co-ordinated, or nobody would know who was supposed to be carrying out which responsibilities. The group's leaders are in charge of co-ordination; they need to ensure that, in delegating tasks, they transfer enough power to guarantee that the job will be done, but not so much that they lose control. For example, if a manager is allowed to spend a certain amount of money on his department, and allocates too little to one particular group of subordinates, he will effectively prevent them from succeeding. But if he gives them all the money, he will have abdicated responsibility, since all his other subordinates will have to ask that sub-group for finance, rather than asking him. Similarly, if a child is made responsible for his parents' relationship, by being told repeatedly, for example, that unless he behaves the parents will separate, the child effectively becomes the head of the family. This might prove too great a strain, leading to the child's mental breakdown, or produce a very effective little dictator. If the parents eventually separate, the child may feel that he is the cause and have to suppress deep and intolerable guilt.

The first time power is delegated to somebody is usually seen as a test of his reliability. If he fails to live up to expectations, he will be less likely to be given this responsibility again. If he succeeds, however, because he is a capable person in this respect, he will be given further opportunities to exercise such power. The result is that a group encourages specialization. Whatever the members are good at is what they tend to be asked to do most often. But they avoid being given responsibilities they cannot carry out effectively. In a family, for example, one child may be seen as a capable cook when he produces an acceptable meal in an emergency. He becomes labelled as 'good at cooking', and is asked to do more, thus gaining practice and becoming specialized. Each new speciality a child attains gives him a wider choice of ways to win approval. A label limits this choice, so the 'cook' may surprise everybody one day by refusing, saying he hates cooking. What he hates is being restricted by the label of 'good cook'.

In some families an 'outcast' child may repeatedly be given tasks without sufficient resources to complete them, thus 'proving' that he is a failure. Similar cruelty can occur between partners, when they do not wish to stay together but cannot admit this to one another. They each prove to their own satisfaction that the other is beyond redemption, saying they have 'tried everything', but having made sure each time that they never tried hard enough.

The way power is delegated and responsibilities are shared in a group tends to become a habit. If something works, there is no particular reason to change it. After a time practices may become so accepted that they turn into traditions, liked for their own sake, however inefficient they may seem in the light of changed circumstances. This happens because any routine improves with practice; it becomes more reliable and predictable, and helps the members know what is expected of them each time. Power sharing in a group develops into a recognizable structure, rather than a series of improvisations or panic measures.

In a power structure certain features are particularly important. Whoever has most power has the highest real status. This may not be the person who contributes most money; it might also be the friendliest person, the person most members are afraid of offending, the most attractive person or a favourite of the most powerful member. Each group develops its own style, and allocates ceremonial status to whoever personifies this, as when a country with a high divorce rate chooses a president whose family life seems to symbolize the ideal family; or when a medical society chooses as its president the most eminent practitioner. Ceremonial status can therefore be given without power. The person with the most power is the one who gives permission for major resources to be used, and who also has the freedom not to give permission. His approval is more important than that of the group.

57 Leadership

Good leadership depends more on what the leader does than who he is

The ideal qualities of a leader are traditionally thought of in terms of personality. A good leader is seen as stronger or cleverer than his followers. He can foresee danger, and is clever enough to protect the group from it. He is a good judge of the talents of others, uses his wisdom for the benefit of the group and is not easily deceived. He is respected by his followers and can inspire them by his eloquence and example. He is respected or feared by the leaders of rival groups. He can temper justice with mercy, because he knows when exceptions can be made to the rules in such a way that the other members will accept this. Not only are these qualities habitually thought of as personality traits; they are often seen as superhuman, mysterious or magical, as having a quality of 'charisma', so that it becomes difficult to see the leader as an ordinary person.

The personality of the leader is important to the group he leads. However, modern studies of leadership have concentrated more on the way groups work than on the personal qualities of the leader. The purpose of the group is to carry out certain tasks; research shows that the role of the leader within the group relates to these tasks and to the management of resources which will further the objectives of the group.

French policemen receive their orders. In a disciplined group, the exercise of power is based on established methods of communication, yet there is still room for individual variations in the style of leadership.

Political and spiritual leadership. (above) Pope John II on a visit to Kenya. (below) President Brezhnev at the funeral of President Tito of Yugoslavia. The spiritual leader draws his influence from the unity and enthusiasm of the members of his church, and wields moral rather than military power. The political leader represents the material wealth and military might of his country, and is listened to because of this power.

Looked at from this perspective, the successful leader will be the person with the clearest ideas about the group's purpose, or, where there are several objectives, about the different priority of each task. He is in a better position than other members to understand the power structure and organization of the group, and has more ways at his disposal of maintaining, strengthening and altering this system. He is also the person with most to lose. The leader is seen as the most representative member of the group. He is more responsible than the others for what it does, and he is its chief representative in any relationships his group has with other groups.

In each of the main group activities – defining the nature of the task before the group, organizing the system, maintaining the power structure and representing the group to other groups – the leader produces types of behaviour which mark him off from his followers. As a result of these behaviours he is able to maintain and enhance his own status. If the group members feel that they have benefited from this, they will regard him as a good leader. If he gains at their expense, with no consequential benefit to them, he will be judged as a bad leader.

Task definition

The leader is the person who is usually most closely identified with the main tasks of the group. His title often emphasizes this primary purpose: Divisional Manager, Chief Salesman, Team Captain, Platoon Commander, and so on. From time to time there may be disagreement about the priority to be given to different primary tasks. The leader will be the person who finally settles these arguments. In most groups there is also a tendency for the secondary objectives of the members to get in the way of their main purpose as a group. For example, a group of managers may show more concern about the quality of the food in the executive dining-room than over their sales figures. On such occasions, the leader brings the group back to the most important matter in hand. Because there is always a danger that secondary tasks will interfere with the main purpose, the leader is often careful not to be identified with secondary tasks. He is therefore less likely to mix socially, and on equal terms, with the followers in the group. Of course, this may be misunderstood, being seen as a rejection of the ordinary members. Accordingly, the leader often produces token acknowledgements of the secondary aims, as when a general visits the troops and stops here and there to joke with individuals who are expected to smile just because he is the general.

System maintenance and organization

Power systems need constant maintenance because each member belongs for his own reasons; he experiences these directly, and with more force than the more remote needs of the group. Each member will tend to put his own needs first, and if there is a conflict between these and the needs of the group the power structure is threatened. The leader plays a key role in holding the group together and reducing such threats. First, he must make sure he is recognized as the leader. This is done by means of status symbols and high status behaviour. The symbols of status emphasize that he has more power than his followers without forcing him to use this power. In a company, for example, the top man

Team leadership: a group of managers enjoys a joke from its leader. This helps to maintain the cohesion of the group, at the same time strengthening the members' acceptance of its purpose.

will have the largest salary, and therefore not only the biggest rewards but the most to lose if the company fails. He will probably have the most expensive house, the best office, the most secretaries and the largest car. He will show high status behaviour by the way he communicates with a lower status person. For example, he will use a tone of voice which prevents familiarity and does not allow for argument, and he will insist on being addressed by his correct title. Another part of his high status behaviour is that he will be seen as having the power to give and receive rewards and punishments on behalf of the group.

The leader also has the greatest say in who does what to achieve the group's objectives. If he encourages initiative, he also makes sure he controls the effects of what is done. The leader is also the most conformist member of the group: he must not be seen to break the rules of which he is the main custodian. He must also bear in mind that any leader who demands more self-sacrifice than he gives will need more absolute power over his members to force them to accept this.

Representing the group

A group always has relationships with other groups. For example, a committee may set up a sub-committee, and have a parent-child kind of relationship, with the smaller committee dependent on the larger for all its powers. Some groups form fraternal alliances with 'brother' organizations. All groups are affected by the activities of more powerful groups with similar aims. The leaders of a set of groups which have relationships with each other also usually have private discussions in which they treat one another differently from the way they would in public. In public, for example, they are careful never to be seen straying from the policies accepted by their members. In private, they can safely negotiate without direct reference to their members' views, provided that they do not commit themselves finally to a change of policy they cannot later 'sell' to their members.

58 Pulling Rank

Showing you have a higher status helps you win power struggles

Everybody's power struggles are different. It is therefore very difficult to give a detailed analysis of how they are won or lost. Nevertheless, certain principles can be described which apply to all power struggles involving a threat to status inside a group. The purpose of this chapter is to apply the analysis of group needs given earlier to the question of winning and losing battles.

Power struggles concerning status are won by the first person to stimulate the other into showing submissive behaviour. The general name for this kind of 'victory' is 'pulling rank'. The effect of the victory is that the winner is then able to do what he wants, without opposition from the loser. This can be a matter of great importance or something relatively trivial. In a power struggle, one side tries to use a resource, while the other side tries to prevent somebody from using it. Resource use follows the normal five-stage sequence outlined in chapter 5, namely, identification, security, commitment, specialization and

In a dispute after a traffic accident, the man on the left tries to pull rank by identifying himself. The sceptical look on the face of the woman beside him shows that he has not yet won the dispute.

achievement. In contributing to a group, you gain status by helping the group meet these needs. To pull rank on somebody, therefore, you have to show that you are more important than he is in respect of each of these needs.

Identification

Power struggles are often resolved at the identification level. The question which the attacker poses to the defender is, 'Do you know who I am?', thus implying that he is important. This can be expressed non-verbally, as when one person looks at the other in a dominating way or dismisses him with a glance. The submissive behaviour which ends the struggle at this level is characterized by the reply, 'I'm sorry, I didn't recognize you.' Many examples could be given from family life or the internal politics of business organizations. In the family, parents stress their own authority by controlling the way children speak to them. There is often a right and a wrong way to address elders and betters, and a mother may tell her child, 'Don't speak to your father like that.' 'How dare you talk to me like that?' is another way of stressing identification status.

A power struggle between dinghy and whaling ship. Conservationists from the Greenpeace ship 'Rainbow Warrior' put their own safety at risk to prevent the killing of whales. Their defiance eventually forced the Icelandic whaler to let the whales go free.

A moment of triumph for a tennis champion. Björn Borg holds the trophy aloft after a lengthy Wimbledon final, a power struggle in which only superior specialized skills can achieve victory.

Security

Power struggles can begin and end at the identification level, but sometimes those which are not won and lost over identity become security battles. The attacker in effect poses the question, 'Do you realize I have the power to make life difficult for you?' He seeks the submissive response, 'Please don't pick on me; I'm not important.' Security battles turn on the fact that, within the power structure of a group, everybody at a certain level of status is in effect licensed to attack those lower down, as long as this does not harm the group as a whole.

Any evidence you give that you are willing to cause trouble if you do not get what you want is a security-level attack. There are many variations in the way this can be done, such as threatening to report somebody to higher authority. In the family, a weak parent may threaten discipline on behalf of a stronger parent by saying, 'Wait till your father comes home!' A child may get his own way just by being a nuisance for long enough. When you complain about the quality of goods or services, you may need to show that you will not leave until satisfied. Both sides may be deadlocked if they show that they will not be disturbed by threats, however long they last and whoever they come from: 'I don't care who you are and how long it takes, but you are not getting what you want.' The deadlock is broken when one person says, 'I'm sorry, I didn't really mean what I said' or 'I'm sorry if I wasted your time', or leaves because he has run out of time.

Commitment

Both the attacker and the defender may stress their commitment to the group. Each says he is simply doing his job, acting not for himself personally but on behalf of others; if he does not obtain what he wants, a great many other people will be angry. The question the attacker

'Eyes front! Don't answer back!' These female army recruits will soon learn that they cannot win power struggles with their superiors. Each recruit will be treated as a negative asset to the whole squad unless she obeys orders without question.

poses to the defender is, 'Do you realize that if you resist me you will have to fight the whole group I represent?' The submissive response he is looking for is, 'I'm sorry, I didn't know how important it was.' (Variations on this include, 'I had no idea they wanted it so badly' and 'Nothing personal, I just didn't understand.') The battle at this point is also about popularity, and one method an attacker can use is to suggest that the defender will lose status with his own group: 'If you don't let me have what I want, I shall destroy your own credibility with your friends.'

Specialization

At this stage of the battle, the submissive response which is being sought is, 'I'm sorry; you know best.' Some power struggles begin at this level with an attack on a person's expertise. This throws doubt upon his identity, trustworthiness, and credibility as an expert. As a result, this kind of power struggle often turns upon whether the attacker can show that he has been right before, because an expert generally keeps his powers only as long as he succeeds. In the family, for example, parents may foster the legend that they always know best, and be so successful that they do not have to prove it every time. They can then win an argument simply by saying, 'I am your parent' (identification) instead of having to say, 'I know best because I am your parent' (specialization). Some power struggles with adolescents arise when the young person no longer accepts his parent's authority. The parent may refuse to see this as a challenge to his own expertise, preferring to treat it as an identity threat, and ask, 'Who do you think you are?'

Achievement

Power struggles end with the achievement of victory. The submissive behaviour of the loser is often characterized by the attitude of, 'I didn't expect to win anyway.' In effect, he has lost control of the disputed resources, and readjusts to the new level of his expectations by accepting this loss. If victory is not conceded in this way, the power struggle is usually either suspended or diverted into a fresh struggle over something else.

SECTION FIVE
SEX AND SEXUAL RELATIONSHIPS

Recent discoveries about the nature of the human sexual response provide the starting-point for this section, which goes on to consider the way social control of sexuality affects all relationships. The agent of control is the family, which teaches the avoidance of certain 'taboo', or forbidden, kinds of sexual behaviour.

The connection between sex and love is considered next, and this is followed by a detailed consideration of the marital relationship, including sexual problems, jealousy, extra-marital affairs and marital breakdown. The final chapters look at how we can recover from the loss of a partner and our need for self-love.

59 Sex and Sexuality

Sex is only one part of a person's sexuality

All human beings are sexual. That is to say, each one is either male or female biologically, and relates to other people in a sexual way. The biological basis of sex is that at conception every egg carries twenty-three chromosomes, one of which is roughly in the shape of the letter 'x'; every sperm also carries twenty-three chromosomes, but in some sperm instead of an 'x' chromosome there is a larger one, roughly in the shape of a letter 'y'. When a baby is conceived, it will grow into a boy if the sperm carried a 'y', and into a girl if the sperm carried an 'x' chromosome.

The most 'acceptable' aspect of being sexual is having children, yet most of our sexual activity is designed more for pleasure than for conception.

Biologically, the differences between male and female are mainly to do with the different role each sex plays in reproduction. As far as relationships are concerned, however, the biological process of conceiving and bearing children is only one manifestation of sex, and by no means the most important. People are sexual all their lives – from before birth, throughout childhood and adolescence, in adult life, through the middle years, into old age and until they die. In our society the fertile years in a woman are between the ages of twelve and fifty. Men are fertile from around thirteen until the glands which produce sperm atrophy with age, and this can be well into their seventies. An 'average' woman of seventy-five will therefore have been capable of bearing children for about half her life, and an average man capable of fathering children for slightly longer. Yet the biological product of these fertile years will probably not be more than two or three children, if any. It cannot therefore be argued objectively that sex is mainly a matter of reproduction; for half our lives we are sexual but infertile, and for the other half we are sexual and fertile, but produce very few babies. In an 'average' marriage, for example, beginning when the couple are twenty-five, and counting only until they reach the age of fifty-five, sexual intercourse once a week would not be considered abnormal. This suggests a total of around three thousand episodes of sexual intercourse to produce fewer than four children. Sex from the couple's point of view is certainly not mainly about having babies. Similarly, the sexuality of children, adolescents and adult men and women is expressed in many other ways.

Before considering in detail how sex affects relationships it is necessary to make a clear distinction between the biological and the social aspects of sex. The simplest way is to distinguish between 'sex' and 'sexuality', and then to spell out the connection between them.

Sex refers to two broad categories of human activity. First, a person's sex means whether he or she is biologically male or female, in other words, whether or not this person is the product of a conception involving a 'y' chromosome. As a result of this difference, some people are identified as male and some as female, according to the presence or absence of a penis or a vagina. Secondly, sex means the use of the penis, the vagina and other sex organs to stimulate part or all of the reproductive cycle.

Sexuality is the term used to refer to any human activity which differs according to which sex you are, or which involves the use of sex. For example, a person's sexuality may be expressed through being a son or daughter, father or mother, husband or wife, male lover or female lover, grandfather or grandmother, father- or mother-in-law, and so on. Your sexuality is how you show what sex you are or want to be, either by yourself or in the presence of other men and women.

The connection between sex and sexuality is, first, that sex is only one aspect of sexuality. This shows in several ways. Sex roles are not dependent on the sex or age of a person. A man is perfectly capable of behaving in a motherly way towards children, women and other men. A child can also take a parental responsibility towards his own parents, by looking after them when they are tired or ill, for example, or by showing concern for their welfare in the way he criticizes them, as when a child advises one of his parents not to smoke. A woman can take on

Childhood sexuality. Sexual arousal is just as normal among children as among adults. The pleasure felt by this small boy in building a card house is added to by his sexual excitation, both oral and genital.

the role of father towards children, men and other women, and also compete with men and women by producing actions which in our culture are more normally associated with masculine behaviour.

Relationships of a sexual nature between men and women need not depend on sex in the normally accepted sense of the word. A marriage in which there is no sex can still be a marriage. Two people can be sexually attracted to one another and develop a lasting relationship without explicit sexual contact. This happens, for example, in cases where a man or woman has a long-standing friendship with another person of the same sex. It is also common between opposite-sex friends. Moreover, the relationships in the family are sexual, without all the members of the family having sex together (brother with sister, for example, or parent with child).

The reasons for these variations in the way sexuality is expressed is that sex is controlled and organized in relationships. Through the use of his sexual activities, one person can reward another or withhold a reward from him; he can also decide whether or not to reward himself. Sex and sexuality are a major source of pleasure; most psychologists would argue that they are the major source of *all* pleasure. The ability to give and experience sexual pleasure is part of the normal biological inheritance of every individual. It is therefore a highly valuable natural resource, and one which every person can use in power, trading and loving relationships. Its use is under the personal control of its owner. Whether you give it or not, and whether you take it or not, very largely depends on you. For this reason, throughout your life, other people seek to control your use of your own sexuality and your access to theirs.

60 The Sexual Response

The four stages of human sexual activity

In the field of human sexuality the most important discovery in recent years has been the way in which the human sexual response sequence works. This discovery was the result of thousands of observations under laboratory controlled conditions by William Masters and Virginia Johnson. There are two reasons why it is relevant to relationships. The first is that a person's sexual relationships are among his most important. Secondly, since all relationships are concerned with the control of sex in some form, it is useful to see in detail what is being controlled.

The human sexual response occurs in four stages, known as the excitation, plateau, orgasmic and resolution (or resting) stages. The response sequence is the same for all men and women, regardless of age, sex, and racial or cultural differences. As will be made clear later, however, the time spent at each stage is subject to wide variation.

Excitation stage

The first external sign of sexual excitement in men is the erection of the penis. It increases in size and begins to protrude from the body. This may be the result of physical contact with the penis or it may be due to a sexually stimulating sight or train of thought. It occurs usually in a few seconds and a small penis may double, or more than double, in size; larger ones tend to keep the same length. The reason for the change is that more blood is flowing into the penis than out, causing its spongy tissue to swell and thicken. In women, the first sign of sexual excitation is the lubrication of the vagina. Again, onset is usually within half a minute of stimulation. The lubricating fluid is not produced by glands, but by a 'sweating' action on the walls of the vagina. This is also accompanied by a change in the blood flow to other parts of the sex organs, notably the clitoris. This organ is situated just above the entrance to the vagina. Like the penis it consists of a very sensitive tip, packed with nerve endings, and a thinner shaft. Similarly, the size of both tip and stem vary and bear no relation to the person's capacity for orgasm. As with the penis, the clitoris thickens due to engorgement; this is, of course, less visible, because the clitoral shaft is hidden inside the body. The lips around the vagina may also thicken or open out. In men and women, other signs of sexual excitement are enlargement of the breasts and the erection of one or both nipples.

As the excitement stage proceeds two other major signs can be noticed. The penis begins to reach its maximum size, and simultaneously there is a lifting of the testes inside the scrotal sac. The vagina now swells internally, particularly the outer one-third, so that it becomes narrower and firmer; this part forms what is called the 'orgasmic platform'. The inner two-thirds grows wider, ballooning out to form a cavity around the entrance to the womb. Next, the clitoris lifts up inside the body, often taking the tip with it, so that when the orgasmic platform is stimulated, this will stimulate the clitoris, too.

Plateau stage

During excitation the pulse rate speeds up and blood pressure rises; as the plateau stage is reached these become even more marked. In many cases there will be no sharply defined moment when excitation is complete and the plateau begins, but all the developments noted above now reach their maximum intensity. The penis reaches its full size, and the testes are about twice as large as before excitement began; the orgasmic platform is as tight as it can become, and the clitoris is fully withdrawn and completely swollen. The womb also enlarges. Muscles all over the body tense, and there is a general heightening of sensitivity of every part of the skin. The body seems to gather up all the available value of its physical resources, ready for a massive expenditure of energy upon the pleasure of the orgasm.

Orgasmic stage

At some point during the plateau stage a 'point of no return' is reached, signalling the onset of orgasm. The body characteristically shows a series of rhythmic contractions, varying in number from three to upwards of a dozen, although twenty-five have been recorded. The contractions last a regular four-fifths of a second. They appear in the female body as contractions in the uterus, sweeping from the top downwards (like a weaker form of birth contraction) and in the vagina, as a series of spasms in the orgasmic platform. Pulse rate, blood pressure and breathing rate reach a peak. The body may sweat and blush all over. A man ejaculates a few moments after he first feels his orgasm: sperm is pumped out of the end of the penis as the result of a complicated reaction triggered off by a special fluid from the prostate gland. Muscles all over the body also produce spasms: the face, is often contorted into positions similar to those which would otherwise indicate pain.

Resolution stage

During the resolution stage of the sexual response sequence, the sexual organs and the rest of the body return to their original resting positions. Throughout the body, muscular tension relaxes, and in the sex organs blood which was previously dammed up begins to flow back into the main blood circulation system. The clitoris reverts to its unstimulated position, but it usually takes half an hour to return to its resting size. The penis loses its erection in two stages: the first is quite rapid but leaves the penis still notably enlarged; the second is slower and more complete. The nipples also lose their erection. Pulse rate, blood pressure and breathing all return to normal.

Three further points are worth noting. First, the orgasmic stage, and the resolution stage following orgasm, cannot take place unless the plateau stage is reached. Lubrication of the vagina is therefore not in itself an indication that a woman is ready for orgasm. Secondly, the excitation stage does not commit the body to the 'point of no return' and can take any length of time, with a return to the resting state possible throughout. Thirdly, the number of orgasms possible within the plateau stage depends on the individual's skill and experience; a woman is naturally more able than a man to experience many orgasms within the one plateau stage because a man's orgasm depends on the collection of prostate fluid, and this is a comparatively lengthy process.

61 Sexual Control

Society controls the way people use sex

The control, or lack of control, of the sexual response has an important part to play in relationships. It operates in several ways. First, there are major social controls on how people behave sexually, both in public and in private. Secondly, in any two-person relationship one person may seek to control the other's sexual response. Thirdly, individuals can institute self-control. Social control is negative – it is designed to decrease interest in sex. The other forms of control may work either to increase or to decrease sexual arousal. To understand how this is possible we will need to return briefly to the four stages of the response which were described in chapter 60.

The four stages of the sequence can be divided into two halves. One half, the orgasmic and resolution stages, is a relatively uncomplicated reflex action. That is to say, once a sexually aroused body reaches the 'point of no return' some kind of orgasm, however mild, will take place, and the sex organs will return to their resting state as a result. This half of the response is, like other reflexes, under the automatic control of the 'sympathetic' nervous system. However, excitation before the 'point of no return' is affected by the 'parasympathetic' nervous system; as we saw in chapter 60, this part works to collect and conserve bodily resources so that there will be a surplus ready for emergency use. During the early stages of excitement, therefore, the response is capable of being controlled. We can often tolerate a certain amount of pain from hot bathwater, rather than be forced immediately to withdraw our hand from the bath. In other words, the reflex can be delayed. In much the same way, a person can slow down or speed up his level of sexual arousal, thus delaying or accelerating the onset of his 'point of no return'.

For example, a person who wishes to maintain or increase his desired level of arousal may find that he is distracted by events around him, such as a creaking bed or the thought that he might be disturbed. By concentrating on a sexually stimulating train of thought he can deliberately build up a surplus of erotic feelings and move closer to orgasm. Similarly, somebody who wants to lower his level of excitement can concentrate on distracting thoughts. Nevertheless, these controls require previous experience in training, or 'conditioning', the parasympathetic nervous system; the amount of control varies widely between individuals and many people have more control under some circumstances than under others. It is important to note here that a person's 'hidden agenda', or unconscious self-control, also works by conditioning the same part of the nervous system. Where sex is concerned this conditioning is often a response to social control, which is designed to decrease sexual arousal.

The major social controls upon sexual behaviour in our society are designed first of all to prevent the onset of sexual excitation except under approved circumstances. Where this is not possible, the next line

MAN
ablished 1666

of defence is to slow down the increase in arousal, thus keeping it within permissible levels. Should this fail, a person is expected to exercise self-control; children are therefore taught to inhibit their sexual responses in particular circumstances by regarding some kinds of sexual experience as 'taboo', or forbidden. Beyond this level of defence, self-control might fail. It is therefore assumed that orgasm is the likely result, so control works through the method of reducing the value of the reward. That is to say, an orgasm which is the result of taboo behaviour is not supposed to be enjoyed. For those people who insist on breaking the taboo *and* enjoying their non-approved orgasms, there is a further line of control, in that society regards the relationships leading to such orgasms as illicit and the people who have them as outcasts. Sexual taboos vary widely throughout our culture. Three of the most general and important from the point of view of relationships are the taboos against incest, masturbation and homosexuality. These are examined in more detail in chapter 62. The general process of social control can be illustrated at this point by seeing how it applies to prostitution (less of a taboo in some countries and cities than in others).

The first level of social control is designed to stop people being excited sexually by seeing prostitutes. In some countries, including the United Kingdom, it is an offence for a prostitute to solicit in the street. However, it is not an offence for her to advertise her services under the guise of 'French lessons', 'Model' or 'Masseuse'. Many European countries allow licensed prostitution in city areas designated as 'red light districts', but the second level of control – slowing down the increase in arousal – is more usually contrived by police 'culling' of prostitutes: every now and then a few are arrested to keep the numbers down. Excitement at seeing prostitutes, incidentally, is not exclusively male, and may not necessarily be interpreted as sexual; respectable middle-aged and middle-class females are often amongst those most likely to lose control of their emotions at the sight. This kind of reaction is avoided by limiting permitted prostitution to non-respectable areas.

Self-control works against prostitution in several ways. Girls are taught in childhood and adolescence not to expect to be paid for sexual services past the 'point of no return'. Up to that point there are double standards, and an appropriate gift such as red roses, chocolates or alcoholic drinks can validate petting, at least as far as the lower reaches of the plateau phase. Studies show that young women who go beyond this point are deemed to have 'asked for whatever they get', that is to say, the responsibility is theirs and not the man's. (In the United Kingdom, moreover, if the result is rape, this is not an offence if the man concerned can prove he had reasonable grounds for assuming the woman to be willing.) The self-control system works to make a person feel guilty if he asks for payment, and justified in reacting violently to being asked for one. However, if self-control fails, the next line of defence comes into operation, and any orgasm which results is reduced in value: one is supposed to feel guilty afterwards. In addition, men who go with prostitutes are stereotyped as miserable and unhealthy creatures who are unable to obtain sexual satisfaction 'normally', even though there is not the slightest evidence for this. The final line of defence is to make the prostitute into a social outcast, excluded from respectable society, and stereotyped as incapable of orgasm.

A hostess in a men's club, London. She dresses to encourage her clientele to indulge in sexual fantasy, but she is not a prostitute. This is one of the ways in which society controls the open display of eroticism and at the same time provides a harmless outlet for men who are tempted to break the taboo.

62 Sexual Taboos

The family is the main agent of sexual control

A general description of 'approved' sex in our society would be as follows: sex is acceptable between a man and a woman who are not too old or too young, who love one another, who are married to one another and who either have children or intend to have them. Looked at objectively, the most important of these permissions is that they love one another. There are various controls within society which are designed to encourage approved sex and discourage alternatives. The family is the main social instrument for imposing these controls and for teaching the appropriate self-control.

Three taboos are particularly stressed by the family. They are the prohibitions placed upon incest, masturbation and homosexuality. The control process works along the lines already described, that is to say, by preventing excitation and slowing it down where prevention fails, by inhibiting orgasm if this is reached, by reducing the value of the orgasm retrospectively and by 'outcasting' those who indulge in prohibited orgasms.

Each of the three taboos is relevant to the production of approved sex. Incest, for example, is sex between a parent and his child, between siblings or between near relatives. The most common argument against incest is that in-breeding might lead to defective children. It is also seen to have other drawbacks, such as the likelihood of large age differences where parent-child incest occurs, the increased possibility of under-age sex, and, in the case of sibling incest, the higher chance that early sexual experience will be homosexual. Incest might also lead to two members of the same family loving one another to such an extent that one or both partners might not look for somebody outside the family whom they could marry.

In many families incest is avoided by strong taboos on nakedness. This prevents members of the family from becoming sexually excited by seeing each other's breasts and genitals. Children are inhibited from expressing sexual curiosity by the expedient of being separated at bath times as soon as they begin to notice the difference between brother and sister. Separate bedrooms are also provided at about this age. Fathers tend to avoid being seen naked, although in many families this only applies on occasions when a child might see the father's erect penis. After puberty a son's erect penis is often pointedly ignored by his mother, and many fathers are careful not to see, touch or mention their daughters' breasts. There are very few studies of incest which reaches coitus; they are mainly confined to case histories of people convicted for the offence, which in many parts of the world includes sexual intercourse with an adult stepchild who is more attractive than the spouse. Nevertheless, there is some evidence to suggest that, while some incest takes the form of violent or non-consenting child molestation, most parent-to-child incest is willing, loving, gentle, and only clandestine because society in general treats incestuous people as out-

The taboo on nakedness. As part of an experiment, the reactions of men and women to a 'topless' girl were photographed in a busy street in Copenhagen. The older woman exhibits a typical reaction – disapproval, expressed in a refusal to acknowledge any interest in this unusual sight.

casts. Case studies at a London teaching hospital of daughters pregnant by their fathers have revealed that the mothers often know of the sexual relationship and connive at it, perhaps to take the pressure off themselves. Homosexual contact between brothers, taking the form of mutual masturbation, is so usual as not to be counted as incest.

Nevertheless, masturbation is not generally accepted as an 'approved' form of sex. Young children are often slapped for playing with themselves, or told that it is 'dirty'. Self-stimulation, despite the controls, remains quantitatively the most important form of orgasmic behaviour among human beings. However, since prevention is virtually impossible, the taboo works mainly through devaluation of the orgasm, and this is reinforced through mild outcasting. Thus, although a child may be told that masturbation can stunt his growth, ruin his eyesight and give him acne, these warnings are not widely believed, and the usual result is that masturbation proceeds in secrecy and shame. There is no evidence that it affects any aspect of social, physical, sexual or intellectual growth; indeed, teaching adults to masturbate is now the most commonly accepted procedure as the first stage in the medical treatment of most sexual dysfunctions, particularly lack of experience of orgasm amongst women. Consequently, attitudes generally are changing in favour of encouraging the practice. The resulting orgasms, however, are still widely and mistakenly seen as a poor substitute for 'real' sex, which means with somebody you love and to whom, preferably, you are married. One notable exception to this attitude is indicated by a

An intimate moment in a relationship. These two men have accepted their homosexuality, yet the widespread taboo on homosexuality will create problems for them which heterosexual couples will not have to face.

recent Danish study which shows an increased acceptance of private masturbation by wives and husbands separately. At the other extreme, case studies in the United Kingdom suggest that old people (particularly old men) living in institutionalized care are frequently deprived of privacy in which to masturbate and are not dealt with sympathetically when forced to do this more openly.

Perhaps the most far-reaching of taboos in our society, however, is that against homosexuality. People who are homosexual are often not regarded as 'complete' men or women. There is therefore great pressure in many families to prevent children behaving in ways which do not fit into the stereotype of the 'real' male or female. Signs of masculinity in girls, and femininity in boys, are discouraged as soon as they arise by the parents insisting on a different attitude or a change of activity. Thus a boy is often discouraged from playing with dolls, and a girl from being a 'tomboy'. The taboo against homosexuality may also explain why some methods of sexual intercourse between 'real' men and women (particularly penis in vagina sex) are 'approved', while others (such as mutual masturbation, anal intercourse and oral contact) are not: the latter are, of course, available to homosexual lovers while penis in vagina sex is not. The most deeply rooted control against homosexuality, however, is the development of 'homophobia', or fear of being seen as homosexual, taught in the family by the inhibition of man-to-man sexual kissing and hand-holding. It is now widely accepted that only a small proportion of the population are not to some degree bisexual, and that most people are heterosexual by choice rather than by nature. One might therefore reasonably argue that the social training towards heterosexuality is often motivated by parents who are repressing their own natural bi- or homosexual impulses.

63 Sexual Attraction

In a competitive society attractive people have an advantage

We live in a society which has a general view as to what is, and is not, attractive. People who fit the standard idea of beauty are seen as more likely to succeed. This has been demonstrated by many psychologists. In one American study, a large number of men and women were asked to rate a series of photographs for attractiveness. These were then presented in random order to a second, similar group, who were asked to assess the chances in life of the people in the pictures and to rate their personalities. The people who were considered attractive by the first group were rated by the second group as more sensitive, kind, warm, interesting, strong and responsive. They were seen as more likely to get highly-paid jobs, and to have happier marriages. They were not, however, seen as likely to make better parents, perhaps because they might be more interested in having affairs or succeeding at work.

This association between being attractive in the conventional sense and being more likely to succeed in a competitive society begins early in life. Several studies have shown that quite young children are more popular if they look attractive to their schoolmates. One study of nursery-school children aged between four and six set out to find which children were the most popular in the class, and also asked a group of adults not connected with the school to rate photographs of the children for attractiveness. The most popular children in the class turned out to be those chosen as most attractive in the photographs. In another study, American college students were asked to mark an essay. Each student was given the same essay, but a different photograph was attached each time. The highest marks were given when the photograph was of an attractive person.

Competitiveness in attraction is probably seen at its extreme in a beauty contest. The girls who win can often expect hard but rewarding work as models. Market research taught the advertising agencies long ago that the best way to sell is to have the product associated with sexually attractive people. This applies not only to goods, but also to people: they are more likely to be seen as attractive themselves if seen with somebody who fits the stereotype of beauty. The basis of competitiveness is that some people have more valuable resources than others. In a competitive society, where most sexual activity concentrates on arousal rather than consummation, sexually attractive looks are particularly valuable. People can be turned into sex objects, and the standard of sexual beauty separated from whether a person is interesting in other ways. Sex can become a question of performance, and looks may be something to be rated on a points scale

One consequence of this is that men have their own general ideas as to what women admire in a man. A famous study by a New York newspaper showed that this may be rather different from what women really admire. The men thought women would be 'turned on' most by a tall man, with a muscular chest and shoulders, muscular arms and a

large penis. The women actually preferred small, sexy buttocks, slim figures, flat stomachs and various looks in the eyes, such as 'interesting' or 'kind'. Fifteen per cent of the men mentioned the large penis they thought women wanted; only two per cent of the women mentioned the penis at all. Several studies have shown that men divide fairly easily into those who prefer breasts, those who prefer buttocks and those who look for legs to turn them on. Sporty, extrovert types have been consistently found to prefer women with large breasts, while more submissive introverts prefer women with small breasts. Similar studies of female preferences are less common; those which have been conducted suggest that women who are interested in competitive sport tend to prefer large men, and that smaller women prefer larger men. It is also standard practice in computer dating companies to match couples so that the man is taller. Men clients who prefer taller women partners are very rare.

It is widely believed that women are much slower than men to become sexually excited. As a result men are expected to take the initiative in sex, to be 'only after one thing' and always to be ready sexually at the slightest provocation. They are therefore supposed to be more inclined to treat women as sex objects than women are to treat men as such. A fact which lends further support to this belief is that men appear to be the main consumers of pornography.

There is some evidence that men masturbate more often than women, and that more men masturbate than women. The latest studies, however, show consistently that this is not a 'natural' difference between the sexes, but has its origin in early sex training. In a recent German study, for example, men and women brought into the laboratory were shown a series of slides, ranging from 'soft-core' pornography (a person of the opposite sex in a one-piece bathing costume) to 'hard-core' (represented by a couple described as 'in coitus showing genitals, and not in the face-to-face position'). Before seeing the pictures, the participants completed a questionnaire about their work, social and political attitudes, and sexual history. Twenty-four hours afterwards they were asked to report the effect of the pictures on their feelings of arousal and on their subsequent behaviour, to see if it had made them more sexually active. Only small changes were reported, and the main difference between men and women was that more men had masturbated. Otherwise the women's reports showed more or less exactly the same range of responses: they liked what they saw just as much as the men did. In a similar study, where an erotic story was read out, men and women were equally aroused sexually. The details of these and other experiments, some of which directly measure penile erection and vaginal lubrication, show that men and women have the same range of sexual readiness for arousal.

Two views of human attraction. The Mississippi couple (left) laugh together, confident of their mutual attractiveness; though neither conforms to a stereotype of beauty, onlookers will probably find them attractive too. By contrast, the conventional beauties on display at the Miss World contest in London (below) seem synthetic and asexual.

64 Sex and Communication

Using the first stage of the sex response in communication

Sex plays a much larger part in our everyday relationships than many people realize. This is because everybody is sexual, but has nearly always been trained in childhood to regard only a certain part of the human sexual response sequence as 'sex'. As a result many of us fail to give and receive small amounts of sexual pleasure for fear that we will be indulging in something we have been taught is not approved. The best way to illustrate this point is by analogy – comparing the response sequence to a hill.

Suppose you are riding a bicycle, skiing, and you reach the top of a hill. The downward slope is gentle at first and you could stop very easily; if you did so, and turned back to the top, you would scarcely notice the climb. Beyond this gentle slope, some distance away, the hill starts to descend more steeply. Here you could stop quite easily, but would have to climb back. Past this, the land falls away into a deep valley, and if you went this far you would start to get carried away. Somewhere along here is the 'point of no return'. On your bicycle or skis you would have to let yourself go, and finish by shooting up the other side of the hill, carried along by your own momentum.

Most of our day-to-day relationships are concerned with the first part of the sexual response sequence – the gentle slope where we can give and take very small amounts of sexual pleasure without even realizing that we are being sexual. Mild amounts of pleasure are gathered together into a small surplus so that you have enough to feel good about yourself, and enough left over to spend on making other people feel good. You get pleasure from communicating with attractive people, and from being treated by them as an attractive person in your own right. When you feel like this, it is easy to find people who look attractive: people of your own sex, even though you are heterosexual; people of the opposite sex if you happen to be homosexual; children and old people, whom you would never consider as sex partners; and animals with big eyes and soft, furry bodies which you can enjoy caressing – with no thought of sex. Nevertheless, all this pleasure is sexual pleasure.

You may also have days when you feel completely unattractive. Everything seems to be an uphill struggle. An unhappy or non-existent sex life is the most usual cause. Your physical resources seem to have no value, or even a negative value. To meet your need to have a surplus of good feelings to spend on somebody else, you will first have to gather a great deal of approval for yourself. Again, you may not recognize that your feelings have anything to do with sex, because you have been taught that only one part of the sexual response is 'real' sex.

The importance of sex in everyday relationships is that each person has a sexual value which can be used to give pleasure. Every human body is sexually attractive in its own right. At the very beginning of the response sequence, where turning back is easy, we can communicate by rewarding people for the attention they give us and collect similar rewards from them. But if we reject our own bodies we also reject our own sexuality. We have nothing of value to give. And the value of what other people offer us fails to come up to our expectations, so we reject that, too.

All communication is sexual. Some of the ways people communicate are sexually rejecting, others are sexually accepting. For example, if you stand too close to somebody and he moves back, he is showing the level of sexuality he is prepared to accept. The rejection is a way of limiting the point at which you might see him as willing to go further down the slope into a less controlled situation. But most of the time you are quite happy to accept this rejection because you had no intention of moving down the slope either. Or suppose you smile at somebody. The warmth of the smile you receive in return may be much greater than you expected. If the other person is a sexually attractive stranger with whom you might like to become involved, you are likely to try to begin a conversation so that you can judge how far down the slope he is prepared to go with you.

A couple communicate their commitment to one another by the giving and receiving of a sexual caress. They have reached a point in their relationship where they can do this without even realizing they are being particularly sexual.

A free gift of sexuality during communication. The girl's happy, open smile is given without obligation, indicating complete acceptance of the other person.

All the non-verbal behaviour people use in conversation can be used to give intense pleasure during orgasmic contact – touch, close proximity, full eye-contact, caressing tones of voice, body movements which are completely co-ordinated, and so on. The difference between the way these behaviours are used in conversation and how they are used in making love is a question of intensity. The pleasures of conversation are more controlled because, first, there is no intention on either side of going too far down the hill. There is another reason, too. In a loving relationship people give without counting the cost. Not all conversations are loving. The free gift of a warm smile can be greeted with suspicion; it might mean that somebody is trying to get you to relax so he can take advantage of you. Until you know what his intentions are you cannot be sure which part of the hill he is aiming for, or whether he simply wants you out of control. You might stop counting the cost while he calculates every move.

Fear of getting out of control is one of the most important products of the way we are taught about sex in our society. The taboos on nakedness and masturbation are reinforced in childhood by teaching people that their bodies are ugly, particularly the parts which give most pleasure, the genitals. Many people learn in childhood that the best way to stop is never to start; they are taught to be suspicious of pleasure, since this is the beginning of the slippery slope. Some people learn that sex has nothing to do with loving and sharing the gentle, early slopes of sexual excitation, and that only the headlong rush of a quick orgasm really counts as sex. For others, love is something which cannot be given freely, even in small amounts, to everybody they meet, but must be saved up for very special occasions when it is safe to take off the brakes.

65 Love

An immeasurable feeling of the value of life

A spontaneous show of mutual enjoyment. Because the couple are in love, all their resources at this moment have unlimited value.

There are some kinds of human experience which are far richer than any words which can be used to describe them. Love is such a feeling. Yet love, or the lack of love, plays such a major part in relationships, particularly where sex is concerned, that its function cannot be understood and discussed without some form of analysis of the feeling.

From a psycho-economic point of view all feelings are explained as a person's awareness of the value of resources. Thus negative or unpleasant feelings indicate a fall in value, while positive or pleasant

feelings indicate an increase in value. Feelings can only be experienced individually. They can be shared through sympathy, empathy and other modes of communication, but one person cannot feel something in place of another. The value of a resource or set of resources depends on who wants them and why. The need for resources differs according to who you are and whether you need the resource to protect a declining standard of life, maintain an existing standard or reach a more satisfactory one.

The feeling of love towards any resource is the feeling of an immeasurable increase in value. When we give somebody love, we do not count the cost; when we receive love and return it, we cannot count the reward. Love is the feeling of value beyond description. It can enhance the value of all the resources in a person's system, so that when two people love each other they may feel that, now they are together, there will be an endless increase in the value of being alive. Previous standards of life seem meaningless as a result. Nothing seems impossible.

As we saw in Section Four, when discussing groups, relationships can form between several combinations of people: between two people, each acting on his own behalf as a free individual; between one person and a small sub-group; between groups; and between people who are seen as representing groups. In each of these situations a person can feel valued beyond his ability to quantify that value. The sense of belonging which someone feels with comrades and friends stems from knowing that in that group his own value is immeasurable, just as their value is beyond measure to him. Families can also feel this way about one another. Part of the feeling of love is the sense of unity, of there being no boundaries to experience because of life's endless abundance and limitless value. This same sense of unity is a major part of the feeling of love experienced by two people in a loving, two-person relationship. They become one system of resources for both to use without counting the cost or being able to measure the reward.

A person's first experience of this sense of unity is in his relationship with his mother. The bond between mother and child is created out of necessity. The two begin their relationship as one system of resources; when a mother holds her baby for the first time, she is usually unable to count the cost of her pain and anxiety and unable to estimate the value of her reward. At the moment when she accepts the baby as hers, and the mother-child bond is established, the unity of their two-person relationship is complete. She will always be his mother; he will always be her child. Yet the value of the baby is out of all proportion to its skills and abilities, and to its physical resources as a person. It lies in the potential each baby has; and in the simple fact that the baby exists and is alive and is an individual.

In adult life the experience of love seems to repeat many of the features of this bonding moment. First, the experience is of a timeless, here-and-now nature. It has a freshness and an immediacy which come from the fact that it is enough to be alive, to be you, because previous standards of life are irrelevant and future standards are unimaginable. Secondly, the potential value of all resources is seen as positive. In other words, every part of you which had doubtful or unknown value ceases to be a source of anxiety.

66 Love and Sex

The advantages of loving in sex

One of the most common claims made about sex is that it is best when you love your partner, and that 'sex for fun' is superficial and only second-best. This argument presents several problems. One is that it is often used as part of the general social pressure upon young people to marry rather than to experiment sexually with many different partners. Most of the present generation of parents in our society received very little sex education in childhood and adolescence, and probably only a small minority of them experimented widely during their own adolescence. Contraception was not nearly so widely available thirty years ago as it is today, and attitudes towards sex not so permissive. When the claim is made by a parent with limited experience, therefore, it may lack conviction. Secondly, there is good reason to suppose that sex is mainly for pleasure, rather than for having babies; it can therefore be fun, whether or not you love your partner. The objective of sex, in marriage or outside it, can be the orgasm alone. Each person experiences his own orgasm for himself. It seems futile to suggest that an orgasm under one set of circumstances is any better or worse than under any other set of circumstances; there are simply different orgasms and different circumstances.

Nevertheless, there are grounds for supposing that sex as part of a mutually loving relationship can be a more intense and enhancing experience than sex between two people who like and respect one another, find one another attractive, but are not committed to the development of a loving relationship. These reasons are set out below, not as a dogmatic series of facts, nor as a moral or ideological argument, but as an extension of the analysis of relationships presented so far.

When two people love one another, they value each other for what they are, not what they do. However skilled a person may be at achieving his own orgasm and helping another person to do likewise, sex is not perfect every time. The more two people love one another, the easier it is for them to cope with the frustrations of imperfect sex. Nor is every partner equally skilled. Valuing somebody for what he is, not for what he does, and being valued in this way yourself means that love matters more than sex, and lack of skill is less important. Two people who are committed to the development of a relationship will not stop trying just because one of them has more to learn about sex than the other – or because both have an equal amount to learn.

Love means that two people value one another's orgasms as much as their own. There is no reason why this should not also be the case between partners who do not love one another. It seems probable, however, that somebody who does not love you will be less likely to value your feelings as much as his own; certainly he will not value all the other feelings you have in quite the same way. When people love one another all the feelings they share can be as valuable and as exciting as their orgasms.

Sex is often about performance and competition. This can be fun. For example, two people can compete to find better ways of pleasing each other than they managed last time. They can improve their performance in the sense of lasting longer at the excitation or plateau phases, having more orgasms than last time, or cutting down the rest period to a shorter one than before and then starting all over again. Loving partners who are committed to staying together, and particularly those who agree not to find alternative partners, know that they always receive their partners' best performances – as well as their worst. They are not competing with somebody they do not know. Previous lovers are irrelevant. More importantly, other lovers do not exist. This means that they do not have to compete or perform at all unless they want to because it is fun. Uncommitted lovers have to give a good performance each time, and are always competing with the last lover or the next one, even if their partners are too polite to say so.

Sex between people who love one another can develop without pressure of time. There is no need to prove anything, not even that they love one another. Even a few minutes can be a timeless experience, because they know it will not be their last time together. Over the weeks, months or years of a lasting, loving relationship they can explore each other's personalities through a growing understanding of their bodies. Sex in a one-night stand can also seem timeless – but only once.

People who are in love probably have more to talk about before, during and after sex than those who are not. Pillow talk is an integral part of sex, but between mere friends it can easily degenerate into polite conversation. To those who are in love, sharing sex also means the time spent sharing the resolution phase to its full conclusion. If you come together mainly for sex, this period can seem like a waste of time; hence the polite conversation.

It is often assumed that people who like sex to be free of any commitment to a lasting relationship are superficial, interested only in their own pleasure and looking for nothing more than a comfortable place to masturbate. But this view of sex is by no means confined to the sexually mobile; many counsellors are familiar with it as a normal characteristic of stable marriages. It is also widely assumed that there is such a thing as 'bad sex'. Assumptions of any sort about the sexual feelings of other people, and judgements about their motives, are probably more revealing about the people who make them than about those who are judged. Love, and orgasms, are feelings. The individual is the only person who can experience his own love, and his own orgasms. Only he can define what in his case is bad sex.

Contrasting attitudes during sexual relationships. When two people love one another, their relationship enables them to regard everything they experience together as valuable, not simply their sexual performance. The couple in bed (right) look less relaxed, less mutually involved, than the lovers in the park (below).

67 Marriage

Marriage takes over where the family leaves off

Marriage is the most important of all two-person sexual relationships. In the United Kingdom, for example, on present population trends, nine out of ten people can expect to marry at least once before the age of fifty. Throughout our society the overwhelming majority of children are born to parents who are married.

Several economic and psycho-economic changes have affected marriage this century. The most dramatic has been the change in the status of women. Working women now play a fundamental role in industry, commerce and the public services. Many of them are married; thus wives have more economic independence than most of their mothers, and certainly their grandmothers, had. At the same time, a general increase in the standard of living has led to increased expectations from marriage. People live longer: some twenty-five years have been added to life expectancy since the start of the century. The availability of contraception has reduced the number of pregnancies a wife expects during marriage. Easier divorce has also added to her independence. The main psycho-economic result has been that marriage is now much more dependent upon the relationship between the spouses, and is today less of an institution, held together by social and economic pressures regardless of the happiness of those concerned, than in former years.

Marriage is still seen as an exclusive sexual relationship, legitimated through a public ceremony in church or by a secular licence. In the United States the average marriage begins when the wife is about twenty-one years old; she will have her first baby within three years, and her last before she is thirty. Her last child will marry before she is fifty, and she will then have about seventeen years on average with her husband before he dies. In Europe the pattern is similar: although there are variations as to the age at marriage, a woman still usually marries in her twenties, and her child-bearing years are completed before the age of thirty in most cases. One effect of the longer life expectancy is that, whereas a marriage in 1911 lasted about twenty-eight years on average, the typical 1967 marriage is likely to last forty-two years.

People marry for a mixture of reasons: so they can have sex without interference, in order to leave home, to have babies, because they wish to legitimate an existing exclusive sexual partnership, to please their parents or friends, because they are in love, in order to make house tenancy or purchase easier, and so on. One accelerating trend this century has been the move away from religious ceremonies to secular ones: in the United Kingdom, for example, the number of civil marriages first exceeded church weddings in the late 1970s.

From the psycho-economic perspective, marriage is the continuation of the aims and objectives of the family of origin by other means. The family, in common with other groups, has a set of purposes which justify its continuance. They usually include obvious factors, such as having somewhere to live, sharing an economy and acting as a focus for the emotional growth of the members, particularly the children. Families, however, vary widely as to their awareness of purpose and the emphasis placed on different objectives. In many cases, objectives are vaguely associated with the provision of similar home circumstances to those under which the parents grew up. Often families exist without conscious, or 'overt', awareness of purpose, while the members pursue unconscious, or 'covert', aims, in response to the hidden agenda.

For example, one wife may see her family life as being aimed at supporting her husband in the career he has chosen, preventing family arguments and looking after her husband's children; these aims will seldom be discussed unless the marriage gets into difficulties. Her view of the purpose of the family reflects that of her mother and is seen as 'what everybody does'. Another wife may see her aim as being the provision of loving support for her children by acting as a good and careful manager of her husband's income, while his career is of secondary importance to her. She will also see this as the normal behaviour of 'every wife'; she is perpetuating the aims she learned from her parents. A husband may see his family as proof of his virility and stability, people he can love and support, a way of achieving a closer relationship with his wife, and so on. Sometimes the covert aims of the family are stronger than its overt aims, and sometimes the reverse is true.

When a person marries, he may choose a partner who will help him pursue either the covert or the overt purposes of his own family, whichever is the stronger. For example, in some families there may be a strong sense of agreed purpose – that the family is a loving and caring unit, which succeeds through the sacrifice of self-interest, and which is largely for the production of physically and emotionally healthy children who can compete successfully in their careers. A child from this type of family will choose a partner who is able to carry on these aims, with the consent of the child's parents. He will tend to conform to the code of the family and select potential partners of whom his family approves, rejecting those who are not approved. The choice of partners will thus avoid conflict.

In a family where the hidden conflict is more important than their superficially agreed aims, the choice of partner will tend to perpetuate the conflict. For example, suppose a family has stayed together for the sake of the children, even though the parents are basically incompatible. The parental aims will often conflict, and this will show in difficulties of communication and acquaintance between the parents. Such parents often unite to oppose their child's choice of marriage partner. In choosing his partner the child continues the hidden conflict, partly because he cannot in any case please both parents, since nothing pleases both of them; and partly because his own hidden agenda leads him to search for a partner with whom he can have a marriage similar to that of his parents. Thus, although the cultural expectation is that a marriage should be 'happy', there are in fact many people who marry in order to continue the state of conflict to which they became accustomed in childhood. Unless each partner grows away from his dependence upon conflict, he will count his uncomfortable marriage as successful.

68 The Marital Relationship

The early, middle and later years of marriage

The marital relationship is undertaken as a life-time partnership, even though in the United Kingdom alone, about a fifth of marriages end in divorce. For the remaining four-fifths, the relationship usually covers the years in which all the main adult tasks are completed: separation from the family home to live with the spouse, the birth of children and their childhood and adolescence, the achievement of career seniority, the marriage of the children in their turn, and the remaining years of

Bride and groom display the public symbols of the wedding – the white dress, the carnation and the shared glass of wine. Their relationship will now be put to a private test, to see if it meets their own expectations rather than those of their families.

Bringing up young children can be exhausting, both physically and emotionally, and may isolate mothers from other people of their own age. These young mothers have temporarily joined forces to lessen the strain. Notice how contact between the adults can continue despite many interruptions.

seniority, retirement and grandparenthood. The marital relationship can, for convenience, be divided into three phases: *the early years*, covering the period before and during the arrival of children; *the middle years*, which last until the youngest child is married; and *the later years*, which end with the death of one spouse.

The early years

The tasks of the married couple during their early years differ according to whether their marriage is based on conformity to the overt objectives of the family of origin, or rebellion against these and conformity to its covert tasks. The former can be called 'conforming' marriages, the latter 'conflict' marriages. First, the early years of the conforming marital relationship will be considered. The 'average' such couple begin their married life during their early twenties, and their last child is born before the wife is thirty. The early years therefore fall naturally into two parts: the time before the first child is born, and from here until the last child arrives.

The partners' first need is to separate from the direct control of their families and to establish their identity as a couple in their own right. The spouse, rather than the parent, is now the most important person in their lives, but difficulties can arise if either of the newly-weds ignores his spouse and asks a parent for advice over housing, furniture, sex, finance, and so on. Some young marrieds from very conforming families

The cycle of deprivation. A child who grows up in poverty is more likely to accept conflict in his relationships and to marry in order to leave home, so perpetuating his parents' conflict-based marriage into the next generation.

have stronger emotional links with their parents than with their partner throughout these first years. Thus, when problems arise in the relationship the dependent spouse may separate and go back to the parental home. Emotional insecurity, however, is often caused by economic insecurity. People in their twenties often have low incomes, and may not be able to afford their own home without parental help. Unless they have a measure of privacy, interference from the in-laws with whom they have to share may cause any difficulties between the couple to be exaggerated out of all proportion. At this stage, there are more likely to be problems over money than over sex. The couple are dependent for their home-making on both incomes; they have to learn how to manage their finances jointly and to share the chores.

Sexual commitment develops and becomes enriched during this time. Traditionally, couples begin married life without much experience. Most of their sexual contacts before marriage will have been with each other, and under relatively constrained circumstances, such as the back of a car, or while the parents were out. There is, however, a surprisingly low incidence of sexual difficulty. Recent surveys in both Britain and America showed that, of wives who had been married for less than a year, about 80 per cent reported their sex life as satisfactory, and 5 per cent had been able to solve the problem by communicating their feelings to their partner. Problems such as non-consummation, premature ejaculation or failure to enjoy sex disappear during the second year, although upwards of 10 per cent of couples are still unsatisfied.

The timing of the first child is often a response to several pressures. It is delayed until the couple feel they can afford to have a baby, since this may mean losing the wife's income, and will in any case increase their committed outgoings. At the same time the conforming couple are often under pressure from in-laws – most often the wife's mother – to have a baby. Wives become 'broody', and husbands too, but both usually accept that it is best to delay the first pregnancy until they have adapted sexually to each other. The most usual way of taking the decision is probably to increase the risk of pregnancy by an increasingly lax use of contraceptives.

The birth of the first child irrevocably alters the psycho-economics of the family; they are now a threesome, and the couple's parents have a new grandchild. Mother-child bonding may to some extent lower the self-esteem of the father, who may not only have to adjust to a period of sexual abstinence and lack of interest on the part of his wife, but may also feel jealous of his baby in other ways. The presence of the father at the birth can often help to overcome this problem. But there is also a new set of reasons why the father can justifiably stay at work longer, and leave his wife to carry out her extra tasks in addition to the ones he expected of his mother when she was at home all day. He now needs to earn more, to further his career, and the company he works for may see his promotion into fatherhood as evidence of his increased capability in handling responsibility. If he feels jealous, he has ample opportunity to transfer his guilt to his wife, and then 'scapegoat' her for not being efficient and helping him more. Fatigue is one of the effects which the arrival of the first child has on the wife; an American study of 1,296 mothers of children under a year old showed they spent 50 per cent more time on housework than mothers of teenage children. Another effect, however, may be boredom, when a wife who has been intellectually active now finds she is expected only to be a mother.

The circumstances surrounding the conflict-based marriage are often dramatically different from those of the conforming marriage. A great many conflict marriages start very early, and the couple may marry with the wife already pregnant. Marriages when the bride is under twenty are much more likely to end in divorce, and when the groom is also under twenty the risk increases still further. The highest divorce risk throughout Europe and the United States is associated with very young couples who marry when the bride becomes pregnant. Couples who conceive during the first three years of marriage are also more likely to divorce later. These couples are also more likely to separate. The third year is the peak year for divorce, but studies show that most separations occur during the first year. In the United Kingdom, from the mid-1950s until the introduction of legal abortion and improved contraceptive services, about one-fifth of all spinsters who married were pregnant, and about one-third of these were under the age of twenty. The present trend is for the average age of marriage to fall, probably because more couples cohabit without marriage, and the 'shotgun' wedding is still a traditional reaction to teenage pregnancy in some sections of society. Thus, of those who now marry as teenagers, more are likely to be pregnant. In the United Kingdom, teenage marriages are twice as common amongst the families of unskilled and semi-skilled workers as amongst the families of non-manual workers.

Starting married life with a baby to support throws great strain on what is often an immature relationship, born out of teenage rebellion, and in the face of parental opposition. Housing is often a major problem, partially solved and partially made worse by sharing with parents. The young mother is often a scapegoated prisoner in the parental home, lacking the status of 'real' wife, afraid of being heard as sexually active through thin walls, criticized if she spends any money on minor luxuries, such as cigarettes, drink or a night out, not really a daughter since she is blamed and outcasted, and under criticism from her own mother about the way she treats her baby. Her husband may constantly be made to feel that he is an unwelcome visitor rather than the husband of the mother of his child. Even if the couple manage to find their own accommodation, this will be expensive for them, they may lack the will or the skill to plan their finances and the standard of housing will be low. Nursery facilities are frequently poor or non-existent, and a teenage bride often has a bad record of consistent employment, so it is harder for her to keep her job than to give it up or lose it. Many such marriages end up as a failed bid to leave home – an unresolved extension of the parental conflict for which the newly married wife can now provide a focus. They may also be associated with child-battering; this is partly a response to fatigue and feeling trapped, and partly a reaction to an overwhelming feeling of inadequacy and an inability to cope. A careful study of 214 parents of children with non-accidental injuries showed that premarital pregnancy, illegitimacy of the baby, absence of the child's father and conflict in the marital relationship are often characteristics of the situation where battering occurs. All these factors are more common in teenage marriages.

The middle years

The marital relationship enters its middle period with the birth of the last child. The average number of children in our society is between two and three, and most are born during the six to eight years from the

Unity and dependence in a family. Several generations are grouped round the elderly couple to show the cohesion of the family group.

The child's school activities are an important focus for the marital relationship during the middle years. The mother is often more immediately involved than the father in providing emotional support for the child.

marriage to the early thirties. To some extent the stresses on the relationship during the middle years are connected with the progress of the children through school, culminating in their leaving the family home to share with a sexual partner in a stable relationship. Its main consolation and outlet for tension is sex. Social scientists have found that marital happiness in the middle years is closely connected with sexual satisfaction. In one American study of 100,000 couples, 94 per cent of those who said they were 'mostly happy' also said that sex in their marriage was either 'good' or 'very good'. Fifty-three per cent of those who said that sex was 'poor' were 'mostly unhappy'.

The most commonly reported sexual difficulties in this period are to do with lack of sensitivity and consideration by partners, notably men. Some are selfish, and do not try to arouse their wives before intercourse; wives cope by resisting their advances or masturbating quietly when the satisfied husband is asleep. Many wives apparently give up orgasm, and accept that sex is not an exciting experience, since it never has been for them. Husbands who make excessive demands without considering their wives' feelings are often the presenting cause of problems reported at clinics; husbands also complain of wives who are 'cold' or insufficiently arousable. Marital sex often seems to degenerate into a repeat performance of impoverished routines, restrained for fear of waking the children; too often, sex is reserved for bedtimes, when both partners are in any case tired, or happier with the lights off. Tenderness short of sex, and other ways of using the first phase of sexual arousal, are increasingly neglected by couples who never saw this as 'real' sex; oral sex is more likely to be rejected as 'dirty' or inappropriate to married love; and spouses who earlier covered up performance anxieties now find it easier to arrange a tacit acceptance of less sex simply by not being good at it any longer.

Sometimes the response to this is adultery; one or two instances of extra-marital sex are usually forgiven within the marriage, particularly if the offender is the husband, and his wife has hidden sexual anxieties or does not much enjoy sex with him herself. Provided he promises not to leave, and convinces her that the affair meant nothing, she does not regard it as serious and after showing her disapproval accepts the situation. (Affairs are dealt with in more detail in chapter 71.)

In many conforming marriages, there is a major switch in emphasis during these years from sex to a wider experience of sexuality, in the role of parent, and also as the son or daughter of someone who has now become a grandparent. A wife with young children often enjoys being mother as a complementary role to that of the breadwinning father. Milestones for the wife can be the point at which her youngest child starts school, her husband's promotions and the time when her eldest child leaves school. However, not all families which produce conforming marriages are completely free of hidden conflicts; once her main childbearing role is complete, the middle-years wife often becomes aware of these conflicts. For example, she may start a period of intellectual growth at this time, and realize that she has become excessively dependent upon a powerful and dominating man with unyielding attitudes. Another wife may find she has chosen a submissive, weak partner whom she had expected to succeed in a career while she became a successful mother; the wife's side of the contract has been fulfilled, but not the husband's. The origins of these conflicts often lie much further back in the formation of the hidden agenda. The couple's own parents covered up similar problems, often by pretending that they did not exist or by not noticing them consciously. The wife with the dominant husband, and the husband with the dominant wife, often choose their partners deliberately for this reason, but then outgrow one another.

Conflict marriages, begun as the result of teenage rebellion, are the least likely to survive into the middle years. Where they do so, trust often breaks down between the partners, and conflicts burst into the open. The children fight for their own autonomy in this period, often by producing delinquent behaviour, but also by becoming withdrawn and shy at school. The self-control of the child becomes the mirror image of the suppressed conflict between the parents. It will resurface in his own sexual behaviour during adolescence and lead to a repeat performance in his own marriage.

The later years

The last phase of the marriage is often dominated by three kinds of crises: problems with the husband's career, the death or illness of the parents of the couple, and problems with their adult children as they marry, refuse to marry, or separate and divorce. By now the family has

The middle years of marriage come to an end when the children grow up, marry and leave home. This couple share a sense of purpose today, but will they still have enough on which to base a shared life when they only have each other to worry about?

emerged as largely conforming or largely based on conflict. If conflict-based, this is often resolved by extra-marital affairs, leading to late divorce and the remarriage of one or both partners. If largely conforming, the husband often faces this period as a declining asset to his employer, while his wife may be blossoming into a new career begun when the children reached their teens. Previously dominant men often react violently to this change in status, directing their anger at their adult children, and refusing to provide emotional support to wives who have their own job problems. Submissive men frequently find a means of escape in hobbies and the membership of voluntary organizations. Some become unreliable handymen who never complete the tasks they have undertaken in the house at their wives' insistence.

In most cases, however, studies suggest that the couple are likely to adapt to the third period with renewed hope and vigour. Sexual contact is often more rewarding, free from the fear of pregnancy and interruption. Money is usually far less of a problem than in the lean years at the start of the marriage. Babies enliven the family unit, but as grandchildren who it is somebody else's responsibility to look after when they are embarrassing.

The love between a couple in the later years of marriage is expressed in the comfortable and familiar gestures they have developed over years of shared crises and triumphs.

The major upheaval which affects most couples at this time is the terminal illness or death of their own parents. A wife is often particularly upset by the death of her mother, and she may find herself really alone for the first time in her life, as her husband fails to grasp the need for a long period of mourning and readjustment. A husband is often equally upset, but is more likely to receive support.

The phase ends with the death of one partner; in our society this is usually the husband. His wife is likely to live for a further twenty years; she is probably sexually active and safe from the risk of unwanted pregnancies, has no major responsibilities, is intelligent and attractive, and unsure as to whether life is just beginning again or has ended for good.

69 Sexual Problems

Why some people do not enjoy sex

Sexual problems between a couple cause difficulties in their relationship, but they are also the result of difficulties. They may originate in feelings which one or both partners are aware of but try to hide. Alternatively, they may be caused by feelings of anger or fear which were used by the parent to control sexual behaviour during the person's childhood. In adult life these feelings are sometimes forgotten, but more often they are ignored or accepted as 'normal', so that the adult is unaware of them, and believes that his feelings about sex are no different from anybody else's. For example, a person may feel disgust at his partner's sexual body scent, or at handling the genitals, and believe that everyone else feels this way about sex scents and organs.

The most common sexual problems are related to the orgasmic, plateau and excitation stages of the conditioned sex reflex. Problems with orgasm occur in both men and women, and may be either temporary or permanent. It should be stressed that sex without orgasm can still be fun, and is not necessarily a problem; if a couple are enjoying sex there is no particular reason why it has to be orgasmic. Indeed the term 'problem' merely means that people attend clinics to ask for help on such matters. Many couples do not ask for help, because they do not need it and are happy as they are.

Non-consummation is one orgasmic difficulty which often comes to light when a couple are infertile. In this case the man is non-orgasmic during intercourse, or feels unable to insert his penis into his partner's vagina. Many men who feel unable to do so present themselves as gentle, unassertive and willing to do all they can to overcome the problem; they have no difficulty in obtaining and keeping an erection during masturbation, or up to the 'point of penetration' during intercourse. The problem lies in the relationship between the couple, and in the feelings they have about sex. The man's excessive patience may be what attracted his partner to him; yet this is often not what it seems at first sight. Frequently the excessive patience covers up strong, hidden feelings of anger, kept in check by a fear of losing control. These feelings can often be traced back to excessive parental control of the child's natural desire to masturbate, or to heavy punishment in response to real or imagined incest. Similarly, the man's partner often received a sexual training in childhood which led her to look for a gentle, undemanding partner, so she could avoid being blamed for having sexual feelings. She has often been taught to believe that sex is what a man does *to* a woman, and her partner's failure to do it to her leaves her free of guilt about the act. Some men penetrate but do not ejaculate; recent studies show that this occurs more frequently than chance would suggest where the man is one of a pair of twins. Psychiatrists believe that this is also due to suppressed anger as a result of childhood training, probably as part of the control in the family against incest.

Orgasmic difficulties among women are common. Sometimes women who have never experienced orgasm are classed as 'cold' or 'frigid'. This leaves them bewildered and angry, because they have no way of understanding orgasm, and do not know what is expected of them. The main cause of their inability is the taboo on masturbation, and this is often made worse by lack of sexual experience or by their experience being limited to insensitive or equally ignorant lovers. It is, however, safe to assume that all women are capable of having orgasms. There is therefore no such thing as a 'frigid' woman, only women who do not want to have an orgasm because of the way they are treated by their partners, and women who have not yet had an orgasm because they do not know how to. The first step is for the woman to be happy with her own body, then to learn to pamper herself and feel and enjoy the pleasure this brings, then to learn to touch and stimulate the lips of the vagina and the clitoral hood. Over a few weeks, or even more rapidly, the woman gets in touch with her feelings, enjoys them and discovers her own capacity for orgasm. She alone can then decide whether she wishes to share this with her present partner or find a different partner.

Male sexual problems associated with the plateau phase often concern timing. Inability to retain an erection is one of the most common problems; there can be few men who have not experienced this at some time. The root cause in childhood is often that the man has been brought up to think of real sex as meaning only penis in vagina sex. His sexual excitement grows but then fades, due to anxiety over a possible inability to 'perform' and to 'satisfy' his partner. The idea that women are only satisfied by intra-vaginal sex is obvious nonsense – although they may connive at this as a result of similar childhood training. Some men ejaculate 'prematurely', in other words, before they consciously wish to. This is caused by a similar childhood control. In cases of loss of erection and premature ejaculation, fear, or a combination of fear and anger, are preventing the person from co-ordinating his sexual response with that of his partner. Both these problems are made worse by a lack of communication.

There are two stages in the treatment of the problem. First, the couple may have to be helped to improve their communication. This partly means helping them to talk about sex, but it also entails enabling them to accept that they love one another whether or not either 'performs' satisfactorily during sex. If they do not accept this, the difficulty will not be resolved. Secondly, the male sufferer can be helped to trace the origins of his fear and anxiety towards sex; this is often found to be associated with fear of women generally. During sex, fear and anger prevent the man switching from the conscious control of his excitation response to the unconscious control required for orgasm. Many men retain control because they see this as the man's duty during sex, and cannot or will not let their partner share responsibility.

It is worth noting also that some people present themselves for clinical help not because they fail to achieve orgasm, or mistime their orgasms, but because they wonder whether they are having the 'correct' number. It is easy to dismiss this, but a mistake to do so, since it signals competitive sex, and is often used by a husband or wife to ask for help with the relationship. One or both of the partners may be competing with previous lovers, or with extra-marital lovers; counselling will help them to sort out their feelings.

between the couple having the affair, but without the guilt of incest.

Friends sometimes 'get carried away' and have sex once or twice, but resist the temptation for the affair to become serious. They try to suppress their sexual arousal, but still need each other as friends; they may feel that as long as they do not talk about having sex together the need will go away. The spouse usually knows about this kind of friendship, and often encourages it, it being assumed that sex between the couple would be very unlikely.

Serious affairs

The most devastating affair from the point of view of the continuation of the marriage is the secret courtship. This often begins after a futile search for an alternative partner covering several unsatisfactory affairs. Sometimes it is a means of escape from a conflict marriage into a conforming one: such affairs are the most likely to result in divorce from the present partner and a marriage between those who have the affair. Sometimes, however, a secret courtship ends before it surfaces; for the married person, the result is a period of bereavement and mourning, made all the more intolerable because he needs his spouse while he grieves, but cannot admit to the affair. The most typical symptoms are depression and increased dependency on the spouse, often accompanied by a renewed sexual fervour, which surprises and delights the unsuspecting partner.

Some affairs last undetected for many years as secret alternative marriages. The partner in the affair often becomes a friend of the unsuspecting spouse and his family. Alternative marriages of this kind meet the spouse's sexual needs by providing two 'half-marriages' instead of one whole one. A typical example would be the married man who has a long-standing affair with a younger, single woman, such as a colleague or secretary. From her point of view the biggest danger is that she is trapped in a clandestine marriage: she cannot have other lovers without provoking terrible jealousy from her first lover because, although he has two lovers, they only count as one. She is never able to express her love openly, and often feels extreme loneliness during public holidays when her man has to make duty appearances at home with his family. Her need to have an affair with a married man is often an expression of a desire to set up a marriage of which her mother would not approve, but which she is too frightened to try for herself. In such cases, the mother typically believes her daughter is still a virgin; but because the mother continues to press for a conforming marriage with a 'nice young man', followed by the birth of children, the daughter hides these sexual adventures, with the double insurance that the affair also has to be kept secret for the sake of the man.

First affairs are often serious, simply because they represent the first full admission that the marriage is not satisfactory. An inexperienced adulterer often feels the need to say that he is in love because, as in his adolescence, sex is approved if it is for love. Yet he is seldom as much in love as he says. Some affairs are serious because they seem to present the one and only chance to escape from marriage. These are the 'infatuation' affairs, a romantic-escapist dream come true. They have little more chance of ending happily than the marriage from which the partner is escaping, and which often began in exactly the same way.

72 Marital Breakdown

Passive and active responses to strain in a marriage

The marital relationship has to survive many strains if it is to last from the early twenties into the sixties or beyond. Success in a marriage is not, however, the mere survival of the relationship, accomplished simply by staying together and not divorcing. The relationship exists to meet the needs of both partners, and of any children they have. For a marriage to succeed, it has to provide a quality of life which is acceptable to both partners and which forms a more than adequate background for the development of healthy, intelligent, adaptable and responsible children. Equally, the failure of a marriage cannot be assumed from the fact of divorce. Couples whose marriages are dissolved usually seek to benefit both themselves and their children; the divorce often helps the family to grow more effectively by being apart than they could by being together.

It would be a mistake, therefore, to see marital breakdown only in terms of failure; nor would it be safe to see failure as always indicated by divorce or separation. A more accurate view would be that all marriages are subject to periodic phases of marital breakdown, some of which lead to an increase or decrease in the quality of the relationship. In some cases the response to breakdown is passive, with the family staying together, and in other cases the response is active, and separation with or without divorce is the result.

This point can be clarified by reference to the analysis of group relationships given earlier. The stability and unity of a group is preserved by displays of approval and disapproval. People show their disapproval by restricting communication and withdrawing from mutual acquaintance. If this does not prevent the threat to the group, the intensity of disapproval rises, and is followed by temporary outcasting of the member who has offended. Should this also fail, outcasting can become permanent, and the offending person is excluded from the full benefits of membership of the group or actually expelled. Sometimes this is not possible either, in which case the group breaks up as members who disapprove resign from it, in effect expelling themselves. All these responses can be seen in the marital relationship during periods of breakdown, but the active expulsion of a member from the group, or the active resignation of one or more members, is what shows as separation and divorce. Responses which fall short of separation and divorce are regarded as 'passive' responses. These responses will be considered first.

Passive rejection of the partner

Criticism by one partner of the other is a normal part of many marital relationships. This can be seen in terms of intensity, frequency and duration. Most couples accept criticism up to a certain level of aggression, expect it to occur periodically after a certain interval from the last bout of grumbling, and expect the disturbance to last for a certain length of time before the matter is forgotten. The first year of marriage usually includes bouts of criticism which are unacceptable, since they are too harsh, follow on too closely from the previous one and last too long. However, this is because each partner is still using the acceptable pattern he learned at home, and which may be different from his spouse's pattern. The couple therefore develop a pattern of their own which contains features of both, and is a compromise established by give-and-take to bring stability to their power relationships with one another. Failure to develop a pattern which is jointly acceptable brings the marriage closer to active breakdown, and this is more likely to occur where the home patterns are widely dissimilar, as with most conflict-based marriages. In a conforming marriage, the two people are more likely to be from similar families and to have the support of their parents and siblings when either spouse over-reacts to criticism from the other. In conflict marriages there is not only a lack of support, but active interference from families to make matters worse.

The early years of marriage lead to a steady stabilizing of this pattern, and it comes to represent the standard of life both partners regard as acceptable. It is also the standard against which criticism is judged. In other words, if disapproval is shown which is more intense, lasts longer or follows more closely than expected after the last bout, the partner being criticized knows he has seriously disturbed the marital relationship. Only a major row will lead to the adoption of a new standard, and even this is likely to be relatively temporary unless one partner goes as far as threatening to walk out.

The major cause of breakdown is likely to be the failure of the partners to adapt to one another's expectations, that is to say, their differing views as to what constitutes an acceptable quality of life. These differences focus mainly on money, social life, the care of property, sex and attitudes to children. Consistent failure by either partner to meet the other's expectations on these matters produces increased criticism; if there is no response, the marriage begins to break down passively through a withdrawal from communication. For example, one partner stops listening to such criticism, and calls it 'nagging'; or the other partner may stop expressing criticism, not because he has changed his attitude, but because he regards the expression of disapproval as a waste of time. Anger on both sides is bottled up, and the couple have taken a step towards growing apart. Nevertheless, each still cares about how the other feels, and they find ways of showing that they care. They often agree to differ on one or two of the above items; outsiders will be told of this in a humorous way, to preserve the outward appearance of unity. In some couples, however, disagreement covers all the key issues, and when this happens a more critical step towards passive breakdown has been taken.

This is signalled by the point at which a couple stop trying to improve their acquaintance with one another. They now cease to care about each other's feelings on matters which they assume will produce disagreement. As a result, they stop self-disclosing. For example, one spouse may be caught spending more money than he should on something of which he knows the other will not approve. The excuse is given that nothing was said 'because it would only lead to a row', but in reality he has ceased to care. Or a spouse may submit to what he sees as an impoverished sexual experience, but not self-disclose, assuming that he will be ignored. A breakdown in acquaintance restores stability without unity. The couple will disagree but will no longer be disturbed by the arguments which they know would take place if they showed their feelings. At the point where *communication* broke down, the couple might have retrieved unity if one partner threatened to leave. But once *acquaintance* has broken down, any walk-out will need to produce a clear commitment to the continuance of the marriage, since not only will they need to learn to talk to one another all over again, but they will also have to learn to get to know one another as each really is; and they might not like each other any longer.

The couple who reach this point have now got to know one another as far as they want to. In many 'happy' marriages, this is as far as they need to, and they accept their view of one another as the basis for continuation, adapting to a lower quality of life than either of them desired at the start of the marriage. Yet there are still problems, notably the children. As a result of the earlier breakdowns in communication, the children have grown up accepting a certain base level of intramarital strife, and are able to recognize a 'normal' pattern of anger by its intensity, frequency and duration. Children are very sensitive to changes in this pattern. But after a breakdown in marital acquaintance, the parents cease to care very much about this pattern. Since they now no longer wish to get to know one another any better, they can revert to the levels of criticism they learned in the family of origin. They may go back to 'being themselves' and stop trying to please one another by maintaining the compromise levels which they used during the early years.

Unfortunately, if the couple quarrel now, it will be seen by the children as a dramatic change in the acceptable level: if the more violent partner reverts to what was seen as only mild anger in his own family of origin, the child may react with fear and bewilderment. Frightened child and more passive partner form a majority in the group, and begin to expel the offending member of the family. The first of these 'expulsion' rows is yet another milestone in marital breakdown. The expelled member may react violently against his expulsion: this is his home, and if anybody is to do the expelling it should be him. More usually, he will expel himself, but only temporarily; he may walk out, perhaps, slamming the door, or show one of the righteous anger tantrums his parent used under similar provocation when he was the same age as his own children are now.

The offender may now be expelled from the marital relationship, or withdraw himself, by the ending of sexual communication. If sex still occurs, it is perfunctory or brutal; tenderness will be refused, as this might lead to renewed acquaintance and a seemingly hopeless search to re-establish communication. The so-called 'successful' marriage often continues, with the conflicts po ntedly ignored for the sake of the children. The children now begin to withdraw from communication and acquaintance with their parents, and start to search outside the family for consolation in schoolwork, friendships, independent sexual activity and their own kinds of success. The children who fail at school meet with levels of criticism which are no different from what they expect at home, and may even be milder. They may, however, feel more at home

A Russian couple sit next to one another before their divorce hearing, displaying the extent of the breakdown in their relationship and the personal isolation and sense of failure which result.

by attracting criticism, either at their accustomed level or above it, from police or their peer-group gang leaders.

Once the parents have withdrawn from the sexual side of the marital relationship, the next step will be active withdrawal in the form of separation leading to divorce – or to an attempt to start again.

Separation and divorce

Separation and divorce are the active signs of marital breakdown, making official and public what was formerly unofficial and private. Marital problems are on the increase throughout Western industrialized society; a recent study has shown a steady upward trend in the number of divorces in eleven European countries and the United States. The main reasons are changes in the nature of the family and marriage, and similar patterns of breakdown are found in every area of our society. A recent study in Nigeria has revealed similar trends amongst the wealthier families there, too. Alongside the increase in divorce there has been a rise in remarriage. In the United Kingdom, for example, one in five marriages end in divorce; coincidentally one in five of all marriages are currently between partners of whom at least one is remarrying. Although early marriage leads to early divorce, more than a fifth of all current UK divorces are obtained after twenty years of marriage. In the United Kingdom there is currently one divorce for every three marriages, and in the United States one for every two marriages. Many of these divorces involve people who are marrying for the second time. About two-thirds of UK divorces are between couples with children under the age of sixteen.

The one consistent pattern which can be seen in these statistics is that people are no longer satisfied with marital relationships which retain stability at the cost of unity. Nevertheless, the end of a marriage is still widely regarded as evidence of failure, and separation and divorce create several problems which deserve more detailed consideration.

First, there is a clear association in urban areas between psychological illness in adults and active marital breakdown. A study of self-poisoning in 68 married men and 167 married women showed that about a third of the men's marriages and a quarter of the women's had broken down, and in 17 per cent of the cases the breakdown had occurred less than a month before the suicide attempt. The highest rate for successful suicide is found amongst people who are married but living apart. In England and Wales, the annual suicide rates per 100,000 are 7·8 for the marrieds, 11.1 for the singles, 23·9 for the widowed and 35·5 for the divorced. Secondly, there has been a major increase in the number of one-parent families. In the United Kingdom one and a quarter million children live with only one parent; there are about three-quarters of a million one-parent families, resulting from divorce, separation or bereavement.

The first of these points indicates the importance throughout our society of the need to improve skill with relationships. The breakdown of a marriage is accompanied by an emotional crisis in which the adult finds all his values reduced to nothing, or less than nothing. He responds to the crisis as he would have done in childhood if separated from his mother. Yet throughout this period he receives little therapeutic support. The stigma of failure means that the divorced person often feels unable to ask for help with his emotional disturbance. The childlike nature of the reaction is misunderstood and treated by friends, relatives and society in general as 'childish' rather than natural. Employers may be sympathetic, but often do little to help, and expect the crisis to be over too quickly. Doctors may try to help, but they lack the time and the trained support to provide adequate counselling. In many cases, the best they can do is to prescribe tranquillizers and hope that time will do the healing. Education for the possibility of divorce is virtually unheard of; like sex education a decade ago, it would be seen as encouraging a 'wrong' attitude to marriage (and, in any case, sex education, which is arguably more important, is itself still frowned upon in many parts of the world).

Next, there are the problems faced by the one-parent family. Of particular importance is the provision of high quality pre-school and nursery education. The children who are worst hit are those born to the teenage conflict marriages. They are frequently left to grow up without enough enrichment in their early lives to help them avoid repeating the pattern set then by their own parents. In many countries, it is still too early to see the effects of divorce reform, but it seems likely that society as a whole would benefit if the state provided better facilities for nursery education.

Outside the field of psychology, it is seldom understood that the active ending of any relationship is like a death. The separated family often needs a long period of mourning before a new pattern of life can be established. As the nature of the family changes under the impact of more readily available divorce, perhaps this will become more widely recognized, and the traditional family will gradually relinquish its monopoly of control over education for relationships.

73 Starting Again

After a relationship ends, being sexual again brings new hope

The marital relationship may come to an end with the death of one of the partners or as a result of divorce or permanent separation. In principle, there is no reason why the surviving partner should not start again and develop a new, stable sexual relationship. But he or she may face certain difficulties and will be especially vulnerable at first. We need to consider these problems and to discuss the impact on sexuality of bereavement and divorce.

After bereavement

People react in many different ways to the death of a partner; to some extent this depends on whether it was a sudden or a slow death, and whether the partner was able to be present to say goodbye and provide companionship at the moment of death. A few generations ago people grew up more accustomed to the idea of death than they are today; we prepare for it less adequately. Under ideal circumstances it can be a time of great happiness and beauty, a shared mystery, rather than an occasion for shock and dismay. Yet the shock still occurs, and is a natural part of grieving. If there is time to prepare for death, the surviving partner may feel a sense of the completion of life. If not, there will be many feelings of fear and anger mixed up in the sense of loss; some people feel they have been deserted, others that life will now lack all meaning and love. After the fuss of the funeral, friends fade away to leave the bereaved person more alone than ever before, and often stop mentioning the dead partner, as if he had never existed. The survivor knows his true friends at this point; they are the ones who talk happily about the person who died, and accept the loss with thanks for the gains.

The most important gift is a sense of having time. Many bereaved people believe they should get over the death and put the events behind them far too quickly, whereas three, or even four, years are not too long. This reaction is, however, part of the natural process at the end of a partnership, the desire to resign from or expel oneself from a group which no longer meets one's needs. Some people make the mistake of selling up and moving away from familiar surroundings, uprooting themselves from twenty years' worth of relationships, their own and their partner's. Others wish to resign from life itself. These feelings come and go, particularly at night when you may sense the presence in bed of the lost partner, and be unable to accept the reality that this presence is an expression of your need for sexual contact.

Slowly, however, the new identity of the bereaved person begins to emerge, and as the fear fades, a sense of being safe may take over from it. As the weeks and months pass, the desire to die yourself grows weaker; instead of filling in time it is possible to use it, not merely by keeping busy to take your mind off things, but by doing things for yourself again. The first anniversary will provide set-backs, and often casts its shadow over the preceding weeks; anniversaries will always be like this, but the effects fade after four or five years. One way of coping is to buy yourself a present in remembrance, something you would both have liked, and enjoy your melancholy.

The most important sign of recovery is the desire to be sexual again. This can emerge within days, or it can take years. To enjoy your own sexuality is to move towards a stronger commitment to life, and away from your own death. Yet the safest commitment is to sex itself, not to remarriage. People who remarry too soon are no less vulnerable than those who marry too young. It is far better to have a new adolescence, irresponsible if necessary, than to run for shelter to somebody you do not really know.

After divorce

In many ways people react to divorce as they do to bereavement; in both cases there has been the death of a relationship. There may be a sense of relief, as after a long illness, but anger and fear are there, too, and a sense of futility and waste. The loss – whether through death or divorce – of any important relationship means that you will weep alone and need more time than you realize to get used to your new identity.

Both the divorced and the bereaved are vulnerable to the kind person who offers intimacy but does not realize he needs it more than them. People who come to help find they are being helped rather than helping. After divorce, many people will come for sex, amongst them the partners of old friends who you thought were happily married. As your need for sex reasserts itself, it does little harm to become mildly promiscuous; the harm will come from becoming too committed too early. Of course, this may not be a problem; you may have divorced in order to remarry, as the result of a long and partly clandestine courtship. But many divorced people have no ready partner to take over, and feel bitter when their ex-partner has used the last years of the marriage to set up a new home at their expense. This feeling is a hangover from the need to 'expel' yourself from the group; it is similar to the widowed person's desire to uproot and destroy old memories. If it can be used constructively, either through the help of a trained counsellor or in talk with trusted friends, it is far better than using it destructively; your feelings are a place from which to grow and discover yourself as you really are. It is futile to try to use them to alter a past which is now beyond your control.

It will help if you can learn the art of asking for sex; and of refusing offers which do not appeal to you, but without rejecting the friendship of those who find you attractive. The place to start is where you left off: with the level of skill you had developed as an adolescent before the marriage. It may be difficult to find new partners, particularly if you have young children to care for, and even more so if you are short of money and live in the country. But loving sex is still the best answer to loneliness; sex without love is a better answer than no sex at all. One of the greatest dangers, particularly if you had an orthodox or conforming adolescence, is that you might see sex as only concerned with marriage, and feel you have to fall in love and marry in order to be sexual again. If so, you will probably make the same mistakes in your next marriage as you made in the last one.

74 Self-love

Knowing your full sexual value

Sex is for you, for your pleasure, for your fulfilment. It does not belittle sex to have fun with it, only to use it for power. You can share the fun with yourself or with others. But to use it as a free gift of love (whether this is the small pleasure of day-to-day contact with people, using only small amounts of eroticism, or the maximum gift of your full capacity for arousal, plateau, orgasm and resolution), you first have to know it.

You would be wise to spend a lifetime getting to know your own sexuality. Human sexuality is the free gift we all start life with, and the best context in which to end it. Yet because of the way we are taught to deny ourselves the full use of sexuality, few of us even begin to realize our full sexual potential. This potential makes sense of all our relationships, and of each of the main methods we have of starting, continuing, ending and starting again with other people.

Each of the four stages of the sex response is equally important. If any one of them is an impoverished experience, the value of being sexual is less than it might be. The first stage can be shared with anyone; in our culture we tend to save the other stages for special people. But the first stage is also the most often neglected. A love of life and a delight in sights, sounds, touch, smells and the presence of other people are the signs of a healthy capacity to enjoy the first stage. Art, music, poetry, drama and sport are all fascinating experiences to those who

The joy of being alive. A young woman's energy and exuberance is displayed in a spontaneous and unselfconscious expression of delight. She is completely at one with her body, her sexuality and her youth.

are sexually alive and know their own value as sexual beings.

The sex response is also part of the wider process of having babies, being a parent or a child and being a man or a woman. It may be impoverished if it becomes too far removed from loving and caring. In our society the main base for these expressions of sexuality is the family, but the family is also a control system, and often uses more control than is necessary for healthy sexuality. This is why some people fail at sex; but if they use their failures as a starting-point for new growth, and in order to develop insight into their hidden agenda of unconscious control, they can grow faster from their failures than people who never know they have failed.

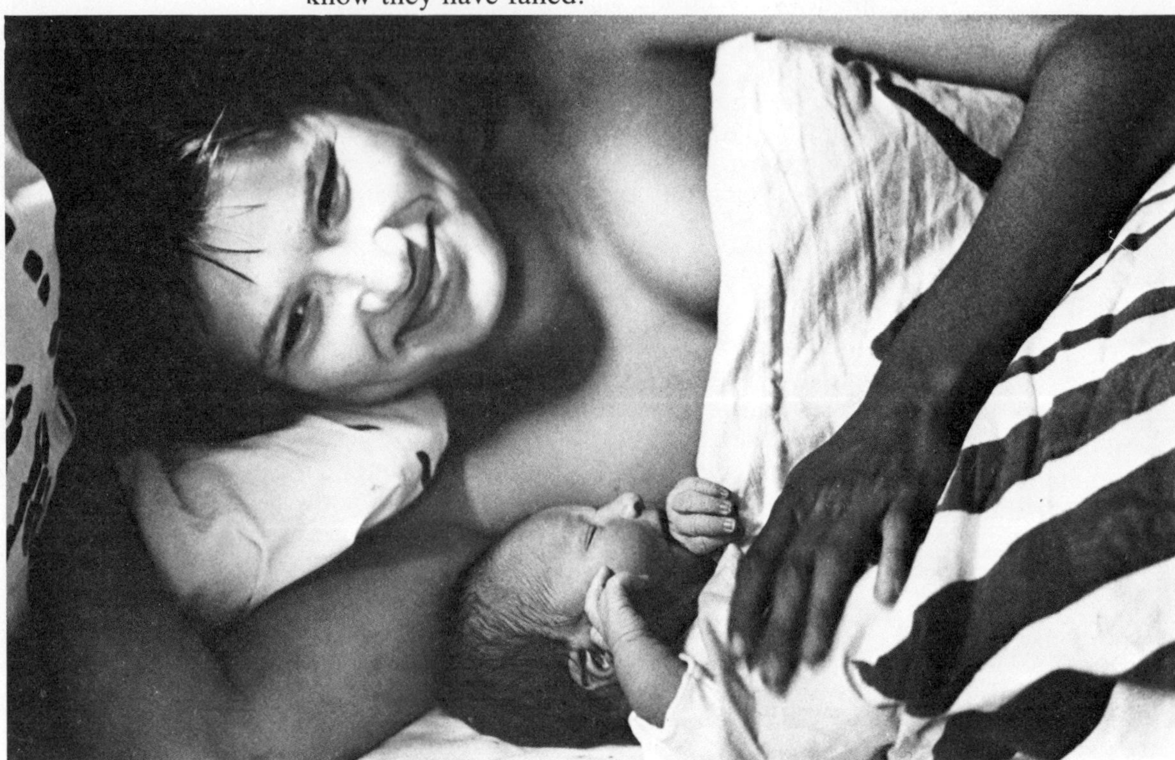

Motherhood: an affirmation of the value of being alive and sexual.

Growth in sexual terms means understanding the value of your own sexuality. This cannot be judged accurately by comparing yourself with others, as if sex were a competition. It can only be judged by each person alone, according to his feeling of preferring life-to-the-full over apathy and death. Masturbation, as the rewarding of yourself by yourself, can be a no less enriching sexual experience than making love with somebody else. It is often said that before we can love others we must love ourselves. Certainly we cannot share the full value of our sexuality unless we have experienced it in freedom from fear, anger and guilt, as a free gift to ourselves. Those who compete sexually miss the point of sex. They also present a danger to others, because the easiest way to win is to belittle the sexuality of others. But a person who has experienced the full value of his own sexuality knows the futility of competition. To such a person, counting the delight is impossible; and if there is no way of measuring the delight on a points scale, there can be no competition.

SECTION SIX
YOU AND YOUR PERSONALITY

The purpose of the final section is to enable you to focus on your own personality and to show how you can improve your skill in relating to others. Key points are described which help you save time and effort, and the different ways in which a personality may be organized and defended are considered in detail. This is followed by a series of exercises designed to help you reassess your own experience in infancy, childhood and adolescence. The 'false economies' which cause most difficulty are also examined.

The section closes with a look at advanced skills in relationships, and considers the future development of these skills – for society in general, but also for you yourself.

75 Developing Your Skill

Key points which can save you time and effort

The purpose of this book is to help you improve your skill in relationships. There are, however, no simple and effortless formulae for achieving this. It is something you have to do for yourself, and which will cost a certain effort on your part. A book can help by stimulating you into thinking afresh about yourself and the people you know; it can suggest ideas and theories, and describe the results of research. But in the end there can be no substitute for action of your own. You alone know what your feelings are, and what you wish to achieve.

Nevertheless, there are certain key points which can save you time and effort in developing your own skill. The first of these is to recognize the importance of relationships. You may tend to treat relationships as a special compartment of life. Something similar happens with mathematics. Some people see mathematics as a specialized activity which has nothing to do with daily life, and can for the most part be forgotten until they need to add up their money. This approach treats 'mathematics' as a 'subject', like something to be learned at school and forgotten later, a phenomenon which is 'out there', to be looked at with interest but hardly to be understood in real terms as part of everyday life. To take this attitude towards relationships would be to see them as an 'interesting topic', rather than as an integral part of what you are. Relationships cannot be separated from what you are, and this is why they are so important.

The second key point is to arrive at a better appreciation of the complexity and variety of human behaviour. Most of us grow up with relatively stable families around us. We accept these conditions as normal and right, and may be inclined to spend the rest of our lives judging other people by the yardstick of our own early experience. This is not necessarily dangerous, provided we can avoid seeing behaviour which is different as 'morally wrong' just because it is different; the strength of many families lies in their ability to teach the child to know 'right' from 'wrong', but their weakness is often that they neglect to teach the child that 'different' is not necessarily bad. Because of the way we grow up, therefore, we may easily fail to recognize how *unalike* people are. In the bustling, competitive world of twentieth-century industrial society, we may feel that there is no time to acknowledge or respect differences. We simply assume that other people are like ourselves and blame them if they later turn out to have 'misled' us. One major step towards improving your skill is therefore to like individual differences for their own sake; this will also help you to value your own difference from other people without feeling self-righteous about being different.

Despite the awesome complexity of human behaviour, there is an underlying unity about it which goes much deeper than any grasp of 'common factors' can possibly illuminate. Relationships provide us with this sense of unity: they help us to belong not just to a marriage, a family, a neighbourhood or a corporation, but to an ever wider structure of groups and systems which adds up to the total experience of the human race, now and in the past. It is worth considering the reason for this unity. Each individual is a system in his own right, a collection of resources which is more than the sum of its parts, just as a tree is more than a collection of leaves and branches, or a planetary system is more than a cluster of planets. The nature of a person is not different in kind from the nature of the human groups to which he belongs. They, too, are collections of resources: organized, purposive, determined to do more than merely survive, integrated, systemic. A person cannot be manufactured out of bits of body and brain; he has to grow from an organic fusion of material which has taken millions of years to create. He is more than the sum of his parts, as a group is more than a mere collection of people. The unity of human behaviour holds good whether we look at one person or the whole world of people, because each human system is essentially the same system looked at in different ways. Perhaps the most important skill you can develop is to grasp the essential unity of human behaviour, despite its infinite variety.

You alone know your own skill. It will save you time if you can acknowledge this. It is impossible to be adult without having acquired a certain skill with relationships. The problem with the study of relationships is that it is generally reserved for those who have problems! There is ample justification for understanding what you are doing and how people relate to one another without the necessity of having a problem to solve. Whatever you want from life, you can only get more of it by forming better relationships. But there is no need to regard your present relationships as failures in order to find an excuse to learn more about them. It will help if you realize that what you have learned already by yourself is more useful to you than anything you can be taught by anybody else. The point of learning more is to build upon what you know already, not to replace it with something else.

The following chapters have a slightly different emphasis from the rest of the book. This is because they are based on the assumption that *you* are now the subject, and that your own personal relationships, rather than relationships in general, can provide the focus of study. Each person who wishes to improve his skill and understanding must start from where he is, not from where somebody else happens to be. In many of the following chapters you will be invited to take part in exercises designed to help you establish a clear starting-point for yourself. You may find that you are simply reading the questions and not answering them, as though they were intended for somebody else. But to obtain the full benefit of the exercise you will have to put each question to yourself and answer it honestly. Those which seem irrelevant or trivial may well be the most important in your case; their apparent irrelevance arises from the way your own hidden agenda is defended. People often protect themselves from experiencing disturbing feelings by avoiding those issues which reawaken painful memories. As a result, their ability to benefit from relationships is restricted. You are urged, therefore, to work through to the end without avoiding any of the questions. When you reach the end of the book, however, it will only be the end of the beginning; you will have been given an introduction to relationships, and the rest will be up to you.

76 Personality

Your personality contains all your resources

There are many different ways of looking at personality. The most common is to regard each individual as having a certain kind of 'character', indicated by 'traits' such as generosity, impulsiveness, kindliness, and so on. According to one estimate, there are 18,000 such 'trait' words in the English language, and probably no less in most European languages. Psychologists, however, tend to see personality as something more complicated. They analyse individual behaviour according to a set of logically connected ideas which explain why people act as they do. From a psycho-economic point of view, each individual is seen as an integrated set of resources, a 'mini-economy' in its own right. We looked at the way such systems work when considering the nature of groups and two-person relationships. The next step is to apply the same analysis to individual personality.

We saw earlier that a group owns and controls resources which it retains inside a boundary. An individual also owns resources and has boundaries. First, his physical resources are contained inside his skin. Secondly, his actions take up a certain amount of space, and last for a limited period of time. In other words, his behavioural resources operate within boundaries similar to the spatial and temporal boundaries we saw when we looked at groups. Thirdly, an individual owns objects – the property resources which help to support him physically and behaviourally. These are contained within his territorial boundaries. (A person's home, or the space allocated to him at work, are examples of individual territory.) Fourthly, the boundaries of his social resources are determined by the groups to which he belongs.

Every group has its internal economy; this works as a 'closed' system, so that money, approval and disapproval circulate inside the group for the use of members only. Similarly, each individual is a closed economy. Most of us, for example, have money which we can spend on ourselves, allocating different amounts to various activities. This money belongs to nobody else, and is kept in a closed system. We also have feelings which nobody else can feel on our behalf. A person's feelings show him the value of his resources from moment to moment; whether he reveals them or not is his decision. In order to survive, a group must have dealings with other groups in its external economy. Similarly, an individual has to incorporate new resources from outside, not only to stay alive, but also to maintain what he judges to be an acceptable standard of life. For example, we have to ensure that we obtain food and water; that our behavioural resources are protected by sufficient clothing and shelter; and that we have the tools necessary to use our skills. We need to obtain money and other property, and to replace the friends we lose. We grow by obtaining surplus resources and keeping them inside the boundaries of our system.

We have also seen that a group has purpose, organization, membership and leadership. These are necessary because a group only contains a limited amount of resources. Each factor contributes to the group's ability to survive at the standard of life it regards as acceptable. The individual also has purposes, ways of organizing his actions and the equivalent of 'membership' and 'leadership' internally.

It is obvious that, in general terms, every individual needs to have a purpose of some kind in everything he does, even if this is to behave in a deliberately aimless manner. (Abraham Lincoln, for example, once declared, 'My policy is to have no policy.') In the broadest possible psycho-economic terms, the purpose of all individual behaviour is to meet needs as completely as possible, that is to say, to have enough for ever. On a more specific, day-to-day basis, we all tend to interpret the actions of ourselves and others in terms of purpose. We frequently ask why people do things. When we cannot see the point of an action this may puzzle or annoy us. To be in two minds about what to do next, or to be aimless, hesitant, worried or indecisive, is dangerous: when we lose our sense of purpose we cannot work out how to use our resources, and they suffer a temporary loss of value as a result.

Every individual needs organization within his personal economy. The human body is an integrated system and human skills depend on organized behaviour. Personal territory is usually organized so that

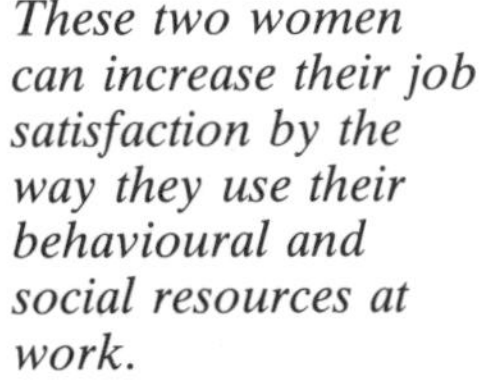

These two women can increase their job satisfaction by the way they use their behavioural and social resources at work.

people can find the objects they want when they are required. When we looked at the organization of power in a group, we saw that methods which are successful tend to become traditions which are retained. Similarly, we all develop habits, repeating patterns of action which have proved rewarding in the past in the expectation of obtaining similar rewards each time. Many of the habits an individual develops begin early in life; some are designed to avoid crises, and persist long after the probability of a repetition of the crisis has faded to zero.

The members of a group contribute their different skills and abilities towards the maintenance of the group as a whole. Each member is himself a resource which belongs to the group. The various skills, abilities and resources which make up an individual's internal economy are the equivalent of the members of a group. This is not a recent idea: in one of La Fontaine's fables, the different parts of the body quarrel and the man concerned nearly dies of starvation until his head takes charge. Children often think of their bodies in terms of 'little men' who issue instructions and have conversations telling different parts what to do. From a psycho-economic point of view each individual has many different resources; like the members of a group, they can be considered separately as single resources, or in sub-groups or sections; be seen as representative of a part or the whole of a person's behaviour; or be regarded as a complete system, as, for example, the personality.

A group has leadership; so also does the personality. Although scientists have not yet satisfactorily explained the nature of 'mind' and its relation to the body, we are all aware of having a 'self' which acts as the leader or co-ordinator of the resources contained inside our individual systems. The 'self' directs and controls the resources at its command in order to further the purposes of the individual economy.

Although these two people are engaged in a similar activity as they wait for a train, they show very different personalities because of the individual ways in which they organize their visible resources.

77 Your Relationship with Your 'Self'

Self-awareness depends on internal communication and acquaintance

Your most important relationship is with yourself. To understand this relationship we have to distinguish between your 'personality', meaning all the resources which make up your individual economy, and the 'self' which acts as leader, manager or co-ordinator of the system. For centuries philosophers have urged people to 'know themselves'. It would be more accurate to argue that you need to know your own personality; the part of you which is capable of doing this is your 'self'.

Before looking in more detail at the relationship between the 'self' and its system of resources, it is worth considering why you can benefit from understanding your own personality. The main reason is that in any relationship you have with somebody, you own and control half the resources you can both use. These are the resources in your own system. But you can only use them effectively if you know what they are, and what they are worth. Secondly, if you understand your own system you are much more likely to be able to understand other people; we are all physically similar, and tend to organize our resources in much the same way. The main difference between individuals is not that they use different methods of organizing their resources, but that they own and control resources of different kinds, and value their resources in ways which may be unlike your own system of values.

We saw earlier that the four main responsibilities of a leader are system maintenance, system control, representing the group in its dealings with other groups and task definition. The next step is to consider each of these responsibilities in turn as they apply to the 'self'. At this stage in the argument, they will be looked at in general terms so as to show how a person's internal economy is organized. Later they can be examined in more detail to show the range of individual differences which arise from the various ways in which people value their resources.

The 'self' has the task of maintaining its own system of resources. We decide for ourselves, for example, when and how much to eat, exercise, sleep, and so on. These actions contribute to the maintenance of physical resources. Yet the 'self' is not fully in control of physical resources; if you feel threatened enough, fear will take over and force you to run away, or perhaps you will feel angry whether you want to or not. At other times, the hidden fear or anger which you have been taught not to feel overrules your conscious control of your resources. You may, for example, exercise to the limits of your physical capacity, without a clear idea of why you are jeopardizing your health in this way; or work too hard and not exercise enough, without knowing why. Some people eat, smoke or drink too much, apparently unable to exert 'self-responsibility' for the care of their physical and behavioural resources, perhaps due to fear or anger of which they are not fully aware.

The leader of a group controls his system; similarly, the 'self' has the

Even in rehearsal, the ballet dancer Rudolf Nureyev must give all he has. Like many dedicated people, he uses all his resources to their maximum value.

task of system control. For example, you decide for yourself how much importance you place on the different categories of resources you own – physical, behavioural, property and social. You may regard having friends as more important than being clever, feeling healthy or owning property. Or you may consider physical fitness and having friends as less important than acquiring good financial investments.

You have to decide how you represent your system to the outside world – the image you adopt in order to be seen the way you want to be seen. This may conflict with the way you feel inside, as when a person feels afraid but hides this, or feels angry but looks pleased. Some people feel that they are valueless, but do not show this; others feel that they are the sole controllers of resources which are priceless, but they keep this judgement hidden.

The most important responsibility of the 'self', however, is task definition. The leader of any group may lose control if he has no idea of the purpose of his group, or if his idea of its aims is at variance with those of the other members. The 'self' decides its priorities to suit its purposes. It can forgo pleasure or tolerate pain in order to carry out its aims, just as a leader can persuade his followers to put up with hard work and small rewards now in order to obtain a bigger reward later.

The relationship between the 'self' and the personality for which it is responsible depends on an internal system of communication. When we looked at communication in Section Two, we saw that people are 'broadcasting' the whole time, and that a relationship begins when one person becomes aware of another's signals. Similarly, you have feelings the whole time which your 'self' can treat as 'signal' or 'noise'. This set of feelings is your general 'mood'. To become aware of any particular feeling, you have to spend a little energy from your surplus to identify it. At the cost of more energy, you can think abut the feeling; and by increasing this expenditure further, you can talk to yourself 'inside your head', or 'think aloud'. When you communicate with yourself, you will duplicate the conditions outlined earlier in chapter 35 as the best way of developing acquaintance – only this time you will be getting to know yourself. Self-disclosure within the internal system of the personality plays a very important role in self-acquaintance.

78 The Control of Personality

The positive uses of 'internal defences'

A system must be controlled to keep it stable and united. Otherwise it will fail to achieve its purpose and ultimately cease to exist. In Section Four we saw how this applies to a group. If a member acts against the interests of other members, they first punish him by restricting communication; if this does not have the desired effect, they suspend acquaintance; should this also fail, either they expel the member or he expels himself. The control system of a group works through approval and disapproval.

Something very similar happens with regard to personality. The equivalent of the group members are the resources which make up the individual's system. Each person restricts his behaviour internally to remain stable and to use these resources in an integrated and unified manner. A simple example will help to illustrate the principle involved. Suppose you were at this moment to scream at the top of your voice. You are 'capable' of doing so, in the strict meaning of the word: you have the necessary resources. But if you decide not to, there are probably very good reasons why. However good you may be at screaming loudly, there are many circumstances where to do so would be unwise, so you restrict your use of this capability.

When you are able to do something, and it is the right time and place to do it, your 'self' approves the use of the necessary resources. If you are being attacked, and a scream will summon aid, you will approve the use of your ability to scream. This ability (which under most circumstances would be of negative value) can be used at the right time and place because its value then changes from negative to positive.

If we now consider the whole of your personality, we can see that it consists of a great many resources which you could use, but do not use. The things you are most likely to do are those of which you approve internally. The kind of behaviour of which you do not approve is the least likely to be used by you. Generally speaking, people internally approve of the actions they are good at, and disapprove of those at which they are not so good. For example, somebody who is good at cooking will approve of his own ability as a cook, but if he is bad at decorating, he will not approve of his own efforts in this direction.

There is, however, an important exception to this general rule. Some of the things you may be good at (such as stealing, lying or cheating) are not approved of because you are not the kind of person who behaves in this way. Suppose, for example, that you are not a violent person. If so, this is not because you are incapable of violence, but because you do not approve of your capacity for violence. You have therefore rejected this capacity, in much the same way that a member is expelled from a group, so that, as far as the group is concerned, that member has ceased to exist. To be violent would be to behave in an uncharacteristic way; you would lose the unity of your behaviour and regard yourself as unstable, so you *prefer* to see yourself as 'incapable' of violence. Similarly, although you might make an excellent thief, liar or cheat, you prefer not to be such a person, and may regard these capabilities as non-existent in you.

This system of approval and disapproval is a normal part of everybody's personality. Freud was probably the first person to develop a theory to account for it; in his theory of personality the system is known as 'ego defence'. Freud's followers have since refined the theory, and it is now widely accepted that there are four main kinds of defence, called 'denial', 'projection', 'displacement' and 'fantasy'. It is important to emphasize that ordinary, normal, healthy people with no problems all use these four kinds of defence; without such defences they would not be stable people producing integrated, unified behaviour.

Denial occurs when we refuse to acknowledge that we are capable of a certain kind of behaviour. We say we 'cannot' do something, when it would be more accurate to say we 'will not'. The things we are most likely to deny vehemently are those we are good at but strongly disapprove of, such as those in the above examples. In effect, the 'self'

Spectators watching a demonstration by homosexuals seem uncertain how to react. They probably cannot imagine themselves ever behaving in the same way as the demonstrators, having long ago 'displaced' their ability to do so.

which is denying a certain capability is refusing to feel, think or talk about this part of the personality. Internal communication on the matter is suspended. If there are parts of your own personality you would 'prefer not to think about', this shows that you retain your stability and unity of action by exercising denial in respect of the resources involved. Denial is often the basis upon which people 'resist temptation'. Thus, 'Don't tempt me' is an expression of denial.

Projection occurs when we act out of character because somebody else has 'made us' behave like this. Suppose, for example, that you do not like politicians or door-to-door salesmen, and then meet one who is so charming that you are 'forced' to like him. This is due to projection. If you did not 'project' the responsibility for your uncharacteristic reaction onto the other person, you would not be able to recognize your own behaviour. You would not want to 'know yourself'. Or suppose you disapprove of uncontrolled anger, but meet a clever manipulator who 'makes you' angry. Your loss of control will turn you into the sort of person you do not wish to get to know, so you suspend self-acquaintance, project your feelings onto the other person and blame him for the way you feel. In the same way, a group which disapproves of the actions of a member, and needs to go further than a suspension of communication, will also stop trying to get to know him.

Displacement is the equivalent of banishing a member. Other people's actions are sometimes a mystery to you: you cannot understand *how* they can behave like that. This is because you have discarded your own capability for such behaviour. For example, you may feel sympathetic towards somebody who has a problem you have never had, but be unable to see how such a problem could arise. You could never imagine yourself behaving similarly, because you have 'displaced' your ability to do so.

Sometimes, however, none of these defences works, and actions of which you are capable, but which you cannot produce in real life, occur as fantasies. By means of fantasies you temporarily escape from the restrictions of your own personality, and accomplish aims which in real life seem beyond you. This is the equivalent of the way in which a group member may resign if he cannot get what he wants.

The fact that denial, projection, displacement and fantasy are terms mainly used in psychiatry has tended to obscure their relevance to everyday relationships and to the understanding of healthy personality. Thus each of these 'defences' is usually seen as a way of escaping from problems, and of avoiding negative feelings. However, they also have positive usefulness. A few examples will help to illustrate this.

First, let us consider denial in more detail. There is a subtle distinction between not doing something and 'not-doing' it. When you are not doing something, this is simply a statement of fact; but when you are not-doing it, this is a statement of intention not to do it. Suppose, for example, that you tell somebody you are not going out tonight. You could say this meaning that you have made no arrangements but might be prepared to go out if asked. Alternatively, you might mean that you have a firm intention of staying in. To not-do something is to deliberately turn a positive possibility into a negative one. We can express denial verbally in this way; we can also display denial non-verbally. For example, we may find ourselves not-smiling at a joke we think is funny but dirty, or not-waiting for somebody we are only partly waiting for; we can show by our posture and facial expression that we are not-minding being disturbed, or not-caring about the bill for an expensive meal because we like the other person almost enough for his enjoyment to be sufficient reward. Part of the advanced skill of relating to others is the ability to be more positive about our own normal denials, to refuse a little bit, instead of agreeing almost enough. If we are intending not to do something, there is less harm in admitting it than in not-doing it. Equally, it is useful to be able to recognize other people's denials, and to be certain that we have understood what they positively intend to do, rather than what they are partly avoiding.

Projection also has its positive uses, particularly if you are able to listen to what you say and to catch the hidden meanings. We often reveal a great deal about our inner situation by the way we describe our external one. A good example of this is the marriage counsellor who always began his work with a couple by asking them to chat generally about their home. He would then lead them to talk about home decorating, and ask which partner undertook the various tasks involved. One wife told him, 'First I clean the walls, strip off everything and get it ready for him. He comes along, slaps on the paper, and then leaves me with the mess to clean up.' The counsellor immediately had a hypothesis to work on with regard to the different attitudes of the partners towards sex. By the skilful use of projection in this way we can often hear a symbolic message under the official message. Of course, the symbolic message has to be interpreted with caution. However, as was stated earlier in chapter 29, people often talk about 'it' when what they say would be just as true if they substituted 'I'.

Projection avoids inner acquaintance; it also helps us to avoid mutual acquaintance. Another of its positive uses is therefore to alert us to our need to know our own personality better. For example, when you meet somebody you do not like and do not wish to get to know, this can be a clue as to what you do not like about yourself. If you think about this later, you can reopen acquaintance with yourself, and maybe find that this part of your personality is worth getting to know again. It is an interesting exercise to think of somebody whom you are quite certain you do not like and prefer not to know. Were you ever like him yourself? Could you have become like him if you had not been luckier or more careful? If the answer is an angry 'No', why are you angry? Projection means that somebody or something else is blamed for how you feel; in the case of displacement, there is no sense of blame, just a detached feeling of interest. This also has many positive advantages. First it can help you locate people who have problems which you have but did not know you have. You may have so successfully managed to not-have such problems that you can now not-have them effortlessly. For example, you may have forgotten an earlier time in your life when you were shy, or not very good at your job because you were still learning. As a parent, you may be so successful at not-being young that you have forgotten what being young was like. To be reminded of such feelings helps us to know ourselves better. Any truly successful denial can become a successful displacement. One common example in an elderly person is the casual acceptance that the world is getting worse, and that standards are no longer being maintained. He has been so successful at not-getting disorganized despite his advancing years, and at not-allowing his own standards of perfection to slip, that he really believes he has stayed the same and it is the world which has changed. We can all benefit from recognizing not only our own minor displacements but those of other people, too; and from accepting them rather than trying to change them.

Fantasy also has many positive uses. In modern sex therapy, couples who have stopped enjoying sex are helped to share their fantasies, and to communicate them openly without shame. Many people have power fantasies, in which they rule the world or appear on their favourite television chat shows. The most positive way to use fantasies, however, is probably not to analyse them, but to share and enjoy them.

79 The Organization of Personality

Your internal banking system

Suppose a small business is faced with a crisis, perhaps because an expensive piece of machinery needs replacing. The managing director has to find money from somewhere, but some solutions are clearly impractical, such as not paying his staff or selling his car. The problem is that, although the company has wealth, it is tied up in plant and machinery or consists of money which has already been allocated to a variety of necessities, such as staff salaries. There is no surplus of ready cash. In the day-to-day running of your personality-economy you often face similar crises yourself. You need to find energy, or to produce the right level of skill, but find that you have no readily available surplus.

Finding a surplus inside your own system is very largely a matter of organization. The purpose of this chapter is to look at some of the ways in which the internal economy of the personality is organized, so that you can make judgements about yourself and get to know your own system better. Because every one of us uses denial, projection, displacement and fantasy, we often look for resources outside our system instead of making better use of our internal assets. These 'defence' systems help us to behave in a stable and consistent way, but only at the cost of rejecting many of the capabilities we have, on the grounds that such actions would not meet with the approval of the 'self' in charge.

Current account surplus. Two competitors in a top international dog show compensate for the tension of such a highly competitive event by conserving energy and keeping a credit balance in their current account of resources.

To see how a personality system can be organized, let us consider the small business again. A simplified version of its finances suggests that the company probably has several bank accounts. The 'current' account will contain ready cash for everyday use. This money is carefully budgeted, and when it runs out, the manager has to transfer money from a 'deposit' account. If the deposit account runs out, he can ask the bank to lend him money, and open what is called a 'loan' account. The bank will set a limit to what the company is allowed to borrow, and when this limit is reached, cash can only be obtained by selling off some of the company's assets. When this happens the company will be in difficulties, because it will be forced either to go out of business or to cut down its activities until it can pay off its debts and rebuild its reserves of wealth.

Each kind of account (the current account, the deposit account and the loan account), together with money which is tied up in assets, can be found in the personality. From a psycho-economic point of view, the equivalent of 'money' is 'readily available energy'. People often use considerable amounts of energy in their relationships; but some energy may not be available for a particular relationship because its use might mean depleting savings, increasing loans or selling off assets. This will be clearer if we look at each kind of account in turn.

The equivalent of the current account is the amount of energy you have on a day-to-day basis to spend on other people. In an extreme situation you may have nothing to spare, and, indeed, be in need of energy from other people. For example, when you feel that you are beset by problems of your own, it is difficult to listen to someone else talking about his problems. You want to receive attention and comfort, rather than give it. When life is going smoothly, however, you can keep your current account in credit, and each small contact with other people can be friendly, so that you receive as much energy from them as you give them. A friendly encounter may mean that you receive more than you spend; if this is followed by a less friendly meeting, you have energy to spare over and above the amount with which you started that morning.

Each personality has 'deposit' accounts, containing energy which has been invested in the past so as to keep the person safe. For example, a person may have experienced a period of intense loneliness in childhood, and since then has always made sure he has the necessary resources never to feel lonely again. Or somebody may have had to work very hard at school, perhaps because he was unjustly seen as 'stupid' by parents, teachers or siblings. He is therefore determined never to be seen as stupid again, and carries a special reserve of energy for use on all occasions when this might happen. If someone else suggests that he is inefficient or slow to learn, this energy reserve is released in a flurry of activity, possibly as anger, but perhaps also by a show of cleverness designed to demonstrate that the charge is false. The more energy a person needs for his deposit accounts, the less he can spare for his current spending.

From time to time most of us probably feel that we owe people gratitude, perhaps for favours they have given us, but also sometimes when we are loved by people and do not feel worthy of their love. This is the basis of our loan accounts. Many people have loan accounts in

Current account deficit. For the moment this wife and mother has run out of resources. She must draw on her reserves to carry on, or, if she has none, her family must provide support.

their relationships with their parents: they feel that they have a duty to love them. As a result, the 'love' they give has to be counted, since it is designed to pay off a debt. Of course, love which has to be counted is not real love; you cannot love a person as a matter of duty, but only by giving freely what is yours. But some parents demand gratitude, and they manipulate their child into giving this by persuading him that he is not worthy of the care and attention he receives from them. This may also happen in a marriage, and after a divorce it is important to accept that all emotional debts from one partner to the other have been cancelled. Similarly, when a child leaves home permanently or becomes an adult, the longer he carries around such parental loan accounts, the harder it will be for him to assume responsibility for his own life.

Selling off your assets occurs whenever you have to accept somebody else's view of the kind of person you are in place of your own view. This is never easy; in extreme cases, as when somebody needs therapy for a behaviour problem, the whole personality may have to be dismantled and rebuilt, perhaps by helping the patient return to decisions made early in childhood about the kind of person he is. On a day-to-day basis, many relationships would be happier if we could be more accepting of other people's views of our own personality, particularly when we fail to reach a target we have set ourselves. Most of us can recover from failure more rapidly if we invest less energy in keeping up an acceptable image, and more in understanding other people's reactions to us.

80 A Sense of Purpose

Knowing your purpose in life

Every group is directed, controlled and organized so as to carry out a purpose or set of purposes. The same is true of the personality. An understanding of purpose must therefore form an important part of our understanding of personality. The similarities between a group and an individual can help us with this task. Suppose, for example, that we were to ask a group to describe its purpose. In an efficient, well-organized group with good leadership, each of the members could say why the group existed and describe its main aims. In addition, he would be able to say what his own contribution was to the overall plan, and how his job related to those of the other members. Similarly, a person who is sure of his purpose can say what this is, and also describe the ways in which each of his actions helps him achieve his aim.

Not every group has a strong sense of purpose; similarly, each individual differs in the extent to which he is clear about his aims. Most of us probably go through periods when we are not sure what we want, or why we are doing something. At such times we are inefficient and disorganized, and lack internal leadership. Different parts of our personality seem to be in conflict, like the members of a group disagreeing amongst themselves. Many of us are also beset by feelings of guilt at such times. In an industrial society, it may be regarded as morally wrong to be inefficient and disorganized, and to lack leadership; the ethic of such a society is to approve of efficiency and to disapprove of non-productive idleness.

An understanding of groups can also help us see how a person may lose his sense of purpose. One obvious cause is failure. If a group sets out to achieve something but fails, the members will tend to fight amongst themselves. Similarly, most of us probably react to failure by experiencing a period of internal upheaval and dissension. Sometimes a new sense of purpose emerges from this debate, but at other times we may try to 'banish' the parts of us which we blame for our lack of success, become angry with ourselves and punish ourselves. We may do this by mild forms of self-injury, such as hitting ourselves or banging our hands on the table, or by more extreme forms, such as self-poisoning with alcohol or other drugs.

Some groups lose their sense of purpose for historical reasons: they forget why they were formed in the first place. This may happen when a small firm in a traditional industry becomes set in its ways, and concentrates on the craftsmanship of the product but loses sight of its need to sell. Over the years, as employees come and go, the existence of the firm seems to be its only justification. None of the members thinks about purpose; they stop discussing it, and lose sight of the original aim. Only when the firm is faced with bankruptcy does the question arise, and by then it may be too late to find a new sense of purpose. Similarly, an individual may become so much a creature of habit that he forgets why he developed his habits; when a serious problem faces him, he cannot remember what he originally set out to do.

A group can also lose its sense of purpose as a consequence of success; it achieves what it has set out to do, and then has no further justification for its existence. A campaign committee, for example, may win its fight and then disband. When this happens to an individual, however, the equivalent of disbanding is death, and this may be totally inappropriate, due to the age and health of the person concerned. If the main purpose of your life has been achieved in your early thirties, you may spend the rest of your life without finding another purpose. However, you are more likely to go on looking for a new direction than to commit suicide.

Many groups have a life of their own, and continue to achieve their purpose regardless of who is a member. Thus any institution which has lasted for a hundred years must have completely changed its membership several times. The sense of purpose is handed down from one generation of members to the next, and this feeling of continuity is a valuable asset to the group. Similarly, each individual receives his first sense of purpose from the family in which he grows up. His own sense of identity develops as an expression of this. When you consider your own purpose in life, this can only have grown from an original set of purposes you learned when you were a child. To help you think about this, try to apply the following series of questions to yourself.

What do you consider to be the main purpose of life? One clue to your original set of purposes is to think about how you describe your most negative and your most positive feelings. For example, if you tend to describe the worst feeling you get as 'being unhappy' and your best feeling as 'being happy', it is likely that your role as a child was to be happy. Or perhaps your worst feelings are those of 'failure', and your best ones are called 'success'; if so, you were taught to be a 'winner' and not to be a 'loser'. Some people say that their best feelings are 'contentment', which means to have enough of the things they need; their worst feelings are called 'discontent' or 'frustration'. This may show that their main role in the family of origin was the negative one of not asking for too much. For example, children who grew up in wartime or during a major slump, and children who come from poor families, are often taught early in life to be content with less than they really want, and not to express their frustration when they cannot obtain all they expect. If you regard your worst feelings as being 'bad' and your best feelings as being 'good', perhaps your role was to be the 'good child', the one who was always obedient and courteous, and who conformed to the wishes of his parents. Some children grow up regarding their main purpose as to 'get better', and this may indicate childhood illness. An adult who sees life in terms of 'making progress' may have completely forgotten why this has become a habit, because he seldom thinks about the crucial time in childhood when he was ill.

Another way to approach an understanding of your early sense of purpose is to consider what kinds of actions by other people 'make you' experience negative feelings. People who see their main purpose as to be happy often have a low tolerance of those who always seem to be miserable but cannot be cheered up. 'Happy' people usually understand sadness, and have often experienced it, but persistent and deliberate sadness in somebody else leaves them feeling frustrated. Similarly, those who want to be 'winners' can understand what it feels like to be a loser, but become angry with people who simply do not want to win. If your sense of purpose is connected with being contented, you will probably sympathize easily with people who are temporarily discontented, but be quite unable to tolerate those who have no wish to be contented. Deliberate waste will almost certainly shock and annoy you, as when people persistently neglect their own talents. The 'good' person has often developed an ability to understand rebellion in others, but people who are determined to behave badly on all occasions, and seem to have no sense of proportion about this, usually annoy him. The 'progress seeker' is tolerant of temporary set-backs, but cannot understand people who do not seem to want to do better.

A Portuguese paratrooper about to surrender following the attempted rebellion in 1975. By releasing his accumulated surplus of negative feelings he becomes the opposite kind of person to the one he wanted to be.

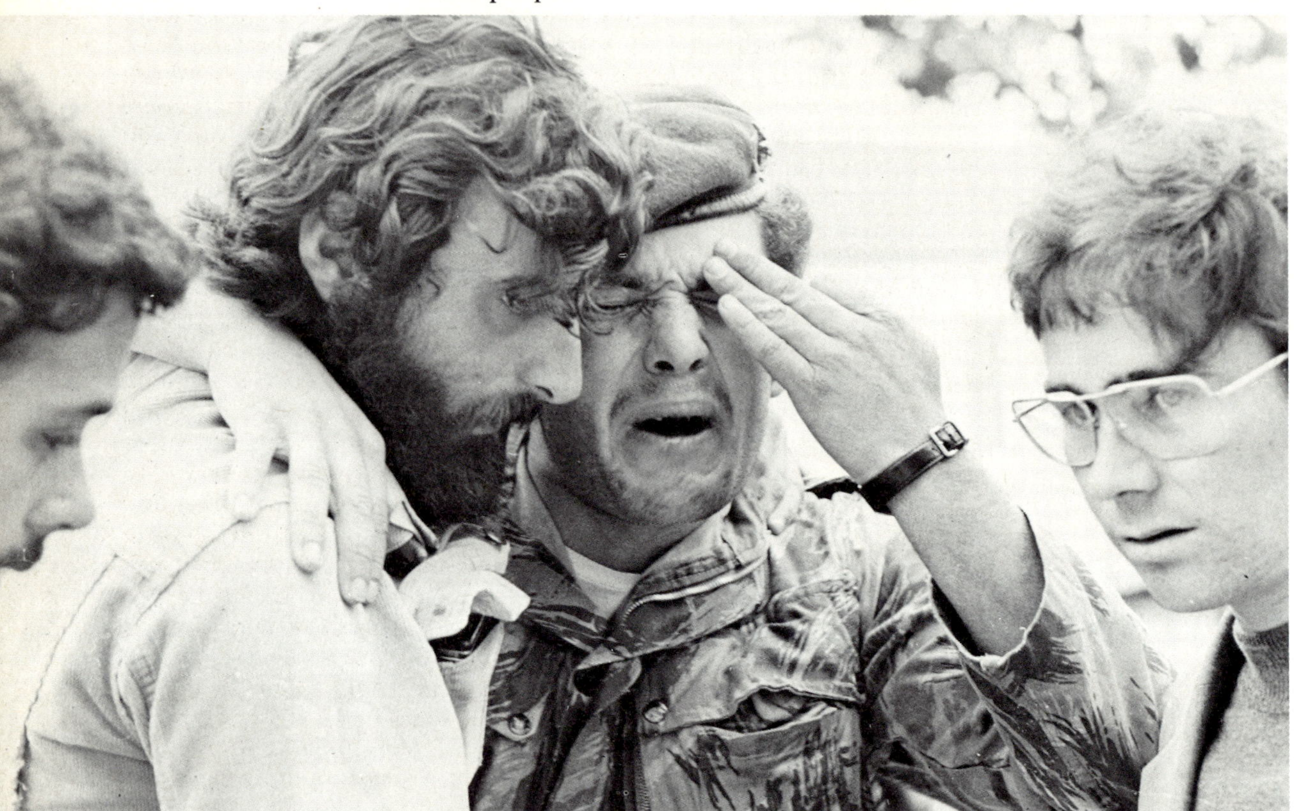

The reason for these reactions is that any sense of purpose is pursued in two ways: first, by collecting a surplus of positive resources, such as things which make you happy, small or large successes, moments of approval for good conduct, signs of progress, and so on; secondly, by avoiding negative resources, such as sadness, failures, minor acts of rebellion and set-backs. Each time a positive resource is collected, it is saved up. When the person has enough resources of this kind for a rise in his standard of life, he spends them. Thus, one of the ways in which a happy-directed person shows that success for him means to be 'happier than ever' (and to make sure this success continues) is to try to stay like this until he can take the feeling for granted, collect some new ways of being happy and thus promote himself to being even happier.

Similarly, a person who wants to be a 'winner' will not be content with one win, but will want to go on winning, each time taking for granted the succeses which had previously seemed so hard to obtain. Each of the other purposes we have looked at is pursued in a similar way, by collecting a surplus and then spending it on a promotion. But a negative resource, such as a sadness or a failure, cancels out a positive one. Each negative experience is a reminder of the kind of person you do not want to be. People who deliberately collect negative resources seem exactly the kinds of people we want to void being like.

Next you should ask yourself what kinds of people you have difficulty in understanding. Many people who have a sense of purpose are quite convinced that everybody else has the same purpose. Thus, if you see the aim of life as being 'happy', you will probably have reacted to the other aims mentioned above by thinking, 'Doesn't everybody want to be happy?' Similarly, if you want to be a winner, you may still be puzzled by the thought that not everybody wants to win and dislikes failure. Those who want to be contented will argue that everybody is looking for contentment: the happy person wants to be contented; the winner wants to be enough of a winner to be contented with his winnings. If your aim is to be good, you may protest that surely nobody wants to be bad at something; if it is to make progress, again, you will see happy people, winners, contented people and good people as all aiming for different ways of making progress.

These examples illustrate the kinds of people you probably have difficulty in understanding – those whose sense of purpose is just as strong as yours, but who want different things. It is often very difficult to accept that not everybody wants the same things as you do. Winners are not interested in being happy or making progress; people who want to be happy are not interested in winning or being contented. For example, a winner who stopped to be happy would slip behind in the race; and if he merely made progress, other people might make more progress than him, beating him to the winning post. Someone who wants to be happy can achieve his aim without winning. He is 'happy' with coming in second or even last (like the tortoise would have been in his race with the hare, in Aesop's fable). Nor does he need to be contented; he claims he can be happy even if there is never enough to eat. A person who wants to be good at something does not care if this wins no prizes, is not content when he does something superbly and hates making progress because this means he is not good enough yet; he wastes no time on being happy about his achievements, but takes them for granted and looks for the next thing to be good at. If your aim is to make progress, you will probably not care about winning or losing, provided you do better than last time. You will perhaps be puzzled by people who seem content even though they are getting nowhere with their lives, be mystified by those who want to be perfectionists and have difficulty in imagining yourself as happy for the rest of your life.

Your own main purpose in life may well not be one of those we have examined, but whatever it is, you can still try to work through the examples for yourself. You might also like to try thinking about somebody else you know, such as a partner, a child or a colleague, and apply the same analysis.

81 Growth

Understanding how your personality develops

Your present personality is the result of a long history of growth. For example, all your present social resources – represented by the people you know today – might be fairly recent additions to your personality, but it is more likely that some of them are old friends or acquaintances, or people you have known all your life, such as your parents, elder siblings or uncles and aunts. Similarly, your property resources may include items you have kept since childhood or early adolescence, such as old photographs of yourself or some of your old school books. If you are married, you probably still wear the wedding ring you were given at the ceremony. But many of the items you possess will be new. Some of them will be with you for only a short time, such as the small change in your pocket.

The process of growth is rather like the way a group changes its membership: old members leave and new ones take over. In a firm, for example, the job of telephonist may have been held by a long succession of people, each doing the same job, but perhaps with some variations in style. Similarly, some of your new friends will be replacements for older ones with whom you have lost contact; they do the same job, but in their own ways. If you are married, your partner may be a partial replacement for a parent, while your best friend may be in some ways a successor to a brother or sister or favourite cousin, filling a similar role in a different style. If you have an old family photograph album, you may be surprised at the similarities between one of your parents and your husband or wife, or between your present close friends and the brothers or sisters with whom you grew up. If, as a child, you lost a parent, a brother or sister, or a much loved relation, you may have spent an important part of your life looking for a suitable replacement without finding one. This is not as strange as it may sound: each of the people on whom you depend is a part of your personality. Because they are all separate people, you may easily forget that they are also resources you need. When a child is separated from someone as a result of that person's death, he may not fully understand what has happened, and for the rest of his life have a vague feeling that somebody is missing. This is particularly common amongst the generation which grew up during the Second World War, because those who died were often said to be 'missing', 'lost' or 'fallen' – all explanations which a child would appear to understand, but tend to interpret more literally than the adults realized. Now in their forties and fifties, members of this generation may still have traces of bewilderment that a 'lost' person has not found his way home.

The capacity for total delight has survived from childhood in most of us. (above) A baby gives free expression to its enjoyment when tickled by its mother. (below) A mother, through expressing her own childlike capacity for delight, encourages her baby to do the same.

Social and property resources change in one of three ways: they may be replaced by something better or by something of equal value, or there may be a loss of value – either because a resource is not replaced or because the substitute is not as good. Growth, therefore, can be positive, neutral or negative. This applies also to behavioural and phys-

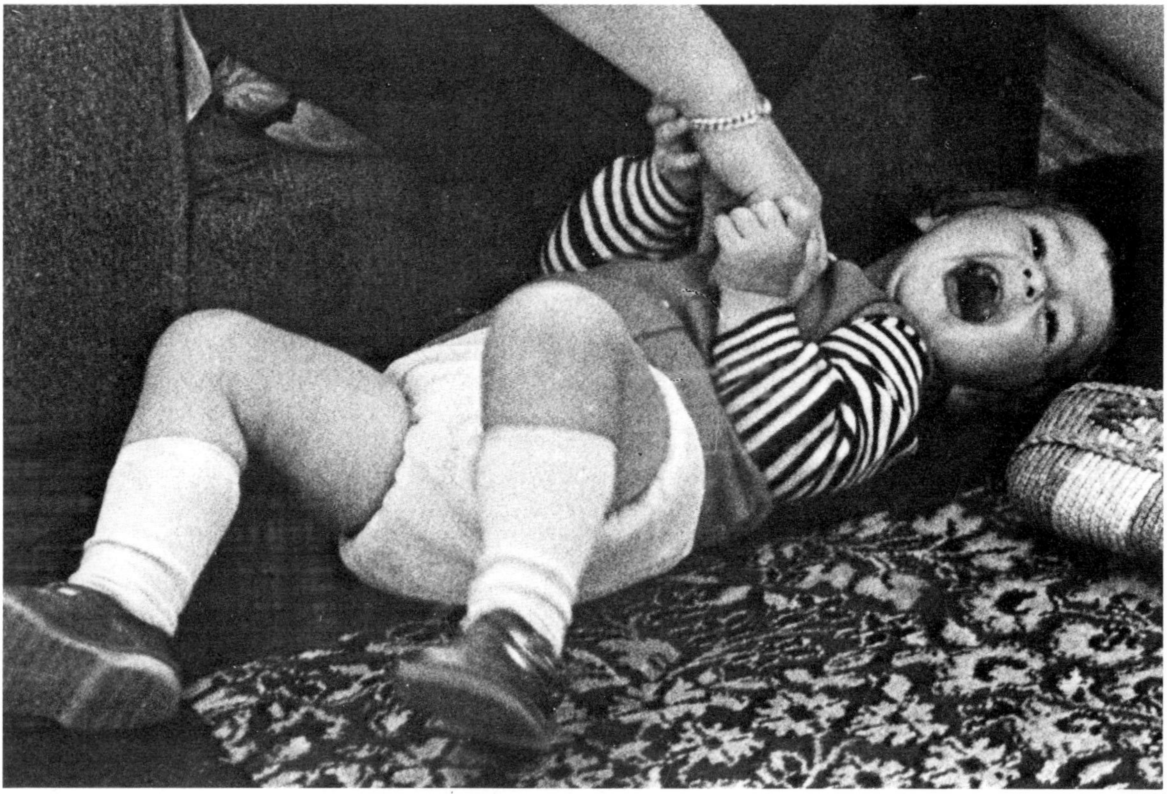

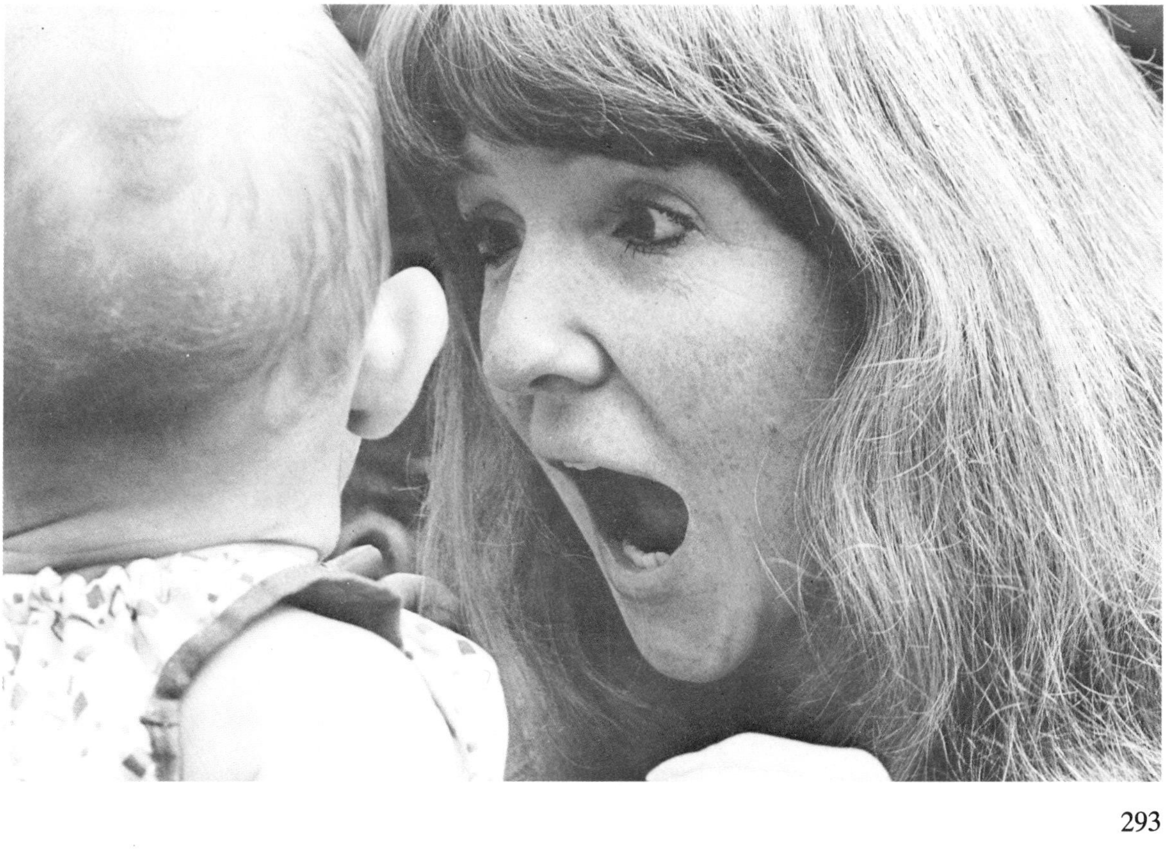

ical resources. Here, too, old 'members' leave to be replaced by new ones, or are not replaced at all.

If we consider physical resources first, these consist of all the cells in your body. The ones you have at present – with one notable set of exceptions – are all replacements. Your skin is continuously wearing out and being replaced; the cells of the heart and the liver, the blood cells, and so on, are not your original 'members' but successors to them. Each is very similar to its predecessor, and does the same job; but there are differences in style, because each cell is also a system, and not a mechanical part, and it has an individual capacity for adapting to its surroundings. The exception is the brain and its set of cells, which do not replicate. There are probably as many as a hundred thousand million cells in each brain; if they were people, they would be enough to populate twenty-five planets like the earth. When the brain is injured, it can often recover, but not by growing new cells. Instead, the remaining cells are reconnected to take over as much as possible of the lost function. At birth a baby's brain is about 350 grams in weight; at the age of twenty, the brain normally weighs between 1,200 and 1,400 grams. This increase in weight is not due to the addition of new cells, but to the growth of nerve fibre connections between cells. In a five-year-old the brain is about 80 per cent of its final adult weight, and in a nine-year-old, about 90 per cent. The growth of the brain is causally connected with the growth of behavioural resources.

You acquired your present behavioural resources, therefore, by a process of growth which was a quarter complete before you were born, three-quarters complete before you were five and nearly finished by the time you were ten years old. Since the cells which are responsible for your behaviour patterns are not replaced by new ones, as an adult you still have behavioural resources which you learned as a child. Some of these skills will be unchanged, as a result of neutral growth; others will have developed and become more valuable; while you will regard still others as of little value now that you have grown up.

A most important aspect of understanding your own personality is therefore to understand your own childhood and babyhood. This is partly an intellectual task – thinking about yourself and your early life. Before starting, however, you might like to demonstrate to yourself some of the early responses which have still survived, using a behavioural method. First, you could try to rediscover your babyhood capacity for total delight. To do this, find a convenient place, lie on your back and try to move as a baby moves, kicking your legs in the air and cooing. If you have somebody who is willing to help, ask him to tickle you very gently, particularly round the chin or neck. If you let your inhibitions go, you will soon be able to disengage your conscious thought processes and react just as you did when you were a baby. Secondly, try standing up and seeing if you can rediscover your childhood capacity for total rage by repeating your childhood temper tantrum actions, perhaps stamping your foot and screaming at the top of your voice. These exercises do not help you feel what it is like to be a baby; they help you *know* what you felt like when *you* were a baby. A third form of behavioural exercise, for which you will need expert help, is the rediscovery of your own birth experience, known as 'rebirthing'. The reflex actions you used at birth are still accessible today.

82 Getting to Know Your Parents

How to work out the circumstances of your birth

Every time you get to know somebody you have an opportunity to get to know yourself, too. Your most important relationships are the ones which help you to grow in your understanding of yourself. You get to know your strengths and weaknesses, and the parts of your personality of which you approve and disapprove. The most important part of your personality is the part which developed in childhood, so getting to know yourself means very largely getting to know more about the child you once were and still are.

You are much more like your parents than anyone else in the world. Your parents' physical resources have determined what yours are like. Your body is a kind of compromise between theirs; your face is a mixture of their faces. If they are tall, you will tend to be tall, and short if they are short. Their behavioural resources also formed the basis of what you have learned. A major contribution to understanding yourself can be gained by getting to know your parents.

A daughter visits her mother at an old people's home. Their relationship can continue to develop, providing both with new insights to help them make more sense of their lives.

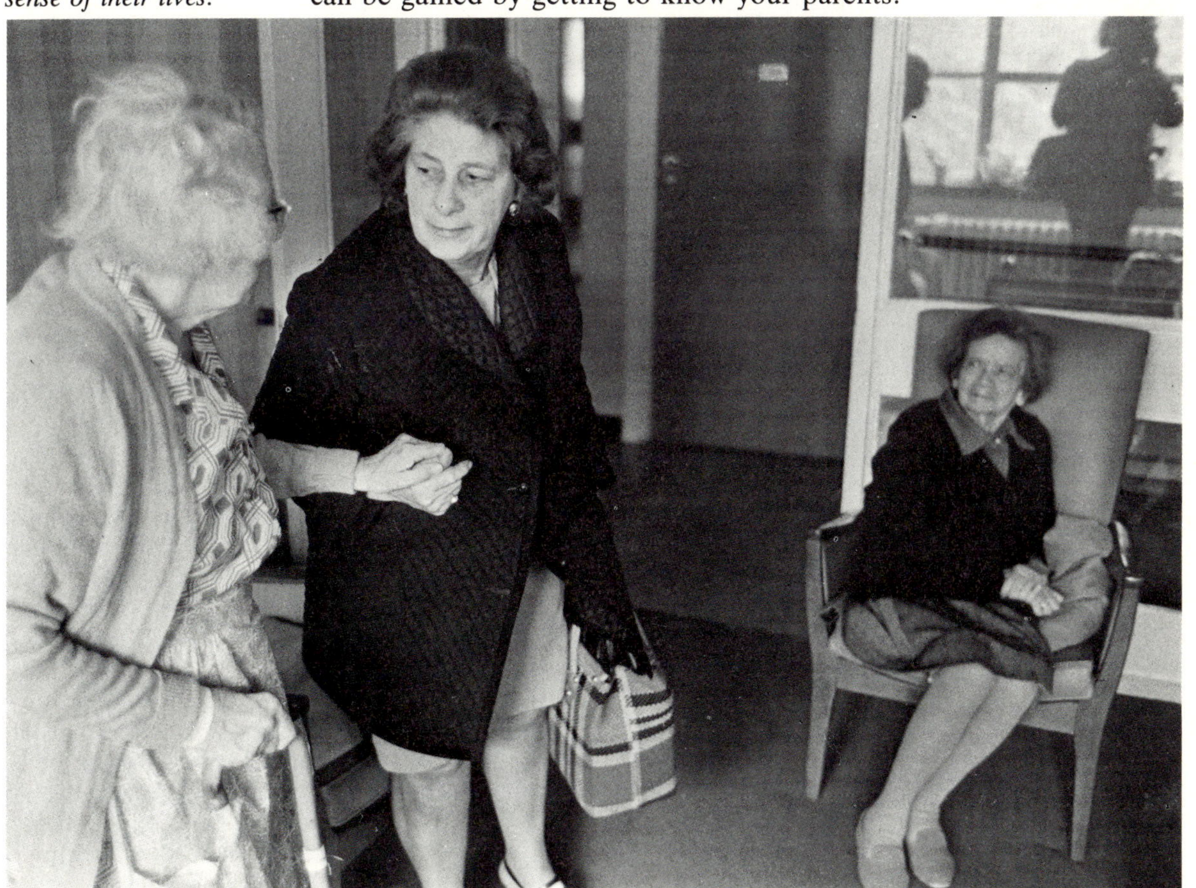

If your parents are still alive, how you set about getting to know them better depends on the kind of relationship you have with them already. You may be lucky enough to have parents who made friends with you as you grew up, so that today you can talk freely with one another as adult to adult. Unfortunately, this kind of relationship between parent and child is still rare. Many subjects are not discussed, including sexual matters and childbirth; parents who faced difficulties while their children were small no longer wish to reopen old wounds, and understandably will not talk about their worst crises. Chapter 35 made several suggestions as to how you can improve acquaintance with somebody you already know well, such as a parent, and you would gain much insight into your own personality and early experience from discussing these matters with your parents.

In many cases this will not be possible, perhaps because your parents are no longer alive or because the relationship between you is not sufficiently safe for such a discussion. However, there is still a great deal you can learn from the intellectual exercise of asking and answering questions. One possible way to start is to write a brief biography of your mother. Try to make a note of all the important events in her life. The following list of questions can be used as a starting-point. When was your mother born, and where? Were her parents living together at the time? Was she the eldest, middle or youngest child? Was she an only child? If she had brothers and sisters, how did she get on with them? What do you know about her school-days? Did she live with her parents until she married or did she leave home before that? How did she meet your father? Did she work after she was married? How old was she when you were born? Were both her parents alive then?

The idea is to try to see your mother as a person in her own right, particularly before you were conceived. When you were a child this would have been particularly difficult for you. A young child usually sees his mother as an extension of his own personality, and not as somebody who had a life before he was born. You are now in a far better position to understand your mother and some of the problems she may have had to face. It will also help if you write a similar biography for your father. The same questions should be included. In chapter 68, when the marital relationship was considered, it was stated that some marriages are more conforming and some more conflict-based. It would be worth trying to understand all the many reasons why your parents chose one another and why they married when they did.

The next step is to consider your parents' probable attitudes to having children. When a woman discovers she is pregnant, she is likely to have mixed feelings. Surveys strongly suggest that more than a third of all pregnancies are unwanted, and if you are old enough to have been born before contraception was practised widely, or if you know your parents had religious objections to its use, this may provide further clues as to your mother's likely reaction to the realization that she was expecting you. But although many pregnancies are unwelcome, this does not mean the baby is unwanted when it arrives. You may have been a 'wanted' baby, but at some cost to your parents' expectations, economically or socially. Even if you were unwanted and not welcomed (as is the case far more often than those people who were 'wanted' realize), you can form a better and more sympathetic view of this now

In our formative years we have to accept the authority of our parents. Later we may be unaware of how much we still depend on the view they had of us, although this may at times have been extremely negative and discouraging.

that you are older. Most parents sacrifice something to have children; if you were blamed for this when you were too young to understand, it is your own life now, and the loan accounts can be closed.

Your parents' experience of bereavement while you were too young to understand can often help to explain their attitudes towards their babies. Did your mother have the support of her own mother during her pregnancies and while you were a baby? Did she have any late miscarriages, stillborn children or babies who died very young? This will be a painful subject for you if it has happened to you; if it has not, but happened to your mother, you will need an effort of imagination to understand how she might have felt about your birth. Your father will have been deeply affected also if one of his parents died near the time you were conceived, or if a baby died.

Negative factors like this are important, however painful, because they are often hidden from young children. On the more positive side, try to work out how your father might have felt when you were born. What factors would have pleased him and your mother? Did he like babies? Was he present when you were born? Would his own parents have been pleased? How do you feel about babies? If you are a man, is this the way you think your father felt about you? If not, how do you account for the difference? If you are a woman, what are the differences between your mother's attitude to babies and your own? Can you account for this?

83 You and Your Name

Your name can provide clues as to your parents' expectations

The first stage in acquiring any resource is called 'identification'. Unless you first identify what you want you cannot obtain it. Throughout your life your personality is identified by your name. But when you were born you were unaware of having a name, and it had to be chosen for you by your parents. When they decided what you should be called, what were they identifying as the part you should play in their lives? What were they saying about what they hoped you would become? This chapter is designed to help you consider such questions about yourself, and also to apply them to other people.

Try to imagine your parents discussing what name to give you during the week or so before you were born. At that time your sex was not known. Did they want a boy or a girl? Some couples want their first-born to be a boy and their second child to be a girl. In some sections of our society, the eldest son is particularly important as the bearer of the family name or for reasons of religious ceremony. A mother who has had several girls may hope for a boy next time, and one who has only had sons will often wish for a girl. In their choice of first names, parents sometimes express some of these wishes. For example, boys' names like Alexander, George and Eric can be made into girls' names such as Alexandra, Georgina and Erica. A girl who is given one of these names can later be called by the shortened form as Alex, George or Eric. Some names apply equally to both sexes. If your name falls into this category, it is worth asking whether your parents hoped for a child of a different sex. Some children are brought up as the sex the parent really wanted, as well as the sex the child turned out to be, as when a mother hopes for a girl for her second baby, gets a boy, but partly treats this son as the daughter she would have preferred. You might also know what you would have been called if you had turned out to be the opposite sex.

Some babies are named after other people. These may be people who are part of the family, such as a grandfather or grandmother, or a favourite uncle, aunt or cousin, or they may be famous people whom it is hoped the baby might be like. Were you named after anybody? If so, whom? A mother sometimes chooses a name for her baby from books or films, particularly if she wants to have a pretty girl for her daughter, and thinks of a certain name as pretty or beautiful. This suggests a romantically escapist view of life, and that her child is part of her fantasy. Alternatively, a name for a boy or girl may be chosen to be deliberately plain and down-to-earth. Children are sometimes named after places. For example, some names represent places where the parents were very happy, or where an event took place which left a deep impression. There are people named after the battlegrounds of the First World War, and even after the nursing homes or hospitals where they were born.

Many children (particularly boys) are named after traditional or legendary heroes. Later in childhood the stories about these characters help the child to identify with heroic deeds, and to fantasize about having the same adventures. Can you remember any stories you heard as a child which included your own name? You may have formed ideas about your purpose in life at that time which still influence you.

Nearly all names have meanings. Were your parents aware of the meaning of the names they gave you? Many Hebrew names express feelings about having babies. Examples are: Abigail (source of joy), Hannah (God has favoured me), Nathan (God has given) and Zachariah (God has remembered). The German name Gertrude means 'spear strength', and is one of many warlike names; some names have poetic meanings, like the Celtic name Clyde, which means 'heard from a distance', or Muriel, which means 'white sea-foam'. Do you know what your name means? When did you find out? If your parents chose it for its meaning, what does this tell you about the way they felt about your arrival in their lives, or about their hopes and fears?

Not everybody likes his name; some people have disliked their names for as long as they can remember. You may have adopted a new first-name for yourself which sounds more glamorous or makes you feel more at ease with other people. With some names it is easy to find a shortened form which you prefer. For example, Elizabeth can become Liz, Betty, Lisa, Bess, and so on. Do you remember choosing a short-form you prefer? If you have strong feelings about any of the forms of your name, where do these feelings come from? When did they start? Do they reflect any of the attitudes of your parents? Some children adopt names for themselves which they prefer, and later drop them. Do you remember doing this? Others grow up without their 'official' names being much used unless they are being reprimanded.

You might also like to consider your parents' first names. How were they named? After somebody? According to what was fashionable at the time? With an unusual name? Did they like their names? Parents in previous generations, and perhaps today, may not have allowed their children to address them by their first names. Does this show a need to be treated as a superior? If so, why was it necessary in the case of your own parents? How old were you when you first learned their names? You may be surprised at the variations between people in answering this question. Some people do not discover their parents' names until quite late in life; others were always encouraged to talk to their parents as equals.

Some names are difficult to pronounce or spell, and others readily suggest a pun which may seem funny at the time but to which the owner of the name has become sickeningly accustomed. In social situations where it is necessary to meet a large number of people in a short time it helps to be sensitive to the feelings people have about their names, and not to embarrass them by making jokes of this kind. Do people make jokes about your name? How do you feel about this? If you make jokes about the names of other people is this because you are more than usually conscious of your own name? You may, for example, have been taught to be proud of it, or you may feel ashamed for some reason. Alternatively, a tendency to joke about the name of another person may result from a need to compensate for shyness, so you get to know his name instead of becoming acquainted with him.

84 You and Your Childhood

Understanding your role in early family life

People often say they have forgotten their childhood. You may remember yours vividly, or be unable to recall most of it. This chapter is designed to assist you to make more sense of what you remember. At the same time, you will be able to use it to look more carefully at your present behaviour to see which of your habitual ways of responding to people grew out of the social situation of your family of origin during early childhood.

The first part of the exercise will work better if you begin by writing down the names of all the children in your family of origin, together with the years in which they were born. If you can remember birthdays, this will also help. Next, work out when each child was conceived, and the period of time between each of your mother's pregnancies. If you are an 'only' child, there are several questions you might like to consider. First, you may not have been the only pregnancy. Secondly, you might have been a baby which your parents tried to have many times before you were conceived. Thirdly, you may be the only child for other reasons, such as an enforced or voluntary separation of your parents, or because your mother and father did not want any more children for health, sexual or social reasons.

Next, consider the role in the family of the eldest child. In a large family, the eldest daughter may become the 'little mother', whose task is to help look after the babies. The eldest son may be the 'little father', who acts as the disciplinarian when the children play together. But the term 'eldest' can be misleading: in families which are spaced out unevenly, there may in effect be two groups of children, forming two sub-families; the eldest of the second sub-family will be called upon to act in the same way as the eldest child of the entire family. A child born several years after the others (for example, one conceived at the menopause, when his mother thought she was no longer fertile) may grow up in effect as an 'only' child, since there will be no other young children within the family.

The first child of any family is always able to identify himself as the eldest, and the influence of this will last throughout his life. His parents are often afraid of 'making mistakes' with the way he is brought up, and for this reason may try hard not to 'spoil' him. Parents often find that the first baby is a greater strain than later ones, partly because the financial impact is greater, but also because they have no previous experience of having babies, and they are uncertain whether to accept or reject advice from well-meaning grandparents or friends. Of course, doing anything for the first time is difficult, and with practice many parents feel much more assured about having and raising babies. If you are the eldest child of several, you could consider how this might have affected your early childhood. The younger children may seem to you to have had a much easier time: being encouraged more, being treated less strictly, or generally arousing fewer expectations from your parents.

If you are not the eldest child, do you know somebody who might be – perhaps a rather dominant person who sticks to the rules and is careful not to be over-indulgent towards himself or his subordinates? If you have children of your own, which of them are most like you in personality? If you are a first child yourself, you may find you are more often in competition with your own eldest than with the others. Do you expect more of this child? If so, why?

Psychologists generally regard the second child as likely to be more rebellious than the others, a view based on the theory of 'sibling rivalry'. This is the idea that the eldest child is a 'little king' for the first period of his life, able to attract the whole of his mother's attention by being very clever or by being ill. But when the second child is born, the eldest is 'dethroned'. The eldest always has to look behind him, so to speak, in case the youngest manages to be as clever, or even cleverer. However, if there are more children, the second child is 'dethroned' in his turn. This child was previously able to compete with the eldest, either by being better at the same skills or by finding ones his older sibling did not value; now he also has to compete with a younger child. While the eldest looks behind him, the middle child has to look in both directions to compete successfully, and may have a hidden fear or show open resentment that both the youngest and the eldest seem to receive favours by virtue of their titles, while he is 'only the second child'. If you are a second child, do you see yourself as a 'rebel'? Do you know any other second children to whom this applies? You may also be able to recall your feelings at the birth of younger children.

The third or last child is more likely to be spoiled; this is the 'pampered youngest' of Adler's theories. A mother is often especially fond of her last child, particularly if she knows it will be the last and if she enjoyed having her babies. Because so many youngest children are favourites in some way, they receive love without any effort on their part, and may take for granted all their lives that they will never have to work hard to be loved; they are loved 'for themselves', not for what they do. The youngest child can often manipulate older children from this position of strength. In power struggles he only has to identify himself as being the 'littlest' to win. Thus he grows up with less experience of the kind of power struggle which is resolved at the 'security', 'commitment' and 'specialization' stages; for him, just being the youngest is a form of being safe, without further commitment or specialization. If you are a youngest child, are you ever accused of lacking commitment or of taking it for granted that you are special – in quarrels, for example?

The only child is at once the eldest and the youngest, and shows a mixture of dominance and being pampered. If this is you, try to work out what kinds of situations you like to dominate, and on which occasions you pamper yourself. You may find that you compete easily with dominant people, but tend to give in as soon as the pressure becomes heavy and you feel in need of consolation. You are more likely to have had a lonely childhood. Are you especially defended against the feeling of being lonely by having a large 'savings account' in this respect?

Recalling childhood incidents about which you still have strong feelings will help you complete unfinished business so that you can be more at peace with yourself.

85 Learning Responsibility

How you may have learned responsibility during childhood

Children have many responsibilities in the family which they have to be taught. Learning to take these responsibilities can be a painful and difficult process, and the learning may still be incomplete when the child leaves home permanently in early adulthood. If the necessary skills are learned satisfactorily they will probably be taken for granted by the person in later life; an adult has usually forgotten how hard it was to learn to read and write, to add up figures, to handle simple equipment like a brush, a vacuum cleaner, a knife or a fork, or to do commonplace tasks such as tying a knot. The skills of handling responsibility are more complicated than these examples. In this chapter we look at some of the stages which a child has to go through in order to learn such skills. This will enable you to recall your own early learning and make fresh judgements about how you exercise these skills today.

Each skill is a resource, and its acquisition follows the familiar five-stage sequence (see chapter 5). The skill of handling responsibility is the ability to be accountable for an action or policy which affects other people. When a child is given responsibility by a parent, this means that he will be judged according to how well he performs in the role of 'adult'; being taught to be responsible is therefore a major part of a child's training for adult life. In general terms, a child in our society has two main responsibilities: to show consideration for the feelings of others and to be successful at school. We will discuss each in turn.

The set of feelings to which a child has to be most sensitive are those of his parents. He therefore has to be able to identify approval and disapproval. In your own case, how did you recognize this? Some parents show their feelings more openly than others; a shy parent, or one who has been taught not to show strong emotion, may present the child with considerable problems in recognizing reactions. A parent who is unpredictable in his reactions causes similar difficulties. How predictable were your own parents? Did you always know if you had done something wrong? How were you punished if you failed to recognize the signs in time? Were you told that you 'never' knew when you had overstepped a limit of some kind?

Children need to do more than identify the danger signals which show they have angered or disappointed a parent; they also need to learn how far they can go. This is the second, or 'security', stage in learning responsibility. Do you remember pushing your own parents to the limits of tolerance by deliberately bad behaviour? What were the signs? How well do you still remember them? If you remember them well, you were probably a rather insecure child, who had to test these boundaries often, and who felt more secure once he knew where he stood. The same habit may still be part of your personality. Does this apply to your own children?

Children who can identify distress on the part of a parent, and feel secure with him, often reach the third stage and build a bond of com-

A young boy and his sister learn to exercise responsibility while their mother enjoys a drink in a London pub.

mitment with the parent. This happens, for example, when a mother is unhappy in her marriage, and the child takes her side when there are marital arguments. The child begins to feel committed to taking responsibility for his parent's feelings. If your parents fought, you may be able to feel a sense of relief by telling yourself that you no longer need to worry about how they feel towards one another. Try it. You may have been committed to keeping your parents together, perhaps in the knowledge that they were unhappy but had said they would stay together 'for the sake of the children'. Now you can relax: if they stayed together, you were successful; if not, it does not matter anyway!

Being able to identify parental feelings, being sure as to how far you could go in upsetting your parents and feeling committed to them however they felt leads to the next stage, the specialization aspect of learning responsibility for the feelings of others. How far were you, as a child, able to see your parents as people in their own right, without feeling embarrassed, threatened or intimidated by this knowledge? Some children are embarrassed to find that their parents are only human, that they tell lies or cheat, that they have the normal bodily functions, that they too can act as children. Did this happen in your case? Do you still think of your parents as special people or have you come to accept them as ordinary people with special qualities? You may be able to recall hurting your parents, and watching them try not to show that they were hurt. Do you ever use the same kind of non-verbal behaviour to show that you are hurt but you forgive? Do you ever catch yourself smiling or wincing the same way either parent did? If so, you may now see how he or she felt. If you have children of your own, do you let them into your own inner world of feelings, or do you restrict yourself to showing them only an official side of your nature, for example, that you are pleased or angry with them in your role as parent, rather than in your role as one equal human being to another?

The achievement of responsibility in childhood is indicated by a happy harmony of feeling between parent and child; both share their triumphs as equals. In babyhood this may have been more common for you than when you became older. Can you remember being 'in charge' while your parents were both out? How did you react? One way to explore this is by writing an account of such an incident, or talking about it into a tape-recorder. You can then analyse what you say, looking for the symbolic meanings that indicate projection or displacement. Pay particular attention to how you felt and how your parents felt. Did you feel 'great', or 'big' or 'much older'? You may have forgotten how hard you tried to be old enough for responsibility. You may still be trying to be old enough.

The procedure for answering questions at school has to be learned, along with other study skills. This teacher is using a competitive procedure, but not all his pupils seem able to benefit equally from it.

Being a success at school

For many children, it is difficult to get used to being at school. When they succeed at this, however, they forget they ever had a problem. Part of the difficulty is that the mother may also find it hard to get used to being without her child during the school day. When her child goes to school for the first time she may feel that he is no longer hers in the same way, that she is older and that she will miss his babyhood. She may transmit her anxiety to the child. Where there are several children in a family, the youngest child is often much keener to start school, and adapts more quickly than his mother. The eldest child may be much more reluctant, for fear that he will miss favours the other children receive during his absence. Do you remember starting school? Were you told that this was like your father going to work? If so, why were you told this?

Some children have to work through the identification stage of being at school over a much longer period than others. When they are at school they are, almost literally, not sure who they are. Other children do not know their names; they easily forget where to hang their coats or where to sit. Nor do they feel safe at school, and they are therefore slow to develop a sense of commitment to schoolwork. If you were slow to complete any of these stages, there may have been quite a long period at the start of your school life during which you felt you were not appreciated for your personal, special qualities. You may, for example, have had a feeling that you were 'there to make up the numbers', and that school was really only for the brighter and more adaptable children, that you were there almost by mistake. You may still be affected by similar feelings when you start a new job or go into any large, strange building. When you emerge from a building like this, do you have a repeat of the feeling of 'being let out of school'? During their early days at school very young children are often unsure about using the lavatory: they do not know where it is, how to ask for help, and so on. Do you recall this feeling, or still feel embarrassed at asking where the lavatories are?

There are both official and unofficial aspects of being good at school. The life of the classroom, with its system of marks and points, examinations, and answering questions by guessing what the teacher wants to hear, is probably one of the most universal common factors in the experience of members of our society. Do you still respond to the 'official' sound of a voice asking you a question to which you are expected to know the answer? Do you also ask this kind of question? The unofficial life at school is the life of the peer group. This means the children of your own age, with whom you played during breaks or intermissions. In the school playground many of us have our first experience of leadership, of being a follower, and of bullying others and being bullied. Do you remember the names of any of the leaders or bullies you learned before you were eight or nine? Were you a bully yourself? Do you remember the names of any of your teachers from this period? Do you recall their faces? All these are traces of the difficulties you faced, and of your eventual triumph in successfully completing the identification stage of this learning process.

The social learning in the unofficial peer group can be far more important to a child at school than the official learning in the classroom. Was this so in your case? You may have underestimated your achievements in this direction, perhaps because they were overshadowed by your parents expecting you to perform well on the official side, while ignoring the social side. Some parents are especially anxious for their child to do well at school, obtain high marks, learn to read and write quickly, perform well in tests and show evidence of being intelligent. Yet they may forget that a child who learns a great deal at school about relating to children of his own age is also doing well. For example, you may recall not telling your parents about some of your school friends and your adventures, feeling this would not be appreciated. You may still separate performance into its intellectual and its social aspects, giving yourself less credit than you deserve for your skill in the latter because of insecurity in dealing with the former.

86 You and Your Adolescence

You are probably still influenced by what you learned at puberty

Your adolescence may be recent or a long time ago, or you may still be an adolescent. In this chapter you will be asked to reassess the changes which occured (or are still taking place) during this period of your life. Adolescence begins with puberty, when a girl starts her menstrual periods and a boy experiences his first sperm ejaculation. A year or so before these signs appear, the hormones which produce them begin to circulate through the child's body and affect what are called the 'pre-pubertal' years, usually between eleven and twelve years of age. Do you recall these years? They are often marked by an increased independence of the child from his parents and family, and by major arguments or sulks. You may also recall childhood friends from whom you parted about this time, and an increased awareness of being more discriminating about people in general.

About a hundred years ago the average age in Europe for a girl to have her first period was probably around 16. In Sweden (where, for special reasons, figures are available) it was about 15.8 in 1886, 15 in 1900, 13.8 in 1950, 12.8 in 1968, and 12 in 1980. A similar trend has been recorded throughout all the countries of the industrialized world. Although no data are available, it would not be unreasonable to suppose that something similar has happened with the onset of puberty in boys. Yet, despite the trend towards earlier puberty, young people have been given social independence later and later: they leave school later and marry later, for example. It is important to note here that the figures given above are average ages; there are very wide individual variations. However, most children are still very much a part of their families when puberty starts. Some families help their children to understand what is happening to them better than others. How much help did you receive?

You might like to consider how you learned about menstrual periods and male ejaculation. If you are a woman, how were you told about periods, and when? Who told you? It was probably your mother, but did you know whether or not your father knew that you had started to menstruate? If you are a man, do you remember your first ejaculation? Who else knew? If nobody knew, did you feel alarmed, lonely, dirty, or just pleased? Women might like to consider how they found out about the male signs of puberty; men, how they found out about menstruation. Before you simply protest that you have no residual feelings of guilt or of all this being 'dirty', remember the defence system we looked at earlier. Did you build any defensive reactions on these topics during adolescence? Do you still have them? One such sign you can look out for is the strength of your feeling that men and women are 'different'. Or that a menstrual flow is altogether a different kind of thing from a seminal emission, the former being 'nasty' and 'dirty', the latter being merely inconvenient.

During puberty and adolescence the young person grows very rapidly.

An adult male requires about 3,000 calories a day; a boy aged between thirteen and sixteen needs 200 calories a day more than this, and during the late teens, the need rises to 3,800. The average amount for a grown woman is about 2,500, and for a girl aged thirteen to fifteen, about 2,800. Do you remember eating more when you were an adolescent, or were you always in too much of a hurry to sit down for a meal? Clashes over eating too much or too little may now be forgotten; or you may have formed eating habits then which are still part of your life.

Were you shy during adolescence? When we looked at shyness in chapter 42, the point was made that a shy person is not sure how to estimate the value or emphasis of another person's signals. You might like to consider your own communication problems during adolescence in this light. Tone of voice signals, for example, depend for their subtle meanings on quite small differences in loudness, or in modulation, thus producing variations we called 'impact', 'pressure' and 'caress'. When a young man's voice changes from soprano to baritone, he goes through a time when his own capacity for voice subtlety is limited. In order to judge body movements, we need a clear idea of the height of the other person; when an adolescent is growing rapidly his ability to adapt to body movement co-ordination is affected, not only by the difference in height but also by clumsiness in movement. Do you remember finding that you were the same height, or even taller, than your mother or father? How did this affect your communication with them? Shyness is also associated with sex; were you shy about people of the opposite sex? Are you still shy with them under certain circumstances? Is this when you feel awkward or clumsy, as you did in adolescence?

One interesting aspect of this is revealed by recent research. During

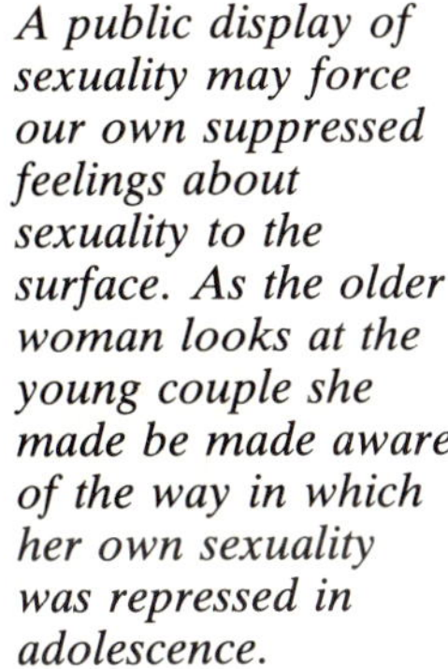

A public display of sexuality may force our own suppressed feelings about sexuality to the surface. As the older woman looks at the young couple she made be made aware of the way in which her own sexuality was repressed in adolescence.

the years of adolescent growth, popularity in a group can be very important. In chapter 50 it was stated that most people are remarkably accurate judges of their own popularity. However, adolescents are an exception to this. In one study, children between the ages of eight and seventeen were asked to rate themselves for popularity, and then to rate their class-mates. These two sets of rankings – how somebody thought he was rated and how the others actually rated him – were then compared. Between the ages of eight and sixteen there were major discrepancies in the supposed and the actual ratings, whereas accuracy of judgement was more or less complete amongst the seventeen-year-olds. The opinion of the opposite sex was more accurately judged at an earlier age than that of the same sex. Not being able to judge how a person feels about you is the basis of shyness; we can see from the research that this inability 'normally' disappears as adolescence progresses. Did you ever resent being told you would 'grow out of' shyness?

Intellectually, adolescence is a time when many of us become aware of the world of ideas and expression, discovering art, poetry, music, politics and religion for the first time, it seems. But there are some parents who feel angered by this, perhaps regarding these subjects as a waste of time. Were your parents like this? If so, you might like to consider your own attitude today. Has it changed since adolescence, or are you as accepting now of new ideas as the adolescent you once were?

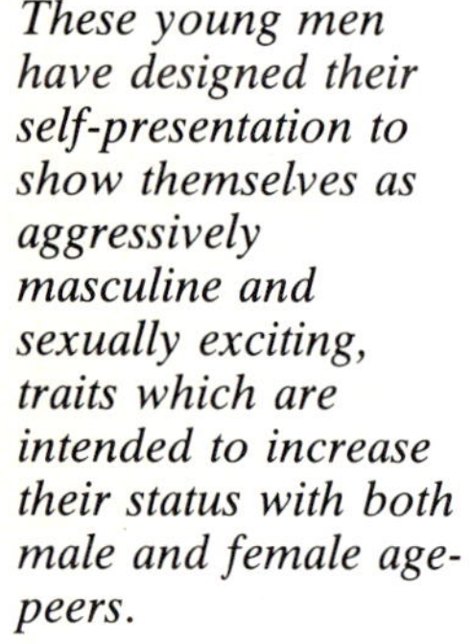

These young men have designed their self-presentation to show themselves as aggressively masculine and sexually exciting, traits which are intended to increase their status with both male and female age-peers.

87 Your 'Self' and Others

How people combine personalities to form a relationship

If you can understand your personality better, you will be able to make better use of your resources. This is usually what is meant by 'knowing yourself'. But it is just as important to understand 'self', as opposed to 'personality'. This is because one of the most common problems in all relationships is the difficulty posed by 'selfish' behaviour. In this chapter you are invited to focus on the word 'self', and to try to reach a better understanding of what it means.

Imagine a man and a woman who have only just met; they are sitting together and talking. Each takes turns to speak, while the other listens. At this moment the man is talking. He refers to his own attitudes towards something by using the word 'myself'. When he mentions what the woman thinks about something, he uses the word 'yourself'. Now it is her turn to speak. She says how she feels, and refers to these feelings using the word 'myself'; when she mentions attitudes displayed by the man, she says 'yourself'. But what do 'myself' and 'yourself' mean? Clearly, they depend for their meaning on who is using them. Both the man and the woman use the same words, but mean very different things.

Knowing the difference between 'myself' and 'yourself' is probably one of the most important of all our early lessons. The distinction may seem obvious to you now, but when you learned to talk in childhood you could speak only for yourself. A child begins to learn to talk at around eighteen months old. Within six months his vocabulary increases tenfold or more. By the age of two he usually knows more than 200 words, and learns new ones almost every day. 'My' is the first of the personal pronouns to appear, followed by 'me', 'you' and 'I'. When a child begins to understand the difference between 'you' and 'me', he has taken a major step forward in developing the concept of 'self', in other words, that there are other 'selves', not just his own. In the case of the man and woman in our example, there could not be a relationship of any sort between them without this simple and basic recognition which is so often taken for granted. However, there is more to this recognition than meets the eye. When each refers to himself as 'me' and to the other as 'you', he is acknowledging boundaries. Each person is dealing with two separate systems of resources, his own and the other person's. Similarly, as outside observers of their conversation, we can refer to 'them', thus indicating that their resource systems are separate from our own.

Let us now imagine that we see the same man and woman holding a conversation a year later. We will assume that they have met many times since we first watched them, that they like one another and have developed a close relationship. Probably the first thing we will notice is that, in addition to 'myself' and 'yourself', another 'self' has emerged. Each of the two people can say what he thinks 'himself', and what the two of them think together, as 'ourself'. In addition to 'I' and 'you', the word 'we' has entered their joint vocabulary as a meaningful description of their joint 'self'. This could have happened at the first meeting, or much later; but it is a significant development. Similarly, when a child learns to talk, the words 'we' and 'us' are a late and important development in his vocabulary. They are among the most common words in any language, but, of all the common words, are among the last to be learned.

The idea that you can combine with somebody else and build a shared 'self' is basic to the skill of relating. So far in this section, we have used the word 'self' to refer to a system of resources with only one person inside the system. The 'self' is the agent for internal communication, providing organization and leadership, so as to direct the use of the resources to meet the needs and further the purposes of the system. But with the man and woman in our example, the 'self' which they refer to as 'ourself' contains not one person, but two. The 'ourself' is the leader of this system, with all the tasks of leadership, and all the defences which every 'self' requires if it is to maintain stability and unity. Similarly, there are systems which contain three or many more people, and each of these systems can have a composite 'self'.

Every 'self' must be able to control resources if it is to survive and meet its own needs; it must also acquire valuable new resources if it is

From her head position, clasped hands and maintenance of body space the girl indicates a reluctance to set aside her individual 'self' in favour of constructing a joint 'self'.

to do more than survivc. When you begin to build a relationship with somebody else, an 'ourself' has to be constructed from the resources which you and that person contribute. These become jointly owned and controlled, so that 'yourself' and 'myself' no longer have the first claim on them. This is reserved for the 'ourself' you build. The resources are mutual. The boundaries which contain them are shared. The system of internal communication upon which your joint personality depends belongs to both of you, jointly and severally. The resources in your shared personality may be of little value to either of you, or they may contain resources so vital that without them you would cease to be the person you are, and be forced to adopt an unacceptably lower standard of life.

Your most important relationships are with the people you love. Here you have constructed an 'ourself' which is recognized equally by both of you, where it is safe for you both to commit resources that are so special you would not be 'yourself' without them. Provided that the resources are equally safe in this way for each of you, you will both be able to go on contributing to the mutual personality, knowing you do not have to count the cost. If your loving relationships are not like this, either you or the other person is being impoverished, because your 'ourself' is worth less than it might be.

'Ourself' meets 'ourself'. Each pair of friends has developed an 'ourself', enabling the partners to act as one unit. The strength of the tie between the same-sex partners will restrict the development of any opposite-sex relationships.

88 The Art of Relationships

You can develop your skill into an art

We are all taught early in life that it is wrong to be selfish. This is partly because a child learns to develop the idea of the joint 'self' out of the conflicts which take place in family life when he is between two and five years of age. We would not know what 'ourself' meant without these conflicts and without being taught to restrict immediate self-interest in favour of benefits from the wider economy of the joint 'self'. It is also partly because many families have less than enough to go round, whether this is money and material resources or love, approval and other non-material resources. When a child is told not to be selfish, this may be because somebody stronger than him (an older child, for example, or a parent) wishes to be selfish instead. The child is being controlled not for his own benefit, but for somebody else's.

In later life most of us learn to be discriminating about when we can be selfish, and when it would be unwise to act selfishly. We come to recognize that selfishness is not automatically 'wrong'. The purpose of any organic system is to grow, and our own personal resource systems are no exception. We have to enrich ourselves, first, to stay alive, but secondly, to maintain an even more acceptable standard of life for ourselves and our dependents. This can be a physical enrichment, such as making ourselves fitter, stronger or healthier; a behavioural enrichment, as when we increase our skills; a property enrichment; or a social enrichment. The whole range of human resources is used in relating, and these can be obtained and absorbed into your personality through power, trading or loving relationships. Absorption is an economic process, an exchange of values. Your rewards can be bigger than, equal to, or less than, your costs.

Skill at making relationships begins in childhood; like all other skills, at first it is a matter of discipline. Out of the early lessons there emerges the craftsmanship stage of the skill, during which we follow the rules and need to think carefully about many of the moves we make. The intuitive, childhood learning seldom takes an individual beyond this level. As we grow older, however, many of us start to see relating not as a craft, but as an art. The artist is a craftsman first, but he becomes so versed in his craft that he can start to extend his discipline beyond the rules, and to modify his approach so as to develop an individual style. In developing your own skill, you too can become a creative artist instead of an imitative craftsman; this is not to belittle the essential discipline of craftsmanship, but to take it a stage further and to build upon it. First you have to know the discipline of healthy relating, and to question it constantly. Learning to be discriminating about your own selfishness is not enough for this development, unless you know the safest principles on which to base your discrimination. The fundamental principle is to avoid 'false economies'.

It is a false economy to have resources which you do not use. They may be stacked away in a 'deposit account', so that you have stores of energy saved up for the rainy day which never comes. Each time you belittle yourself, you are saving up energy for an unnecessary defence. Conversely, every time you pretend to be something more than you are, perhaps by dramatizing your feelings, you are wasting energy. This usually happens because you are afraid to be yourself. Learning to trust your own feelings comes with practice and discipline, by trusting others, and showing your true feelings without either underemphasis or exaggeration if people let you down.

It is a false economy to use resources at less than their true value. Where social resources are concerned, making cheap gains at the expense of someone else is a false economy; people are all valuable in some way, and they will not recognize your value if you do not acknowledge theirs. Where all the other resources are concerned, the most common false economy is to attempt to acquire resources simply by labelling them. All resources can be used in many ways, and to obtain the value of any resource you have to become sensitive to all its attributes. Intelligence and creativity are the skills of finding many uses for resources for which other people see only a few uses.

It is a false economy to reduce the value of a joint 'self' in order to increase your own private value. The art – as opposed to the skill – of relating lies partly in being able to judge what your relationships are worth. You can control up to half their value. Beyond this it is a matter of trust. But the safer you feel as a person in your own right, the easier it is to trust other people. You can feel safer if you carry fewer reserves to pay for your hidden agenda, so that you have a larger surplus to share. The more you have, the more you can give away without being threatened if you later discover that you were wrong to trust somebody.

The art of being selfish lies in avoiding these false economies. It is dangerously selfish to have resources and not use them in a relationship of some kind; it is not selfish to have them and use them, but to restrict their use to people you feel will value them as you do. It is dangerous to use resources at less than their true value, but not selfish to protect that value. For example, any relationship which threatens your minimum acceptable standard of life will eventually destroy your usefulness to the rest of the world. You are better off without such ties, and it would not be selfish to end them.

One of the most common problems which arise from the way we are taught about selfishness is the development of an imbalance between the capacity to give and the capacity to accept love. You may have become over-specialized at taking love, but lack an equal ability to give it. Similarly, you may feel happier loving somebody than being loved. In a balanced personality both capacities are equal. If you give away more love than you receive, and are aware of it, you are probably overreacting to a need to be unselfish. This will lead you to take more than half the responsibility for those relationships in which it happens. The longer you do this the harder it will become to replace the resources you give away, and the more likely it will be that you have to count the cost to yourself. As a result, what starts as your love for somebody will eventually become his power over you. If you find yourself in this situation, the answer is to learn to accept love. You can only do this if you love yourself – if you can accept that each human personality, including your own, is valuable beyond measure.

89 A Sense of Value

Values in the psycho-economy sometimes suffer from inflation

One of the most familiar economic concepts in recent years has been that of 'inflation'. When an economy suffers from inflation, prices rise faster than wages, and people have to spend an increasing amount of money in order to be able to purchase the same items. The cost of living rises, without an accompanying increase in the standard of living. You may not have realized that this phenomenon is also common in the human psycho-economy. It occurs under certain circumstances when an individual spends more and more energy on achieving less and less. The inflationary spiral can occur in several ways within a relationship or within a group. It can also take place inside a person's private personality. The purpose of this chapter is to help you recognize the early symptoms both of inflation and of the reverse process, deflation. First, we will look at inflation.

In the psycho-economy, the equivalent of money is readily available energy. To do anything you have to expend a certain amount of energy; this is the 'price' you pay for what you do. The 'reward' you obtain from the activity is either that your own value increases or that you prevent an unwanted fall in your value. Sometimes the value of what you obtain is worth the price you pay. If something is difficult to do, the price is high; but if the reward is great, the effort will have been worthwhile. Alternatively, if something is easy to do, it costs you little energy and the price is low. Most people like to design their lives so that they can obtain high psycho-economic rewards at low cost to their reserves of energy, but they also usually accept that they have to pay a fair price for most of the valuable things in life.

From time to time most of us probably expect something to be easy but it turns out to be more difficult. We may try to please a group, for example, but find that the members are not as easily satisfied as we had imagined. When this happens, we find that the price has changed. Usually we react by spending more energy. But if this still does not satisfy the members, the inflationary spiral starts. Each time we try harder, they increase the price. The longer this goes on, the more energy we find we are spending for less and less reward. One example of this would be when a group teases one of its members. He expects his efforts to be taken seriously, while the other members are pretending to like what he does, but do not pretend quite enough for him to feel satisfied with his reward.

Inflation also occurs inside an individual personality, and is often the result of growing anger. The angry person finds that he is caught in an increasingly accelerating spiral, in which the price of satisfaction always seems out of reach, so that he doubles and redoubles his expenditure of energy, gaining half and then half as much again of the satisfaction he is seeking as each moment goes by. An angry outburst burns up energy for nothing, or even for less than nothing, if the result is the destruction of valuable resources. But equally, the effect of anger over many months or years, caused by a harboured resentment or hidden bitterness, has the same effect. It may lead somebody to feel that he is continuously making the same effort and getting no reward, as when a person repeats the same mistakes many times. As a result of our early training, many of us are taught to 'keep trying' even if we do not succeed at first, and this determination may lead us into the false economy of an angry, inflationary spiral which pleases nobody, least of all ourselves.

When an economy is suffering from inflation, this may be temporary (or 'acute') inflation or it may be the result of a long-term (or 'chronic') failure. In the case of an acute attack, at least as far as the psycho-economy is concerned, the answer is 'deflation', in which the normal values are restored. When the effort you are making starts to become out of proportion to the results you obtain, the most important safeguard is a sense of humour. If you can laugh at yourself, order will be restored. Equally, when a group teases one of its members, this is usually because they are afraid he has developed ideas about his value which have grown unrealistically out of proportion. If he joins in the teasing and can laugh at himself, instead of taking the false prices seriously, he will be accepted once more as an equal member.

A newly arrived immigrant to Israel is reunited with his relatives, restoring to the family the full value of its psycho-economic resources.

This girl's laughter shows she is relaxed and happy and has no need to defend her opinion of herself. When we need to retain energy because our view of ourselves is in conflict with the opinion others have of us, it is difficult to relax and produce sincere laughter.

The same kind of solution is necessary when long-term inflation affects an individual psycho-economy. The bottled-up anger can be released much more effectively if the energy being used to protect the 'self' from its destructive force can be spent on laughter. Hidden anger can only stay hidden if it is safe from the internal communication system; when you smile to yourself about the causes of this anger, you are reopening internal communication. As a result, you will be able to get to know once more the kind of person you really are, and be able to accept this person. Deflation means 'climbing down' from too high an opinion of yourself and of what you expect from life. It enables you to pay the correct price for your rewards, because it helps you readjust your expectations and bring them back to reality. The symptoms of inflation are an inability to laugh, either within yourself or by sharing your sense of the ridiculous with somebody else.

90 Looking to the Future

You alone are responsible for the success of your relationships

Many of the ideas with which people habitually approach the question of relationships may have worked well enough in the past, but are inadequate for the present and the future. For example, to see people as either friends or enemies, as liked or disliked, or to divide the world into people-like-ourselves and 'strangers', may have been an adequate response when most of the world's population lived in small, isolated villages. Today it seems dangerously inept to restrict our responses to fellow human beings in these ways. In the modern world, communication through radio and television, and through worldwide travel and trade, has turned the globe into a village. We are interdependent as never before. We cannot afford not to get to know strangers, people we do not like and people who are unlike us, just as our ancestors could not afford to have enemies amongst their own kind. There is no sign that the population growth of the present century is slowing down; nor that there will be less travel or media contact between people in the future. The next generation will meet even more strangers than we do. If they are to relate to one another safely and as individuals in their own right, recognizing and valuing one another's individual differences, an improved understanding of the theory and practice of relationships can make a major contribution to human survival.

Learning to communicate with other people more effectively, and to get to know them better, is a matter of skill and can become an art. In the past this was left to chance. Talented individuals emerged naturally from accidental circumstances in their families of origin, able to use advanced relationship skills with no formal learning. It is worth asking how long this may safely be left to chance in the future. A century ago the peoples of the major industrial nations were, for the first time, sending their children to school as part of a benevolent, but compulsory, state-financed education system. They learned basic reading and writing, and simple arithmetic. Their skills at relating to one another were partly developed, because without a degree of improved socialization, the children could not acquire even the most rudimentary numeracy and literacy. Education for relationships is still very largely left to chance, and where it exists, it is for the most part designed to aid other educational objectives, to lead to better and more efficient social control. There is a case for educating people to improve relationships for its own sake.

The institutions through which we organize our society are changing under the impact of technological development; marriage and the family are those most obviously affected. Higher living standards, easier divorce and better contraception are only a few of the causes of these changes. The traditional attitudes towards sex outside marriage and towards divorce were to condemn and not to try to understand. These attitudes are untenable today, and may be dangerous tomorrow. The world's population is not only expanding more rapidly than ever before, but is also becoming younger. This trend is most marked in the less developed areas. But even in the industrialized countries, where there are more elderly people, the young will increasingly look for personal rather than traditional solutions to their problems. In the future, their natural competitors will be people of their own age, now growing up in less stable circumstances. If we wish for a stable future, people must be helped to learn how to find this for themselves, and not merely be controlled or exhorted by their elders.

All this may seem very distant from the daily business of meeting people and getting on with them, yet the connection is closer than it might seem. Human behaviour is not the product of many millions of different systems, but of one system which our unpractised perceptions lead us to see as many systems. The psycho-economic approach to relationships helps to emphasize this unity. The resources you call your own are in your charge, but it is debatable whether they are entirely yours. They form an integral part of the whole social and economic structure of a global society.

Nevertheless, when you set out to increase your skill, you do so alone. You alone have the final responsibility for your own part in the human psycho-economy. Your feelings are your own. Your standards must be set by you, and you alone can judge whether you are meeting them or falling behind your expectations. If you are to realize more of your potential it has to be by your own efforts. But it goes without saying that any improvement in your own relationships will benefit the rest of us.

A boy stands apart from the crowd for a moment, learning more about himself as an individual and about the complex set of relationships which surrounds him. As he grows he will increase his awareness of his unique place in the world psycho-economy.

Index

For an illustrative reference to a subject not covered by a textual entry, the page number is in *italics*.